KETO CLARITY

YOUR DEFINITIVE GUIDE TO THE BENEFITS OF
A LOW-CARB, HIGH-FAT DIET

Jimmy Moore
with Eric C. Westman, MD

Victory Belt Publishing Inc.
Las Vegas

This book is dedicated to everyone who still needlessly believes the conventional wisdom about nutrition even though it's never helped them lose weight or get healthy . . . and very likely made things considerably worse!

First Published in 2014 by Victory Belt Publishing Inc.

ISBN 13: 978-1-628600-07-0

Printed in the USA

RRD 0114

Important Medical Disclaimer for *Keto Clarity*

Jimmy Moore and Dr. Eric Westman (hereafter referred to as the "Authors") are providing *Keto Clarity* (hereafter referred to as the "Book") and its contents on an "as is" basis and make no representations or warranties of any kind with respect to this Book or its contents. The Authors disclaim all such representations and warranties, including, for example, warranties of merchantability and fitness for a particular purpose. In addition, the Authors do not represent or warrant that the information accessible via this Book is complete or current.

The statements made about products and services have not been evaluated by the U.S. Food and Drug Administration. They are not intended to diagnose, treat, cure, or prevent any condition or disease. Please consult with your own physician or healthcare specialist regarding the suggestions and recommendations made in this Book.

Except as specifically stated in this Book, neither the authors, contributors, nor other representatives will be liable for damages arising out of or in connection with the use of this Book. This is a comprehensive limitation of liability that applies to all damages of any kind, including (without limitation) compensatory damages; direct, indirect, or consequential damages; loss of income, or profit; loss of or damage to property; and claims of third parties.

This Book provides content related to topics about nutrition and health. As such, use of this Book implies your acceptance of the terms described herein.

You understand that a private citizen, without any professional training in the medical, health, or nutritional field, coauthored this Book. You understand that this Book is provided to you without a health examination and without prior discussion of your health condition. You understand that in no way will this Book provide medical advice and that no medical advice is contained in this Book.

You understand that this Book is not intended as a substitute for consultation with a licensed healthcare practitioner, such as your physician. Before you begin any health modification program, or change your lifestyle in any way, you should consult your physician or other licensed healthcare practitioner to ensure that you are in good health and that the advice contained in this Book will not harm you.

If you experience any unusual symptoms after following any information contained in this Book, you should immediately consult with your healthcare practitioner.

You understand that the information contained in this Book should not be used to diagnose a health problem or disease, or to determine any health-related treatment program, including weight loss, diet, or exercise.

You understand that there are risks associated with engaging in any activity described in this Book. Any action you take implies that you assume all risks—known and unknown—inherent to lifestyle changes, including nutrition, exercise, and physical activities—as well any injuries that may result from the actions you take.

You hereby release the Authors and the publisher, Victory Belt Publishing, from any liability related to this Book to the fullest extent permitted by law. This includes any damages, costs, or losses of any nature arising from the use of this Book and the information provided in this Book, including direct, consequential, special, punitive, or incidental damages, even if the authors have been advised of the possibility of such damages.

Your use of this Book confirms your agreement to the above terms and conditions. If you do not agree, you will not utilize this Book and will request a full refund within the time frame specified in your contract of sale.

Contents

How to Use This Book

Think of *Keto Clarity* as your introduction to looking at nutrition and health from an alternative and yet equally viable dietary perspective that you probably haven't heard a whole lot about before. The information contained within these pages shares the truth about the critical role a low-carbohydrate, moderate-protein, high-fat diet—in other words, a ketogenic diet—can play in improving your overall health and reversing the ill effects of many medical ailments and chronic diseases. When you face opposition for choosing to eat this way (and you will), let this book be a comforting source of encouragement and advice on your journey to better health.

So many of the foundational principles of a healthy diet that have long been held true in our society are not based on any kind of scientific evidence, and they simply don't work for real people in the real world. Like our previous book, *Cholesterol Clarity*, this book will give you full access to the latest science in plain English, featuring many prominent scientists, physicians, dietitians, and researchers who are speaking up about the therapeutic use of ketones for a wide variety of purposes in improving health.

Be willing to question everything you've ever believed to be true about nutrition and embrace this new dietary paradigm, whose supporting scientific evidence is mounting. It's only a matter of time before the information you will learn about in this book becomes the new normal. This is the cutting edge of nutritional health, and in *Keto Clarity*, you get a front row seat.

Introduction

Have you ever wondered what to make of all the mixed messages about what constitutes a healthy diet? One week the news tells us of a study showing, for example, the tremendous health benefits that come from consuming coconuts and coconut-based foods, like coconut oil. But then a couple of months later, we're inundated with breaking news headlines about a new study that shows coconut foods contain too much saturated fat and will thus clog your arteries and give you heart disease. It's so much to take in; how in the world can the average person, busy with work and family, try to make sense of it all? Trust me, I've been there. I used to weigh over 400 pounds even though I thought I was doing all the right things nutritionally—they just didn't work for me, no matter how hard I tried.

My name is Jimmy Moore, and I transformed my own weight and health by doing nearly the exact opposite of all the things I'd been told to do my entire life to be healthy.

The Government Is Wrong: Testifying on the 2010 Dietary Guidelines

On July 8, 2010, I was one of only fifty American citizens to present oral testimony in Washington, DC, about the proposed Dietary Guidelines for Americans, 2010. These guidelines are released every five years and represent the official policy of the United States government for healthy eating. They are inserted into every part of American society through food stamps, school lunch programs, and even food allowances for members and families of the US military.

Yes, it's a big deal, and that is why I thought it was important enough for me to travel all the way to Washington, DC, on my own dime and share my point of view with the Dietary Guidelines Advisory Committee. Of the fifty people who testified before the committee at the US Department of Agriculture (USDA) on that hot summer day, only two of us were there as individuals—most of the rest were representing some special interest group (the soy lobby, the dairy lobby, the egg lobby, the salt lobby, and so on).

The vast majority of those who were testifying did so with extremely drab, boring, and monotone speeches about why their proposals should be taken under consideration blah, blah, blah in the official Dietary Guidelines. You could really tell their hearts weren't in it; they were simply paid to be there and put on record what was in the best interests of their corporate clients. Authentic testimonies were few and far between that day.

After enduring this agony for a couple of hours, it was finally my turn to share my three-minute remarks as speaker #26. I wanted to get the attention of the panel members, who had been looking down and taking notes through most of the testimonies, only occasionally glancing up at the parade of lemmings that was being ushered in front of them. I nervously but confidently stepped up to the microphone to share an impassioned speech with them (without the aid of any prepared notes) about how my life had improved dramatically because I had refused to accept the ideas that they were promoting to the American people as the only way to attain optimal health. I spoke from the heart because I've lived what I was sharing with them and have witnessed the power of my message in the lives of so many who follow my work. I don't remember much about the actual testimony I was giving because I was so caught up in the emotions of the moment. But one of my friends who was there said that when I began to speak, every single member of the Scientific Advisory Board and the government leaders looked up at me to listen intently to what I had to say.

Here are those remarks verbatim, according to the court reporter at the USDA:

Hi, my name is Jimmy Moore and I am from Spartanburg, South Carolina. I have a website called Livin' La Vida Low-Carb. And in January of 2004, I started on a low-carb diet because after years of frustration trying to follow the Dietary Guidelines that you guys put out every five years, I was failing. It was not working for me. I was a 410-pound man, high cholesterol, high blood pressure. I was in really bad shape at the age of thirty-two, and it wasn't until I was able to think outside the box and go beyond what my government was telling me was healthy that I was finally able to get my life back and my health back. And today I stand here not just on my behalf, but [on behalf] of the hundreds of thousands of people that read my blog [and] listen to my radio show. They are real people, and I wanted you to see a real person whose life has been changed by not doing the things that you told them to do, [by] eating more fat, eating less carbs, not worrying about cardiovascular exercise until I fall out. Those things didn't work for me. And it wasn't until I could find what did work for me that I finally realized, you know, the experts on this panel may not be the true experts in this whole thing.

We really need to get away from one set of guidelines for all Americans. I propose that you have multiple guidelines that people can choose from, multiple options, because we don't all wear the same shoe size. I wear thirteens. Everybody wear thirteens in here? No. The same goes for our diet. We need to have a diet that will [cater] to the metabolic needs of the individual, whether they have obesity, whether they have diabetes. Those are the things that need to be considered. And if we do those things, then I think we are going to be better off.

Otherwise, we are going to be here five years from now with the same people testifying, everybody coming before you with the exact same lobbying for all these things. And what is going to change? I daresay obesity is going to be worse, diabetes is going to be worse, heart disease is going to be worse, and I am going to ask you, "Why?"

It was gratifying to hear from so many people who came up to me after my testimony to share their appreciation for what I had to say. That was what made it worth all the effort to be there. In fact, one security guard asked me if I had a business card so he could check out my blog to learn more about the work I was doing. He said that he could tell there was something about me and my story that was different from most of the others who testified. That was an awesome confirmation that choosing to speak from my heart and letting the words flow freely was the right choice. I'm so glad I did!

I have no grand illusions that what I said that day made any difference at all in what eventually became the 2010 Dietary Guidelines for Americans. But I am so happy that I testified and represented all of the people out there who have been harmed by what the USDA and Department of Health and Human Services have said is a healthy diet. I hope that by 2015, when we debate the next set of dietary guidelines that will become the basis for MyPlate (formerly the food pyramid), these governmental bureaucrats will have seen the writing on the wall about the effects of their devotion to heavily promoting grains and demonizing fat. We're approaching a tipping point when it will become next to impossible for them to ignore the science. Hopefully this book will help move that process along a little quicker.

Think about it for a moment: if the USDA were a business and the state of public health reflected their profit margin, they would have gone bankrupt many years ago. In just the past few decades, the rates of obesity, diabetes, heart disease, and other chronic illnesses have gotten considerably worse. And do you know what's most shocking about that? The spike in all of these ailments coincides almost perfectly with the implementation of the government's Dietary Guidelines in 1980. Coincidence? I think not.

There's a saying that insanity is doing the same thing over and over and expecting different results. And that's precisely what has happened to national nutritional policy in the United States in recent years. The government ignores studies that don't fit within a preconceived template of a low-fat, low-salt, calorie-restricted, high-carb, plant-based diet. But this one-size-fits-all approach to eating does not work for the large segment of the population that is dealing with obesity and other metabolic chronic health issues. In fact, the statistics prove that this message has been an utter and dismal failure for America, and it's time for the USDA and Department of Health and Human Services to realize the error of their ways.

My Story: Veteran of Every Fad Diet and Still 400 Pounds

I'm sure glad I found my way off of the roller coaster ride of nutritional guidelines and poor health a decade ago. In January 2004, when I was thirty-two, my weight had gotten up to 410 pounds. I grew up in a family that was always dealing with weight issues. My mom was on every low-fat diet program that was ever invented, and we always had rice cakes and skim milk in our kitchen. She finally became so frustrated by her inability to lose weight that she elected to have gastric bypass surgery in December 2003. I remember thinking at the time that if my next attempt to lose weight wasn't successful, I would likely follow in her footsteps. Thankfully it never came to that.

Decades of poor eating habits, little exercise, and a general sense of apathy about trying to live healthy had all caught up to me, but I thought that my weight was just the genetic hand that I had been dealt and there was absolutely no hope for ever overcoming it. It's a truly helpless, trapped feeling to believe that you will always be fat and unhealthy and there's nothing you can do about it. And that's exactly the way I had felt for most of my life.

Don't get me wrong, though; I had still tried all of the diet trends, including drinking Slim Fast, taking Dexatrim pills, and eating rabbit food all day long—but none of them seemed to help. In 1999 I tried an ultra low-fat (almost no-fat) diet because we have always been taught that eating fat makes you fat. I did surprisingly well on it and lost 170 pounds in just nine months. But there was one major problem: I was constantly hungry, which made me feel irritable, tired, and like I was going out of my mind! My wife, Christine, will tell you I was "hangry"—so hungry that it made me angrier than the Incredible Hulk! And my stomach was so bloated and big, I felt like I was a lot *worse* off than I was before my weight loss. One day Christine asked me if I would go to McDonald's and get her an Extra Value Meal, and I asked her if I could have a Big Mac meal "just this one time." Well, anyone who has ever been fat knows exactly what happened next.

That was the end of my low-fat diet. I gained back all of the weight I had lost and then some, until I made my way over the 400-pound mark for the first time in my life towards the end of 2003. Christine was becoming increasingly worried about my health, and for good reason. Although I didn't have any major health problems at the time, I was on prescription medications for high cholesterol, high blood pressure, and breathing issues. Even before that, in 1999, when I watched my brother Kevin deal with the ramifications of a series of heart attacks that nearly killed him, I knew I needed to find a way to become healthy that would be effective, safe, and sustainable over the long term. But getting to the point of desiring sincere change took a series of events that began in the fall of 2003.

At the time, I was a substitute teacher filling in for a middle-school English class. As I began writing instructions on the chalkboard for the lesson that day, I heard a voice yell out from the back of the room, "Man, Mr. Moore is really fffffffaat!" There were about two seconds of dead silence and then the loudest, most raucous roar of laughter you've ever heard. Ever so slowly I turned in the direction of the boy who said it and nervously joined in the laughter—mostly to keep from crying!

That was the first spark that led me to seriously look for a way to get my weight and health under control for good. Other signs that I desperately needed to do something about my obesity soon followed. There were countless reminders in my daily life that change needed to come quickly: constantly ripping the back side of my pants getting in and out of my car, having trouble getting up off the couch without assistance, not being able to go to the movies or fly on an airplane because I couldn't fit into the seats, and, most disturbingly, the judgmental looks on the faces of the people I encountered. It was all waking me to the reality that I had gone too far in allowing myself to reach this point.

One prominent and lasting memory is from the annual Fall Festival at my church. There was a rock-climbing wall there, and I was watching kids and adults alike scramble up and down that thing like they were Spider-Man. Of course, I thought to myself that it looked pretty easy and anyone could do it. So I stood in line to try my hand at scaling the wall for myself. After strapping on all the safety lines and gear to begin my climb, I stepped up to that wall and reached high for something to grab on to. When I attempted to step on one of the lower rock ledges, I had trouble lifting myself up because of my weight, and my foot slipped almost immediately. I tried again, and this time my foot slipped off and turned sideways, causing some minor pain in my ankle. I looked around at the crowd of people who were watching my every move and embarrassingly had to forfeit my attempt to climb the wall. That event remains an indelible experience in my mind, and at the time it was a blazing sign that something drastic had to change in the very near future. But what could I do that would be any better than all my futile attempts to lose weight in the past?

Just thinking about going on yet another diet made me sick to my stomach. It's considered common knowledge that to lose weight, you have to cut your calories, reduce the amount of dietary fat you consume, and exercise more, committing yourself to spending hours on the treadmill every week. So the default weight loss plan that so many of us fall into is a low-fat, low-calorie diet with regular trips to the gym several times a week.

But I vividly recalled the intense hunger and frustration that I experienced when doing that in 1999, and I realized there had to be a better way. It was fortuitous that my mother-in-law decided to get me a diet book for Christmas that year. Does any other son-in-law get weight loss books from their wife's mom as a holiday gift? I sure did! And in retrospect, I'm so glad and grateful for that year's Christmas present, which changed the course of my life forever. Thanks, Libby!

Turning It Around: Finding Dr. Atkins' Low-Carb, High-Fat Approach

My mother-in-law had given me diet books for Christmas in the past as a not-so-subtle reminder that she thought the man her daughter married was fat and needed to do something about it. I pretended that this wasn't hurtful, but it was. Hey, I knew I was a very large man and needed to get my weight under control. I just needed to find a healthy plan that would work for me. But that year, she gave me just the plan I needed to make that happen. The book was *Dr. Atkins' New Diet Revolution,* which outlined the diet created by the late, great Dr. Robert C. Atkins. I had heard so many things about this diet, good and bad, but I had never taken the time to actually read the book. Now that I owned it, I had no excuse not to find out what the Atkins diet was truly all about.

Funny enough, back in 1999, when I was doing that virtually no-fat diet, one of my friends asked me if my weight loss was the result of the Atkins diet. "Are you kidding me?" I responded. "No, that's one of the most unhealthy ways you could possibly use to lose weight." In fact, I added, "I would *never* do a low-carb diet like Atkins because it's too unhealthy." Famous last words. It just shows my ignorance and stubborn refusal to open my mind to other possibilities beyond the conventional dietary wisdom. Considering that today I'm best known as the "low-carb guy," there's a certain bit of irony in those words. Never say never.

Reading Dr. Atkins' book from cover to cover in the week between Christmas and New Year's, my initial reaction to the concept of a low-carb, high-fat diet was utter contempt. How on God's green earth can you eat more fat, like butter, full-fat cheeses, and red meat, without negative consequences to your health? Doesn't this Dr. Atkins guy know those things will clog your arteries, give you heart disease and cancer, and ultimately kill you? And what did he mean, cut way down on carbohydrate-based foods? Who could ever live without bread, pasta, sugar, and starchy foods? Aren't they what give your body the energy it needs to operate? What a complete and utter farce of a nutritional plan! Again, ignorance is bliss, and it all has a humorous twist looking back on this now over a decade later.

After mulling the book over during the next couple of days, I came to the stark realization that every single previous attempt I had made to lose weight involved cutting down on my overall fat intake, avoiding saturated fat in particular, eating lots of "healthy" whole grains, and counting every single calorie I put in my mouth. While this way of eating resulted in some initial, nominal weight loss, it always ended with my going back to my old eating habits and ultimately getting right back to the weight I was before I started (and eventually even heavier). I wanted to avoid that trap this go-round, and the low-carb, high-fat diet was the one weight-loss strategy I had never really tried before. Although I'd said just five years prior that I'd never go on the Atkins diet, here I was, primed to make it my New Year's resolution to lose weight on the famous low-carb approach.

On January 1, 2004, I took the plunge and started on the Atkins diet. It was a complete shock to my system. Up to that point, I had been consuming, on a daily basis, two whole boxes of Little Debbie snack cakes; big plates of pasta; sausage, egg, and cheese biscuits from McDonald's; honeybuns and giant chocolate chip cookies from 7-Eleven; and sixteen cans of Coca-Cola. Yes, I was a bona fide carb addict, through and through. I was easily consuming well over 1500 grams of carbohydrate in my diet every single day, and I didn't even think twice about it. Is it any wonder my weight got up to over 400 pounds?

Now I was suddenly shifting my diet from that ungodly amount of sugary, processed carbs down to just 20 grams a day. If you don't think that will have a physiological effect on your body, let me tell you—it does! I've never taken any drugs in my life, but if this comes even close to what it feels like to detox from crack cocaine or heroin, then remind me to never start.

Thankfully the pain of transitioning from my old diet to the Atkins diet only lasted a couple of weeks before I began feeling energetic and alive again. It was as if a dark cloud of despair had been lifted from my head and I realized that this was what "normal" was supposed to feel like. For the first time in my life, I began to feel hopeful that I was going to finally grab back the reins and take control of my weight and health.

Thanks mostly to repeated messages by the mainstream media, the Atkins diet has a reputation for being all about consuming gobs of meat, eggs, cheese, and bacon every single day. Contrary to popular belief, that is *not* the Atkins diet—not by a long shot! While the Atkins diet is too complicated to describe in just a couple of sentences, we'll talk about it in more detail in chapter 2. For now, know that Dr. Atkins did not write about just cutting your carbohydrate intake, eating "low-carb" packaged foods, and consuming only meat, eggs, and cheese.

So how did being on the low-carb, high-fat Atkins diet work for me? By the end of the first month, I had shed a total of thirty pounds. Holy cow! At the end of the second month, when I'd started going to the gym to do something with all this extra energy I suddenly had surging through my veins, another forty pounds were gone. By the end of one hundred days, I had lost one hundred pounds, and I knew something special was happening.

Words cannot describe how I felt going through this incredible journey, and I truly will never be the same again. Although it wasn't an easy road by any stretch of the imagination, I am so thankful I found the healthy low-carb lifestyle, because I went on to lose a total of 180 pounds in one year. More important than my weight loss, though, is the fact that low-carb living gave me my health back. All of those prescriptions I was taking for high cholesterol, high blood pressure, and breathing problems were history within nine months of being on the Atkins diet. Who says your health doesn't improve on the low-carb lifestyle? (We'll have plenty more to say about that later in this book.)

Let me express here my incredible gratitude to Dr. Atkins for helping to change my life through his diet. Since I read his book, my life hasn't been the same. I'm honored and blessed to have a very popular health blog and three highly respected iTunes health podcasts dedicated to spreading the message of low-carb living.

Though I never had the privilege of meeting Dr. Atkins in person, none of the success I have seen would have been remotely possible without the inspiration and education that came from that amazing man. His legacy is still making ripples in the world over a decade after his tragic death due to an accidental fall on an icy New York City sidewalk. His memory lives on in those of us who have picked up the baton and continued the race for low-carb living. God bless you, Dr. Atkins, for saving my life and the lives of millions of others who are still benefitting from your passionate zeal about low-carbohydrate nutrition and what it can do for our health.

And hats off to Jackie Eberstein, a registered nurse who worked with Dr. Atkins for three decades in his New York City clinic and who continues to teach about low-carbohydrate lifestyles today. Additionally, Veronica Atkins has been instrumental in continuing the legacy of her late husband by creating the Veronica and Robert C. Atkins Foundation and funding research professorships at prominent universities around the United States, including the University of California, Berkeley; the University of Texas, Southwestern; Columbia University; the University of Michigan; Washington University; and Duke University.

Giving Back: Showing Others How I'm "Livin' La Vida Low-Carb"

As 2005 rolled around and people began to comment on my very noticeable weight loss, they wanted to know how I did it. After telling my Atkins low-carb weight-loss success story at least a bazillion times, I finally decided I would create an online journal or website to talk about what I did and help others find the same success I did. I had barely even heard of a blog when I decided to start one in late April 2005, but a friend of mine told me how incredibly easy it was to set one up and start writing right away. Sharing my thoughts in written form had been a passion of mine since high school, long before the Atkins diet was ever on my radar screen. So it only made sense to combine my enthusiasm for and skill with the written word with my newfound commitment to healthy living the low-carb way. It was a match made in heaven, and I was ready to take on the world! And I've never looked back.

Almost immediately people began flocking to my new blog, which I dubbed *Livin' La Vida Low-Carb*. The blog's readership has grown exponentially since it first went online in April 2005, and it now reaches nearly 200,000 visitors each month. I've always been excited about educating, encouraging, and inspiring others who are overweight, obese, and unhealthy to do what I did. Because I've been there myself, I am able to share firsthand experiences of the struggles that come with being a sick, morbidly obese man, what it took to climb out of that hole, and the triumphs I experienced when I did. It's my passion to be a beacon of hope for those who think, as I once did, that they are destined to be fat and unhealthy forever. Never, ever give up!

In October 2006, I began doing what I'm perhaps most famous for when I started my iTunes podcast, *The Livin' La Vida Low-Carb Show with Jimmy Moore*. It has since become one of the top-ranked health shows on the Internet today with nearly 900 episodes featuring mostly informal interviews with the best and brightest names in diet, fitness, and health. I have two other iTunes podcasts—*Low-Carb Conversations with Jimmy Moore & Friends* and *Ask the Low-Carb Experts*—that I also use to spread the message of healthy living far and wide.

In August 2013, I released my book *Cholesterol Clarity: What the HDL Is Wrong with My Numbers?* with an internationally acclaimed publisher, Victory Belt Publishing. It features the expertise of my coauthor, Dr. Eric

C. Westman, an internist and researcher from Duke University in Durham, North Carolina, as well as exclusive interviews with twenty-nine of the world's foremost experts on cholesterol. I've been privileged to foster some truly meaningful relationships with a virtual who's who of everyone who matters in the world of health. That includes Dr. Westman.

I first met him in person at a low-carb nutritional health science conference in Brooklyn, New York, in January 2006. I had been blogging for less than a year but had an intense desire to learn more about low-carb eating, which had helped me shed the pounds and given me my health back, so I could share it with my blog readers. I was invited to a symposium put on by the Nutrition and Metabolism Society, which featured extremely technical lectures from medical doctors, diet researchers, and various other experts. My eyes were completely glazed over by the medical jargon being thrown around. My education in political science and English wasn't much help as I tried to make sense of it all.

When one of the lecturers started talking about a treatment concept known as PEP-C during his talk, the gentleman to my right leaned over to me and whispered, "Shouldn't that be a Diet PEP-C?" That man was Dr. Eric Westman. Right then and there I knew there was something special about him. As I got to know him and heard the story of how he initially got interested in low-carb diets, I realized he had a similar drive to get this message out to the people who needed it most. And it was his experiences with patients like me, who found success in achieving weight loss and regaining their health by reading Dr. Atkins' book, that led Dr. Westman to seek out answers about why the diet worked so well. That search led him to contact Dr. Atkins directly back in 1999.

Dr. Westman wrote a letter to Dr. Atkins, who called him and personally invited him to see how he treats patients with nutrition. So he took a trip to New York City to visit the Atkins Center for Complementary Medicine and observed how Dr. Atkins and his staff were helping patients suffering from obesity, diabetes, and many other chronic health issues using low-carbohydrate nutritional therapies as part of their medical treatment. Seeing all the incredible health improvements Dr. Atkins was getting in his patients, Dr. Westman asked if he would be interested in funding a study to scientifically demonstrate the effects of a low-carb, high-fat diet. He agreed, and Dr. Westman began to conduct the very first clinical trial on the Atkins diet.

The findings from the original pilot study, which followed fifty people on a low-carbohydrate diet over a six-month period, were presented at the American Heart Association's annual meeting in Chicago, Illinois, in November 2002. It showed that patients on a low-carb, high-fat diet lost weight and improved their cholesterol levels. But Dr. Westman wanted to see how the results he was witnessing compared to those on the popular low-fat diet. So he followed up the pilot study with a full-fledged randomized, controlled trial consisting of 120 people who were taught how to follow a low-carb diet or a low-fat diet and adhered to it for six months. What he found was that both groups showed improvement, but the low-carb diet was better for weight loss and improved metabolic syndrome best. The results of that study were published in the *Annals of Internal Medicine* in 2004 and paved the way for a bevy of groundbreaking research on carbohydrate-restricted diets.

The Next Step: A Ketogenic Diet

So you might be thinking right about now, "Your story of transforming your weight and health is great and all, but what the heck does all of this have to do with the title of your book, *Keto Clarity*? I haven't heard anything about that yet!" I'm so glad you asked. Once you understand our own experiences with nutrition and the positive impact that it can have on your health, then you'll be ready to learn why a low-carb, high-fat diet may be just what you need to improve your health—and that is where the idea of keto (short for *ketogenic*) comes into play. Just as we did for cholesterol and heart disease in *Cholesterol Clarity*, we're going to make the ideas behind keto and the reasons it works easy to understand and apply to your own situation.

We'll cut through all the massive amounts of confusion that have been brought on by widespread misinformation about keto. Yes, this book will likely rock the very foundation of everything you thought you knew about nutrition and health. But now that you've heard how we became interested and involved in closely examining the low-carb, moderate-protein, high-fat, ketogenic diet, it's time to share some of the knowledge, experience, and wisdom we have gained along the way to help you in your pursuit of optimal health.

The truth about ketogenic diets deserves to be told because it very well could be the missing piece of the puzzle for you, a family member, or a friend. There's never been a book like this one that puts together all the pieces about practical ways to implement a ketogenic diet for optimizing health. Think of this book as your definitive guide to the health benefits of a low-carb, high-fat diet. Let the reeducation process begin.

Let's Meet the Keto Experts

Through my podcasts, I have had the privilege and honor of interviewing hundreds of the best and brightest experts on a number of important health-related topics. Therefore, when I decided to write this book, I knew exactly who to reach out to for the latest information about ketogenic diets and their effects on health. It gives me great pleasure to introduce these twenty-two experts from around the world. You will find their quotes throughout the book in sections labeled "Moment of Clarity."

Zeeshan ("Zee") Arain, MBBS, MPHTM, FRACGP

 Dr. Arain received his medical degree from Monash University in Melbourne, Australia, and his Masters of Public Health and Tropical Medicine from James Cook University. Dr. Arain works as a general practitioner and is the team doctor for the Melbourne Football Club in the Australian Football League (AFL), one of the most elite professional sporting organizations in the world. He has a particular interest in the role of nutrition and exercise in the prevention and treatment of chronic disease and obesity. Dr. Arain has personally treated hundreds of patients using a well-formulated low-carbohydrate, high-fat, ketogenic diet to manage a variety of medical conditions, including diabetes, polycystic ovary syndrome, obesity, hypertension, epilepsy, gastroesophageal reflux disease, and irritable bowel syndrome. He has given several public lectures on nutritional ketosis and is in the process of developing a research study in this field. On a personal level, he has been in nutritional ketosis since 2012. Learn more about Dr. Arain at SouthYarra-Medical.com.au/doctors/5/dr-zeeshan-arain.

Bryan Barksdale

Bryan is pursuing his MD at the University of Texas Medical Branch and completing his PhD in neuroscience at the University of Texas at Austin. He is interested in the application of nutritional and lifestyle interventions, with a particular emphasis on ketogenic diets, in the treatment of neurologic diseases. He is the founder of the Austin Primal Living Group (Meetup.com/ Austin-Primal-Living-Group). Learn more about Bryan at his blog, *From Bench to Bedside*: FromBenchToBedside.wordpress.com.

Dominic D'Agostino, PhD

Dr. D'Agostino is an assistant professor in the Department of Molecular Pharmacology and Physiology at the University of South Florida, where he teaches neuropharmacology, medical biochemistry, metabolism, and nutrition physiology. His research is focused on developing and testing ketogenic diets, calorie-restriction diets, and ketone supplements as metabolic therapies for neurological diseases and cancer. His laboratory uses in vivo and in vitro techniques to understand the physiological, cellular, and molecular mechanism of metabolic therapies, including radiotelemetry (EEG, EMG), electrophysiology, fluorescence microscopy, confocal laser scanning microscopy, atomic force microscopy (AFM), biochemical assays, in vivo bioluminescence imaging, behavioral testing, and motor performance. Learn more about Dr. D'Agostino at DominicDAgostino.com.

William Davis, MD

Dr. Davis is a cardiologist and author of the *New York Times* bestseller *Wheat Belly: Lose the Wheat, Lose the Weight, and Find Your Path Back to Health*, the book that first exposed the dangers of genetically altered, high-yield wheat. He is a graduate of St. Louis University School of Medicine, with internship and residency training in internal medicine at Ohio State University Hospitals, a fellowship in cardiovascular medicine at Ohio State University, and advanced angioplasty training at Metro Health Medical Center and Case Western Reserve University Hospitals, where he subsequently served as director of the cardiovascular fellowship and assistant professor of medi-cine. He presently practices cardiology in suburban Milwaukee, Wisconsin. Learn more about Dr. Davis at WheatBellyBlog.com.

Jacqueline Eberstein, RN

Jacqueline was the Director of Medical Education at The Atkins Center for Complementary Medicine until Dr. Robert Atkins' death in 2003. She began working with Dr. Atkins in 1974. Her experiences were wide-ranging and included educating physicians, physician assistants, nurse practitioners, and nutritionists on the principles and protocols of the Atkins Lifestyle and complementary medicine. She contributed to a number of Dr. Atkins' books, newsletters, and other media outlets. In 2004 she coauthored the book *Atkins Diabetes Revolution,* and she continues to lecture, write, and consult on the Atkins philosophy both nationally and internationally. She is a regular attendee and lecturer on The Low-Carb Cruise and is currently a featured writer for *Carb-Smart* electronic magazine. Because of her extensive experience following the Atkins Lifestyle, she is one of the foremost authorities on low-carb, high-fat, ketogenic diets. Learn more about Jacqueline at ControlCarb.com.

Maria Emmerich

Maria is a wellness expert in nutrition and exercise physiology who has a passion for helping others reach their optimal health. She struggled with her weight throughout childhood and decided to study health and wellness so she could help others stop wasting their time being discouraged with their outward appearance and not feeling their best mentally. Maria understands the connection between food and how it makes us all feel on the inside and out. Her specialty is neurotransmitters and how they are affected by the foods we eat. She has authored eight books, including her 2013 release, *Keto-Adapted.* Weight loss is often a side effect of using diet to treat any number of health problems, including metabolic syndrome, alopecia, Hashimoto's thyroiditis, autoimmune diseases, gastrointestinal issues, and many other conditions. Learn more about Maria at mariamindbodyhealth.com.

Richard Feinman, PhD

Dr. Feinman is a professor of cell biology (biochemistry) at the State University of New York (SUNY) Downstate Medical Center in Brooklyn. He is a graduate of the University of Rochester and holds a PhD in chemistry from the University of Oregon. Dr. Feinman's original area of research was protein chemistry and enzyme mechanism and their applications to blood coagulation and hemostasis. His current interest in nutrition and metabolism, specifically in the area of diet composition and energy balance, is stimulated by, and continues to influence, his teaching in the medical school; he has been a pioneer in incorporating nutrition into the biochemistry curriculum. Dr. Feinman is the founder of the Nutrition and Metabolism Society (NMSociety.org) and former co-editor-in-chief of the journal *Nutrition & Metabolism*. Learn more about Dr. Feinman at FeinmanTheOther.com.

Nora Gedgaudas

Nora is a widely recognized expert on what is popularly referred to as the "Paleo diet." She is the author of the international bestseller *Primal Body, Primal Mind: Beyond the Paleo Diet for Total Health and a Longer Life.* She is also a highly successful and experienced nutritional consultant, speaker, and educator who has been widely interviewed on national and international radio, popular podcasts, television, and film. Her own podcasts are popular on iTunes, and numerous free articles on her website receive a wide readership. She maintains a private practice in Portland, Oregon, as a board-certified nutritional consultant and a board-certified clinical neurofeedback specialist. Learn more about Nora at PrimalBody-PrimalMind.com.

Ben Greenfield

Ben is a coach, author, speaker, ex-bodybuilder, and Ironman triathlete. He holds a master's degree in exercise physiology and biomechanics from the University of Idaho, and is a certified sports nutritionist (C-ISSN) and a certified strength and conditioning coach (CSCS). He has more than a decade of experience teaching professional, collegiate, and recreational athletes from all sports how to be healthy, inside and out. Ben is a consultant for WellnessFX, the host of the *Get-Fit Guy* and *Ben Greenfield Fitness* podcasts on iTunes, and the author of more than a dozen programs and books for optimizing health and performance, including his 2014 release, *Beyond Training: Mastering Endurance, Health, & Life.* He also trains and mentors physicians, personal trainers, and physical therapists from around the globe via his Superhuman Coach Network (SuperhumanCoach.com). Learn more about Ben at BenGreenfieldFitness.com.

John Kiefer

John is a physicist turned nutrition and performance scientist. He's been researching, testing, and verifying ideas about nutrition and physical performance that are often accepted unquestioningly for over two decades, and he helps others—record-holding Olympic gold medalists, power lifters, top-ranking aesthetic athletes, MMA fighters, and even Fortune 500 CEOs—apply his results for top performance. He's the author of two dietary manuals, *The Carb Nite Solution* and *Carb Back-Loading;* the free exercise manual *Shockwave Protocol;* and an ultra low-carb recipe book, *Transforming Recipes.* He's considered one of the industry's leading experts on human metabolism and macronutrient cycling and manipulation. Learn more about John at Body.io.

William Lagakos, PhD

Dr. Lagakos received a PhD in nutritional biochemistry and physiology from Rutgers, the State University of New Jersey, where his research focused on fat metabolism and energy expenditure. His postdoctoral research at the University of California, San Diego, centered on obesity, inflammation, and insulin resistance. Dr. Lagakos has authored numerous manuscripts that have been published in peer-reviewed journals, as well as a nonfiction book entitled *The Poor, Misunderstood Calorie.* He currently serves as a nutritional sciences researcher, consultant, and blogger. Learn more about Dr. Lagakos at CaloriesProper.com.

Charles Mobbs, PhD

Dr. Mobbs is a professor of neuroscience, endocrinology, and geriatrics at Mount Sinai Hospital in New York. He earned his Bachelor of Science degree in life sciences at the Massachusetts Institute of Technology and his PhD in cellular and molecular science at the University of Southern California with Dr. Caleb Finch, and he carried out his postdoctoral research with Dr. Donald Pfaff at Rockefeller University. His recent awards include 2010 Outstanding Mentorship at Mount Sinai, the Glenn Award for Basic Research in Aging in 2012, and Delegate, China Strategic Alliance of Prevention and Treatment Technology for Diabetes, Consortium of Chinese Central Government, University, Research, Institute, and Government in 2013. His research, which focuses on neuroendocrine and metabolic mechanisms of aging and age-related diseases, is described in more detail in a 2011 PBS documentary called *A Life-Saving Diet?* (http://video.pbs.org/video/2146699556). Learn more about Dr. Mobbs at Neuroscience.MSSM.edu/Mobbs.

Mary Newport, MD, FAAP

Dr. Newport graduated from the University of Cincinnati College of Medicine in 1978. She trained in pediatrics at Children's Hospital Medical Center in Cincinnati and in neonatology, the care of sick and premature newborns, at the Medical University Hospital in Charleston, South Carolina. She has provided care to newborns in Florida since 1983. She is currently taking leave to focus on writing; caring for her husband, Steve, who has early-onset Alzheimer's disease; and spreading the message about ketones as an alternative fuel for the brain. In 2008 she wrote an article that went viral on the Internet, "What If There Was a Cure for Alzheimer's Disease and No One Knew?" That article led to the publication of her 2011 book *Alzheimer's Disease: What If There Was a Cure? The Story of Ketones,* which conveys the story of a dietary intervention that has helped her husband and many other people with Alzheimer's and certain other neurodegenerative diseases, as well as the science of ketones as an alternative fuel for the brain and how to incorporate medium-chain fatty acids into the diet. Dr. Newport is a highly sought-after international speaker on the therapeutic use of ketones. Learn more about Dr. Newport at CoconutKetones.com.

David Perlmutter, MD, FACN, ABIHM

Dr. Perlmutter is the #1 *New York Times* bestselling author of *Grain Brain: The Surprising Truth About Wheat, Carbs, and Sugar—Your Brain's Silent Killers.* He is a board-certified neurologist and fellow of the American College of Nutrition who received his MD from the University of Miami School of Medicine, where he was awarded the Leonard G. Rowntree Research Award. He is a frequent lecturer at medical institutions and has contributed extensively to the world of medical literature. He has been interviewed on many national television programs, including *20/20, Larry King Live,* CNN, Fox News, *Fox and Friends, The Today Show, Oprah, The Dr. Oz Show,* and *The CBS Early Show.* He is the recipient of the Linus Pauling Award for his innovative approaches to neurological disorders and was awarded the Denham Harmon Award for his pioneering work in the application of free radical science to clinical medicine. He is the recipient of the 2006 National Nutritional Foods Association Clinician of the Year Award and was awarded Humanitarian of the Year by the American College of Nutrition in 2010. Dr. Perlmutter serves as medical director for the Dr. Oz Show. Learn more about Dr. Perlmutter at DrPerlmutter.com.

Stephanie Person

Stephanie is a self-taught expert on low-carb, high-fat, ketogenic diets. She began learning about the therapeutic effects of ketosis when her mother, who suffered from a terminal brain tumor, was given only six months to live. Stephanie's mom turned to a ketogenic diet, and not only did she beat that cancer, she's been thriving since 2007 because of those nutritional changes. Today, Stephanie is an active proponent and personal user of a ketogenic lifestyle. She recommends it with her personal training clients of all ages and shares encouraging YouTube videos about the benefits of ketosis (YouTube.com/FitSk8Chick). Learn more about Stephanie at StephaniePerson.com.

Ron Rosedale, MD

Dr. Rosedale is an internationally known expert in nutritional and metabolic medicine and founded the first metabolic medicine center in the U.S. in 1996 in Asheville, North Carolina. His interest in metabolic medicine began when he was a student at the Feinberg School of Medicine, Northwestern University, where he worked with one of the world's experts in the epidemiology of diet, cholesterol, and heart disease. Dr. Rosedale is a pioneer in applying concepts based on the biology of aging to reversing diabetes and heart disease through a nutritional approach that he developed to improve the cellular response to insulin, leptin, and mTOR. He has published a highly acclaimed book, *The Rosedale Diet*, and has been featured in many magazine and newspaper articles and dozens of radio and television interviews. For the last two decades he has lectured worldwide, including keynote presentations in Russia, Belgium, Brazil, Germany, and India. One lecture in particular, "Insulin and Its Metabolic Effects," has achieved worldwide acclaim. Learn more about Dr. Rosedale at DrRosedale.com.

Dr. Keith Runyan, MD

Dr. Runyan is a physician in private practice in St. Petersburg, Florida, who specializes in internal medicine, nephrology, and obesity medicine. He practiced emergency medicine for ten years before starting his private practice in 2001. In 1998, he developed type 1 diabetes at the age of thirty-eight. Although, his diabetes was fairly well controlled with intensive insulin therapy, he was plagued with frequent hypoglycemic episodes. In 2011, while training for an Ironman-distance triathlon, Dr. Runyan was looking for a better way to treat his diabetes and perform endurance exercise, and he decided to give the low-carb, high-fat, ketogenic diet a try. In February 2012, he began the diet for the treatment of his diabetes and learned that this diet was also effective for the treatment of numerous other conditions, including obesity. He added obesity medicine to his practice and became board-certified in obesity medicine in December 2012. Dr. Runyan completed an Ironman-distance triathlon on October 20, 2012, in a state of nutritional ketosis and feeling great. Learn more about Dr. Runyan at DrKRunyan.com.

Thomas Seyfried, PhD

Dr. Seyfried received his PhD in genetics and biochemistry from the University of Illinois, Urbana, in 1976. He did his undergraduate work at the University of New England and also holds a master's degree in genetics from Illinois State University. Dr. Seyfried was a postdoctoral fellow in the Department of Neurology at the Yale University School of Medicine and then served on the faculty as an assistant professor of neurology. Other awards and honors have come from such diverse organizations as the American Oil Chemists Society, the National Institutes of Health, the American Society for Neurochemistry, and the Ketogenic Diet Special Interest Group of the American Epilepsy Society. Dr. Seyfried is the author of *Cancer as a Metabolic Disease: On the Origin, Management, and Prevention of Cancer* (John Wiley & Sons). Dr. Seyfried's research focuses on gene and environment interactions related to complex diseases such as epilepsy, autism, brain cancer, and neurodegenerative diseases. Learn more about Dr. Seyfried at BC.edu/schools/cas/biology/facadmin/seyfried.html.

Franziska Spritzler, RD

Franziska is a registered dietitian and certified diabetes educator who strongly supports the use of carbohydrate-restricted diets for people struggling with diabetes, insulin resistance, obesity, and other endocrine issues. She personally follows a very low-carbohydrate, ketogenic diet for blood sugar control and has seen improvements in her health as a result. At the end of 2013, she left her position as an outpatient dietitian at a large veteran's hospital in order to go into private practice, where she uses a low-carbohydrate, whole-foods approach. She is also a freelance writer whose articles have been published online and in diabetes journals and magazines. Learn more about Franziska at LowCarbDietitian.com.

Terry Wahls, MD

Dr. Wahls is a clinical professor of medicine at the University of Iowa and a staff physician at the Iowa City Veterans Affairs Hospital, where she teaches medical students and resident physicians, sees patients in traumatic brain injury and therapeutic lifestyle clinics with complex chronic health problems that often include multiple autoimmune disorders, and conducts clinical trials. She is also a patient with a chronic progressive neurological disorder: secondary progressive multiple sclerosis, which confined her to a tilt-recline wheelchair for four years. She credits the Wahls Protocol, which is based on functional medicine, with restoring her health, enabling her to now ride her bike five miles to work every day. She released a book in 2014 about her experience called *The Wahls Protocol: How I Beat Progressive MS Using Paleo Principles and Functional Medicine.* Learn more about Dr. Wahls at Terry-Wahls.com.

William Wilson, MD

Dr. Wilson is an experienced family physician with a passion for helping his patients attain optimal brain function. He graduated from Macalester College in 1970 and received his MD from the University of Minnesota in 1974. He completed his residency at Regions Hospital in St. Paul in 1977 and spent over thirty years as a frontline family physician on the Iron Range in northern Minnesota, where he developed his approach to helping patients simultaneously improve their metabolic and brain health by using simple dietary changes. In 2008 he moved to the Boston area, where he now works as a hospitalist and lectures, publishes, and blogs about health. Dr. Wilson was one of the world's first medical professionals to demonstrate that our modern diet loaded with processed food can adversely affect brain function through a revolutionary new disease model he calls Carbohydrate-Associated Reversible Brain syndrome, or CARB syndrome. Using the CARB syndrome disease model as a guide, Dr. Wilson has helped thousands of individuals improve their health and brain function by following his simple and safe treatment protocols. Learn more about Dr. Wilson at CarbSyndrome.com.

Jay Wortman, MD

Dr. Wortman obtained a Bachelor of Science in chemistry and biology from the University of Alberta and an MD from the University of Calgary, and completed his residency in family medicine at the University of British Columbia. His interest in diet research led to a position at the UBC Faculty of Medicine, where he studied the effectiveness of a traditional diet for treating obesity, metabolic syndrome, and type 2 diabetes in the Namgis First Nation. The study was the subject of the CBC documentary *My Big Fat Diet*. Dr. Wortman is a recognized authority on low-carbohydrate, ketogenic diets for the treatment of obesity, metabolic syndrome, and type 2 diabetes. He was the recipient of Nutrition and Metabolism Society Award for Excellence in 2010 and the National Aboriginal Achievement Award for Medicine in 2002. Dr. Wortman currently practices in West Vancouver, where he lives with his wife and young children. Learn more about Dr. Wortman at DrJayWortman.com.

These really are twenty-two of the top-of-the-line experts on the subject of low-carb, moderate-protein, high-fat, ketogenic diets for therapeutic uses. Additionally, my coauthor, Dr. Eric Westman, is a bona fide expert on this and will once again be sharing his thoughts and experience on this subject throughout the book in the "Doctor's Note" entries scattered throughout the book. Here's his first!

DOCTOR'S NOTE FROM DR. ERIC WESTMAN: It's a pleasure to assist Jimmy Moore in translating the science about ketogenic diets into plain language that anyone can understand.

The "Moment of Clarity" quotes, since they're from doctors and experts, can use complex language, but don't let that scare you off. The purpose of this book is to provide a basic explanation of what ketones are, how ketosis works, and what you can do to follow a ketogenic diet. I want to make these ideas so crystal clear that you will want to learn even more about ketosis. To that end, there's a glossary of terms at the back of this book to explain any word or phrase that might trip you up.

Are you ready to gain some keto clarity? Oh yeah—let's do this.

Chapter 1
What Is Ketosis and Why Do You Want It?

MOMENT OF CLARITY I believe a low level of ketosis is actually the natural and most optimal state of metabolism for humans. Historically, our genome evolved to express itself most ideally based upon food sources available for our consumption. Thus, from an epigenetic perspective, the very best way we can communicate with our DNA is to provide it with the signals [that], over millennia, it has come to expect.

— Dr. David Perlmutter

So what in the world is this whole keto, ketone, ketosis, ketogenic thing all about, anyway? It's not a very common concept within mainstream health circles, and it's definitely not often talked about in a positive light. If it is discussed in the media or by health authorities, it's generally within a negative context (as we'll cover in chapter 3). Ketogenic diets have been used since the 1920s to very effectively control seizures in refractory childhood epilepsy. This version of the ketogenic diet uses a four-to-one ratio of fat to combined protein and carbohydrate.

Its association with a century-old therapeutic seizure treatment, along with Dr. Atkins' use of the "k" word in describing his low-carb, high-fat nutritional approach, have led some to label the ketogenic diet as an "extreme" diet. Nothing could be further from the truth. Beginning in chapter 16, you'll see that this nutritional approach has been shown to produce some remarkably positive results for a wide variety of the most common chronic diseases today.

MOMENT OF CLARITY The ketogenic diet was also used as a treatment for epilepsy in the 1920s and 1930s, although the mechanism for its effectiveness has yet to be elucidated. It also fell out of favor with the introduction of the anticonvulsant medication Dilantin in 1937.

— Dr. Keith Runyan

Unfortunately, as is often the case, the general public has not been properly exposed to the truth about ketosis because of some deliberate scaremongering about the dietary changes that are required to induce it. Just as cholesterol is not the culprit in heart disease (as we explained in *Cholesterol Clarity*), ketones are not some kind of toxic substance in your body that you need to avoid at all costs. We will attempt to calm any lingering fears you may have about going keto by explaining in simple English what it really is and why it's actually not a bad thing at all.

DOCTOR'S NOTE FROM DR. ERIC WESTMAN: Even in the medical literature, ketones get a bad rap. A classic paper written by metabolism experts in 2003 was entitled "Ketones: Metabolism's 'Ugly Duckling.'"

A good starting point is to define exactly what ketosis is. Ketosis (pronounced KEY-TOE-SIS) is a metabolic state that happens when you consume a very low-carb, moderate-protein, high-fat diet that causes your body to switch from using glucose as its primary source of fuel to running on ketones. Ketones themselves are produced when the body burns fat, and they're primarily used as an alternative fuel source when glucose isn't available.

In other words, your body changes from a sugar-burner to a fat-burner. Depending on your current diet and lifestyle choices, becoming keto-adapted can take as little as a few days and or as much as several weeks or even months. So "being in ketosis" just means that you are burning fat. Patience and persistence are an absolute must as you pursue ketosis.

Let me be very clear about something I know you're probably already thinking about: yes, this is a completely *normal* metabolic state. In fact, according to pediatric physician Dr. Mary Newport, newborn babies who are exclusively breastfed will go into a state of ketosis within twelve hours of birth, and ketones provide about 25 percent of their energy needs. Actually, 10 percent of the fats in full-term human breast milk is composed of medium-chain triglycerides (MCTs), which the liver converts to ketones. This is one reason why virtually every infant formula sold on the market today contains MCT oil and coconut oil, which "mimic the fats in breast milk." Dr. Newport says this is a clear indication that "from birth, and possibly before that, ketones play an important role."

If you have ever fasted by skipping breakfast after a good night's sleep, then you likely have begun producing trace amounts of ketones in your blood. If you consume a diet with very few carbohydrates, moderate levels of protein, and plenty of healthy saturated and monounsaturated fats, then these ketones will begin to increase until they dominate the way your body is fueled, to the point that very little glucose is needed to function. This book will clearly explain why this is a very good and even preferable state for your body to be in. And it makes sense that we were designed to eat this way, just as our hunter-gatherer ancestors once did.

 **MOMENT OF CLARITY** The superiority of ketone bodies over glucose fuel is clear from the large amounts of sustained energy you experience all day, every day.

— Stephanie Person

Dr. William Wilson, a family practitioner and expert on nutrition and brain function, explained that "throughout most of our evolutionary history, humans used both glucose and ketone bodies for energy production." He said that our Paleolithic ancestors used glucose as their body's preferred fuel when non-animal food was available, but during periods of food shortage or when animal-based foods were their primary source of calories, want to take a wild guess at what was sustaining them? You guessed it—ketones! "Thus, our ancestors spent most of their time in a state of ketosis," Dr. Wilson concluded. He added, "If our early ancestors hadn't developed a way to use ketones for energy, our species would have ended up on Darwin's short list eons ago!"

The Inuit are a perfect example of a ketogenic people that have, for thousands of years, consumed a diet that is very high in fat and very low in carbohydrates while maintaining full energy and stamina. In 1879, Frederick Schwatka, a US Army lieutenant, doctor, and lawyer, embarked on an Arctic expedition to look for records left by two Royal Navy ships that were lost in 1845. Schwatka began his journey in April 1879 with eighteen people, including several Inuit families; enough stored food to sustain them for one month; and ample amounts of hunting equipment. He learned that after a period of adaptation, consuming an Inuit diet with plenty of animal fat would sustain him even during hours of strenuous walking. This was one of the first understandings of keto-adaptation, and today, the process of transitioning from burning sugar to burning fat is known as the "Schwatka Imperative."

MOMENT OF CLARITY Ketone bodies provide an alternative fuel for the brain, heart, and most other organs when serum glucose and insulin levels are low— i.e., on a very low-carbohydrate diet. Ketone bodies are preferred over glucose by the heart and can be used as efficiently as glucose by most portions of the brain. There is a growing body of research supporting their beneficial effects on aging, inflammation, metabolism, cognition, and athletic performance.

– Franziska Spritzler

What Schwatka discovered, before the technology even existed to measure it, was that his body was increasing its production of ketone bodies, which appear in the blood primarily as beta-hydroxybutyrate (BHB). (We'll talk more about the various technologies for measuring the presence of ketones in chapter 8.) BHB is synthesized in the liver and can be used as an energy source by just about every cell in the body, including brain cells. So think of ketones the same way we currently look at glucose, as an energy source. In fact, look at how amazingly similar the molecular formulas for ketone bodies and glucose are. (This is a bit geeky, but it is important for you to see with your own eyes why ketones are used by the body as another fuel source when glucose is not present.)

Acetoacetate (urine ketone)

$$C-\overset{\overset{\displaystyle O}{\|}}{C}-C-\overset{\overset{\displaystyle O}{\|}}{C}-CoA$$

Beta-hydroxybutyrate (blood ketone)

$$C-\overset{\overset{\displaystyle OH}{|}}{C}-C-\overset{\overset{\displaystyle O}{\|}}{C}-OH$$

Acetone (breath ketone)

$$C-\overset{\overset{\displaystyle O}{\|}}{C}-C$$

C	carbon atom
O	oxygen atom
H	hydrogen atom
CoA	coenzyme A
—	single bond
=	double bond

Acetyl-CoA (basic unit of energy in the Krebs cycle, the process by which cells generate energy)

$$H-\overset{\overset{\displaystyle H}{|}}{\underset{\underset{\displaystyle H}{|}}{C}}-\overset{\overset{\displaystyle O}{\|}}{C}-CoA$$

Glucose

$$H-\overset{\overset{\displaystyle H}{|}}{\underset{\underset{\displaystyle H}{|}}{C}}-\overset{\overset{\displaystyle OH}{|}}{\underset{\underset{\displaystyle H}{|}}{C}}-\overset{\overset{\displaystyle OH}{|}}{\underset{\underset{\displaystyle H}{|}}{C}}-\overset{\overset{\displaystyle OH}{|}}{\underset{\underset{\displaystyle H}{|}}{C}}-\overset{\overset{\displaystyle H}{|}}{\underset{\underset{\displaystyle H}{|}}{C}}-\overset{\overset{\displaystyle OH}{|}}{\underset{\underset{\displaystyle H}{|}}{C}}=O$$

The point of sharing these formulas with you is to demonstrate the great similarity in the makeup of these molecules—they are all composed of the same elements (carbon, hydrogen, and oxygen), and they are all about the same size. This allows the body to use all of them as sources of energy. We shouldn't fear one over the other. When you are a sugar-burner, your body uses glucose as the fuel molecule of choice to give you energy to function. But when you shift your body over to being a fat-burner instead, the fuel molecule of choice becomes ketones. Regardless of whether you are using glucose or ketones as the primary fuel, your body still burns other fuels, like fatty acids and alcohol.

So why do you want to reduce the amount of sugar that you burn and transition to a state of ketosis? What benefits do you get from using ketone bodies as your primary source of energy instead of glucose? That really is the million-dollar question. Once you understand why reducing sugar-burning and increasing ketosis can help with certain aspects of your health, you will want to pursue it wholeheartedly.

DOCTOR'S NOTE FROM DR. ERIC WESTMAN: It is not surprising that so much research has centered on glucose metabolism as opposed to ketone and fat metabolism. During the last hundred years or so, since the standards of modern research were developed, most people's diets in the West have included carbohydrate, so it made practical sense to study the effects of carbohydrate and glucose.

Ben Greenfield, an elite triathlete who uses ketosis as a means for optimizing his athletic performance, says there are three primary reasons for entering a state of ketosis: 1) the metabolic superiority of fats as a fuel; 2) the mental enhancement that takes place with adequate ketone levels; and 3) the greater health and longevity that come from controlling blood sugar levels naturally in the presence of higher ketones.

Ketones are actually the preferred fuel source for the muscles, heart, liver, and brain. These vital organs do not handle carbohydrates very well; in fact, they become damaged when we consume too many carbs.

MOMENT OF CLARITY Ketones themselves are a great, and in many tissues—such as the brain—far better, fuel source than the alternative of glucose. I have always found beneficial answers to questions pertaining to health by studying the biology of aging. That is really how I became involved in treating diabetes with a high-fat diet. I became interested in type 2 diabetes as a model for accelerated aging. For over twenty years I have talked about the strong connection—perhaps even causation—between a high-fat, moderate-protein, very low-carbohydrate diet and slowing down the biological rate of aging.

– Dr. Ron Rosedale

Ketosis is also an excellent way to lose body fat. Ketones are merely a by-product of burning fat for fuel. In other words, burning fat generates ketones at the same time. When you are keto-adapted, you generate energy from both your body fat and dietary fat. However, when you consume excess carbohydrates, they turn into body fat, which cannot be easily accessed for fuel. This is why you want to be in a ketogenic state—it's fat-burning nirvana, baby!

A low-carb, high-fat, ketogenic diet is a very powerful and highly effective fat-burning diet that's especially useful for anyone who is overweight or obese. When I lost 180 pounds in 2004, most of the weight I dropped was in the form of body fat. My body was functioning very efficiently on fatty acids and ketone bodies because I wasn't feeding it the high levels of carbohydrates that would have kept it working as a sugar-burner. In chapter 5, we'll share more about how to determine what level of carbohydrate intake is best to get you into ketosis.

MOMENT OF CLARITY Weight issues tend to respond extremely well to a ketogenic approach, too. After all, it's hard to become efficient at burning body fat if you're busy burning sugar and starch all the time. Once those alternative fuels are out of the way, the body is more than happy to switch over to burning ketones and free fatty acids instead.

– Nora Gedgaudas

Here are some of the many health benefits that come from being in ketosis:

- ► Natural hunger and appetite control
- ► Effortless weight loss and maintenance
- ► Mental clarity
- ► Sounder, more restful sleep
- ► Normalized metabolic function
- ► Stabilized blood sugar and restored insulin sensitivity
- ► Lower inflammation levels
- ► Feelings of happiness and general well-being
- ► Lowered blood pressure
- ► Increased HDL (good) cholesterol
- ► Reduced triglycerides
- ► Lowered or eliminated small LDL particles (bad cholesterol)
- ► Ability to go twelve to twenty-four hours between meals
- ► Use of stored body fat as a fuel source
- ► Endless energy
- ► Eliminated heartburn
- ► Better fertility
- ► Prevention of traumatic brain injury
- ► Increased sex drive
- ► Improved immune system
- ► Slowed aging due to reduction in free radical production
- ► Improvements in blood chemistry
- ► Optimized cognitive function and improved memory
- ► Reduced acne breakouts and other skin conditions
- ► Heightened understanding of how foods affect your body
- ► Improvements in metabolic health markers
- ► Faster and better recovery from exercise
- ► Decreased anxiety and mood swings

I could go on and on, but I think you get the idea. Ketosis is something you may want to pursue if you are dealing with weight or health issues and you're not getting the results you desire with your current strategy. Later on in the book, we will discuss various health conditions that are dramatically improved by a ketogenic diet, responding even better to it than to some of the best medications available. It's exciting to think that you could see such amazing progress using nutrition rather than a drug.

MOMENT OF CLARITY I became interested in ketosis because I wanted to satisfy my own curiosity. I'd heard the anecdotes and they were compelling, but would it actually work in clinical practice, would it work for everybody, and how well? I wanted to help answer these questions for myself and the rest of the scientific community.

– Bryan Barksdale

So if ketosis is so desirable, then why has there been such deafening silence or even fierce negativity on the subject from health authorities? It really has received an undeserved negative reputation, which is especially unfortunate considering all the countless lives that it could improve. As with many things in life, it comes down to fear and a simple misunderstanding of what ketosis really means.

Part of the problem lies in the word *ketosis* itself, which closely resembles *ketoacidosis,* a medical term that's used to describe a life-threatening condition in type 1 diabetics. Many doctors scoff at the idea of allowing one of their patients to get into a state of ketosis because they immediately think of all the negative side effects associated with ketoacidosis. This confusion may have allowed many patients to remain in a diseased state when they could have seen tremendous improvements in their health with the use of a ketogenic diet. It's a sad reality that this kind of ignorance happens in the medical profession, with the very people we trust to be our purveyors of knowledge on health.

MOMENT OF CLARITY When I ask patients if they have ever heard of a ketogenic diet, the response is usually a blank stare. If someone is interested in trying this type of diet, they likely won't get much help from their traditionally trained family physician. Most doctors have little training in nutrition, and their only exposure to ketosis is in dealing with diabetic patients and ketoacidosis. As a result, many physicians have an inherent bias against ketosis. That means that most people will need to become self-educated. I believe this book you are reading will go a long way in correcting this information void.

– Dr. Bill Wilson

One of my blog readers is a sixty-year-old man named Chris from Austin, Texas, who shared a story about what happened when he went to see his doctor after being on a ketogenic diet for a while. When he went in for a physical as required by his job, Chris gave a urine sample to the nurse, who discovered the presence of ketones and began lecturing him about how dangerous that was. Chris's physician asked him if he was starving himself, but he explained he was eating a low-carb, high-fat diet. Upon hearing this, the doctor insisted Chris begin flushing the ketones out of his body immediately or else he would risk becoming diabetic. The doctor threatened to fail Chris on his physical if he did not comply.

"I was stunned," Chris told me. The doctor was dead serious.

Thinking back on this encounter , it frustrated Chris that so many other patients who are also trying to use ketosis to improve their health are being discouraged by the very people who have been charged with helping them get better. "It just goes to show you how ignorant these doctors can be," he said. "A simple misdiagnosis about ketones can wreak havoc with a person's livelihood." His doctor's confusion regarding what the presence of ketones during a routine lab workup underscores one of the biggest obstacles facing people who want to go on a ketogenic diet.

MOMENT OF CLARITY Nutritional ketosis is not ketoacidosis. Yet many in the medical profession have a knee-jerk reaction to ketones. Their knowledge is limited and possibly biased. Hopefully the information is this book will educate both consumers and health-care practitioners and ease their minds about a ketogenic diet. It is a safe and healthy tool to address the obesity crisis we face.

– Jackie Eberstein

Here's why doctors are so concerned about ketoacidosis: When diabetics do not get an adequate amount of insulin, their bodies respond as if they are starving. Their bodies think there's no more glucose to be had, either from diet or glycogen stores, and they switch to burning fat instead and ramp up ketone production so it can be used as an alternative energy source. The problem is, these diabetics aren't out of glucose—in fact, they have elevated levels of blood glucose. Insulin is the hormone that allows glucose into cells, and without it, the blood sugar has nowhere to go and accumulates in the bloodstream, even as the body can't stop making ketones. Once levels of the blood ketone beta-hydroxybutyrate (BHB) approach 20 millimolars, a diabetic patient will get very sick and may fall into a coma. Ketoacidosis can even be life-threatening. It's an extremely serious thing and certainly should not be messed around with. But keep in mind this condition only applies to type 1 diabetics and, very rarely, truly insulin-dependent type 2 diabetics.

It would be impossible for this sequence of events to happen to non-diabetics. If you can produce even a small amount of insulin in your body, ketones naturally remain at safe levels. As I'll share about in chapter 9, during my one-year experiment of purposely putting myself into a state of ketosis, I tested my blood ketone levels twice daily, and the highest reading I ever saw was 6.4 millimolar, less than one-third of the level considered dangerous.

MOMENT OF CLARITY Thousands of people are on low-carb diets, and with a substantial part of the medical community looking for harm, none has been found. This is strong, probably irrefutable, anecdotal evidence that low-carb diets are safe. So, we're all engaging in doing the experiments.

– Dr. Richard Feinman

Another key point to keep in mind is that the rise in blood ketone levels that leads to ketoacidosis in diabetics corresponds with a simultaneous elevation of blood glucose levels. But when ketosis is used for therapeutic purposes in everyone else, blood glucose actually drops. This is a major difference that should help put your mind at ease if you are at all concerned about stern warnings from your doctor.

In the next chapter, we'll look at the differences between keto and the traditional Atkins diet. Some people have made the two synonymous, and there are quite a few similarities between them. But we'll help you understand the subtle but very important differences that set them apart.

MOMENT OF CLARITY You may have heard that ketosis is a "dangerous state" for the body to be in. But ketosis simply means that your body is metabolizing a high amount of natural, fat-based energy sources. Ketones are molecules generated during fat metabolism—and that can be fat from the avocado you just ate or fat from the adipose tissue on your waistline.

– Ben Greenfield

Key Keto Clarity Concepts

→ **Ketogenic diets have traditionally been used to treat epilepsy.**

→ **Low-carb, high-fat diets are often characterized as "extreme," but they're not.**

→ **Ketosis causes your body to switch from a sugar-burner to a fat-burner.**

→ **Being in ketosis is a completely normal metabolic state.**

→ **Ketones play an important role in human health from birth.**

→ **Our Paleolithic ancestors were sustained by ketones during food shortages.**

→ **The Inuit recognized the importance of keto-adaptation.**

→ **The molecular formulas for glucose and ketone bodies are very similar.**

→ **Ketones are the preferred fuel source for the muscles, heart, liver, and brain.**

→ **When you're keto-adapted, your energy comes from body fat and the fat you consume.**

→ **Ketosis is something to consider if you're dealing with a weight or health issue.**

→ **The term *ketosis* is unfortunately often confused with *ketoacidosis*.**

→ Medical professionals sometimes think—incorrectly—that having ketones in the body is a harmful state.

→ Ketoacidosis happens when very high ketones occur simultaneously with very high blood sugar levels.

→ Nutritional ketosis happens when elevated ketones occur simultaneously with *low* blood sugar levels.

Chapter 2

What Makes Keto Different from the Atkins Diet?

> MOMENT OF CLARITY The typical protein levels of the Atkins diet are not ketogenic in our research mice and in fact promotes obesity in them. The Atkins diet is not really ketogenic, at least in mice.
>
> – Dr. Charles Mobbs

Ketogenic diets are certainly nothing new in nutrition, and we have the late, great Dr. Robert C. Atkins to thank for that. He played an integral part in the marketing of a low-carb, high-fat nutritional approach for burning fat and generating ketones. When Dr. Atkins first began promoting ketosis in the early 1970s, the methods for measuring for ketones were quite primitive. But thanks to some new technology that has come along in recent years, we can quantify ketone production to make sure you're at a level that will give you the benefits that ketogenic diets promise.

If you've ever followed an Atkins-style low-carb diet, you probably already understand the importance of being in a ketogenic state, in which your body switches from using carbohydrates as a primary fuel source to using fat—both dietary and stored body fat—and ketone bodies. Dr. Atkins was far ahead of his time when he made this key concept the centerpiece of his bestselling books. Despite their popularity, however, the "k" word quickly became taboo because of the confusion between it and diabetic ketoacidosis (as discussed in chapter 1). As much as Dr. Atkins tried to explain that ketosis is something different, the negative stigma stuck. That's why the marketing for the Atkins diet has always focused more on carbohydrate restriction and less on ketosis.

> MOMENT OF CLARITY There was no formal specific ratio of macronutrients we designed for each patient. Dr. Atkins knew what constituted 20 grams of carbs and the order in which he wanted to advance the plan. We watched changes in both breath and urine ketones as well as control of hunger and cravings as we advanced

the carb intake. Of course, improvement in lab values and presenting symptoms were also important markers of a healthier metabolism.

– Jackie Eberstein

This is one reason I believe the phrase "nutritional ketosis" is a much better way of framing the idea of becoming keto-adapted or fat-adapted through the use of a well-formulated high-fat, moderate-protein, low-carb diet—it helps us move away from fears of diabetic ketoacidosis and focus more on how we can control ketosis through nutrition. The term "nutritional ketosis" has become popular in the low-carb community in recent years thanks to a series of books written by low-carb researchers Dr. Stephen Phinney and Dr. Jeff Volek. They first used the phrase in their 2010 *New York Times* bestselling book *The New Atkins for a New You* (written with the coauthor of this book, Dr. Eric Westman). Phinney and Volek continued to use and define the term in their subsequent books *The Art and Science of Low Carbohydrate Living* and *The Art and Science of Low Carbohydrate Performance*. This branding of nutritional ketosis has been the best addition to the low-carb vernacular since we stopped talking about a "low-carb diet" and started talking about a "low-carb lifestyle."

Additionally, although Dr. Atkins talked about ketosis and the role it plays in improving health, he didn't communicate any concrete, practical advice for getting there. There are plenty of benefits to your health that come from being in a state of ketosis, so this understanding is crucial to grasp.

To truly get the health benefits of nutritional ketosis, you need to find the macronutrient mix that is right for *you* (which is what chapters 5 through 7 are all about). We owe a great deal of gratitude to Dr. Atkins for making us aware of the benefits of ketosis. Now we stand on his shoulders by taking that work to the next level and helping people figure out what it takes to produce ketones at the level where they can see the most benefit. A ketogenic diet isn't the same for everyone because we all have varying levels of carbohydrate tolerance, and that tolerance needs to be part of the equation, as you'll soon learn.

MOMENT OF CLARITY The underlying formula is for the most part the same: omit sources of dietary sugar and starch, moderate protein intake to no more than 2 to 3 ounces per meal, and then consume as much dietary fat from a variety of natural sources as desired or required to meet essential fatty acid needs and basic satiety. I also allow for the liberal consumption of fibrous vegetables and greens as a means of providing helpful phytonutrients and antioxidants. These may be consumed raw, cooked, cultured or fermented, or in the form of raw, unsweetened juice. Again, all this needs to be customized to a person's particular needs and tolerances, with careful monitoring of blood ketone levels for continued effectiveness.

– Nora Gedgaudas

So what are the biggest differences between a truly ketogenic diet and the low-carb, high-fat diet that Dr. Atkins made popular? It's a subtle but very important distinction.

Nutritional ketosis, in which the body burns fat to generate ketones for energy, can only be brought on by a low-carb, moderate-protein, high-fat diet. An Atkins-style low-carb diet may or may not meet those require-ments, since its focus tends to be more on restricting carbohydrates as the primary function. The only way to tell if an Atkins diet is inducing ketosis is by checking for ketones, and the gold standard is to measure ketones in the blood.

Traditionally, however, ketosis has been measured with urine testing strips. These strips turn pink or purple in the presence of ketones (spe-cifically, acetoacetate, the ketone body found in urine). But in their book *The Art and Science of Low Carbohydrate Performance*, Phinney and Volek recommend measuring blood ketones (beta-hydroxybutyrate) as a better and more reliable way of gauging ketone levels, allowing you to aim for the optimal range of 0.5 to 3.0 millimolar. We will go into great detail about all of this in chapter 8, but for now, just know that the technological advances in testing are one of the things that has made it possible to determine with greater accuracy if someone on an Atkins diet is in nutritional ketosis.

MOMENT OF CLARITY You won't know if you are in ketosis without checking beta-hydroxybutyrate levels. Until blood ketones are high enough, even more fine-tuning will be required. Over time, once ketosis is achieved, it is not nec-essary to measure all the time unless changes in diet or other stressors like exercise and travel occur.

–Dr. Zeeshan Arain

While it's not necessary to do any testing at all to experience the ben-efits of ketosis, you really are just guessing if you don't. Eating low-carb is certainly an important first step, but it's not the only thing you need to do to make your diet truly ketogenic. We're going to dive headfirst into that with more details in a few chapters, but first we'll see what major health organizations have to say about ketosis in the next chapter. As you can imagine, they have fallen prey to the massive amount of misinformation out there confusing nutritional ketosis with ketoacidosis.

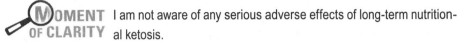 I am not aware of any serious adverse effects of long-term nutritional ketosis.

– Dr. Jay Wortman

Key Keto Clarity Concepts

→ **Ketogenic diets were first popularized by the late, great Dr. Robert C. Atkins.**

→ **The low-carb Atkins diet is subtly different from a ketogenic diet.**

→ **Changing the language we use to describe ketosis can assuage fears about it.**

→ **The Atkins diet never offered practical ways to increase ketone production.**

→ **What it takes to get into ketosis varies greatly from person to person.**

→ **An Atkins-style low-carb diet may or may not generate adequate ketones.**

→ **Without measuring ketone levels, eating low-carb, high-fat is a guessing game.**

Chapter 3

What Do Major Health Organizations Say About Ketosis?

 **OMENT** There is not enough data to prove that ketosis is dangerous.
OF CLARITY

– Stephanie Person

If you've been exposed to what has been most commonly said about ketosis brought on by a low-carb, high-fat diet, then no doubt you have heard such dastardly-sounding terms as "extreme," "toxic," "dangerous," "life-threatening," and "unhealthy." It amuses me to hear this kind of hyperbolic rhetoric used to describe a completely normal and natural metabolic state. But it's disappointing that some of the loudest voices against ketogenic diets are America's most prominent health and advocacy groups, as summarized below.

The positions these groups take on ketosis are all based on misinformation and confusion. We'll spend the rest of this book explaining the problems with their positions and giving you the truth about ketosis and its amazing health benefits. First, though, here's the misinformation we're trying to correct.

American Medical Association (AMA)

The AMA is a highly respected organization dedicated to educating those involved in the medical profession about the latest health information and standard of care. What do they have to say about ketosis? It is characterized as an "abnormal" state brought on by a "deficiency or the inefficient use of carbohydrates." Hoo boy! We'll go down that rabbit hole in chapter 5, but suffice it to say for now that there is no such thing as a carbohydrate deficiency.

Source: American Medical Association Concise Medical Encyclopedia (2006)

MOMENT OF CLARITY There is no such thing as an essential carbohydrate. . . . Anyone who tells you to start eating carbohydrates in order to fix a health problem is totally missing the point.

– Nora Gedgaudas

American Heart Association (AHA)

The AHA is another well-known and prestigious health group whose goal is to share information with the general public about heart-healthy living. They're no fan of saturated fat, which they claim raises your cholesterol levels to the point that you'll get cardiovascular disease. Thus, it shouldn't be surprising that they discourage the consumption of a low-carb, high-fat, ketogenic diet, stating that it is "high in protein," which brings on "a condition called ketosis" that "may cause nausea." Once again, ignorance about this subject matter abounds. In chapter 6, we'll explain how the *moderate* consumption of protein in the ketogenic diet helps bring about the production of ketones for a variety of purposes (and inducing nausea is not among them).

Source: American Heart Association website

MOMENT OF CLARITY I think it has been shown fairly conclusively that it is only the high-fat, not the high-protein, diet that produces the greatest health benefits in combination with a low carbohydrate intake.

– Dr. Ron Rosedale

The Mayo Clinic

The Mayo Clinic, one of the country's premier medical practices and research groups, acknowledges that the body does burn fat for fuel. But they claim that burning fat without consuming large quantities of carbohydrates creates "by-products" of ketone bodies that "build up in your bloodstream."

They admit ketones will suppress your appetite, but warn that being in ketosis will "cause fatigue and nausea." I'm getting nauseated just hearing this unfounded claim about ketogenic diets being repeated by people who should know better.

Source: The Mayo Clinic website

MOMENT OF CLARITY Ketones are an efficient and effective fuel for human physiology without increasing the production of damaging free radicals. Ketosis allows a person to experience nonfluctuating energy throughout the day as well as enhanced brain function and possibly resistance to malignancy.

— Dr. David Perlmutter

WebMD

WebMD has established itself as one of the most trusted websites for everyday people to find quality health information. Want to know what they have to say about ketosis? They say that when you don't consume enough carbohydrates in your diet to produce blood sugar, your body is "forced" to begin using blood sugar that is stored in the liver and muscles before eventually switching over to using ketones and fatty acids for fuel. Although they acknowledge ketosis can bring about weight loss (though they state that the weight lost is "mostly water"), WebMD gives a stern warning that this has some "serious" consequences, including "irritability, headaches, and enhanced kidney work" as well as "heart palpitations and . . . cardiac arrest." Yep, they went there. If this is your current thinking about the effect of ketones on the body, then keep reading this book to get the truth.

Source: WebMD.com

DOCTOR'S NOTE FROM DR. ERIC WESTMAN: The mistaken notion that the weight loss from a ketogenic diet is "just water weight" comes from a study with some significant problems. First, the study was only done for a few weeks—and many studies now show that over a period of months, considerable fat is lost, too. Second, the study showed that the water weight returned when the research subjects started eating carbohydrates again. When you start changing your lifestyle, you are not supposed to go back to eating the same amount of carbohydrate that you did before—which led to the water weight regain!

Medical News Today (MNT)

MNT is a popular online health news aggregator website, and they describe ketosis as "a potentially serious condition if ketone levels go too high." Ostensibly they're referring to diabetic ketoacidosis, but they go on to say that while ketosis lowers hunger, societies around the world are dependent on carbohydrates (not ketones and fat) for energy. If "insulin levels are too low," the website says, stored body fat needs to be broken down and "toxic" levels of ketones are produced, making the blood more acidic and causing damage to your kidneys and liver. Unfortunately, this isn't a joke. And yet this is the kind of misinformation that we find online about ketosis brought on by consuming a low-carb, high-fat diet.

Source: MedicalNewsToday.com

MOMENT OF CLARITY Most doctors are not aware that a ketogenic diet lowers insulin levels and that this directly affects the kidney's handling of sodium and water. Low insulin levels are a signal to the kidney to excrete sodium and water, whereas the high insulin levels associated with a high-carbohydrate diet are a signal to retain sodium and water. Physicians are taught to prescribe diuretics and advise salt restriction in sodium- and water-retaining states such as hypertension and congestive heart failure. But they should be taught the much more powerful effect of restricting carbohydrates.

– Dr. Keith Runyan

Dr. McDougall's Health and Medical Center

I would be remiss if I didn't include the position on ketosis from one of the most outspoken proponents of a vegan diet (as well as a vehement opponent of the Atkins and other low-carb diets), Dr. John McDougall. I interviewed Dr. McDougall on Episode 686 of *The Livin' La Vida Low-Carb Show with Jimmy Moore* podcast in 2013. Google it and listen in for one of the most entertaining examples of what dietary dogma looks like. According to his website, Dr. McDougall believes that carbohydrate is the "body's primary fuel" and that the production of "acidic substances called ketones" will zap your appetite, resulting in a decrease in calorie consumption, nausea and fatigue, and lowered blood pressure. He says this is the same thing that happens to someone during starvation, which is why he describes ketosis as "the make-yourself-sick diet."

Source: DrMcDougall.com

> **MOMENT OF CLARITY** During periods of starvation or fasting, the human brain can very easily switch over to using ketones as an alternative to glucose. As we age, we tend to use less glucose and switch over to alternative fuels in the brain. If we are on a high-carbohydrate diet, which suppresses ketone production, and have no other dietary source of ketones, we cannot expect that our brains will function as well. So many people have at least some degree of insulin resistance, and ketones could provide alternative fuel to cells that are not taking in glucose well, allowing for better cell function and ultimately healthier organs, including the brain.
>
> – Dr. Mary Newport

American Diabetes Association (ADA)

As the leading advocacy group for diabetics in the United States, the ADA certainly has a thing or two to say about ketosis. They describe ketones as "a chemical produced when there is a shortage of insulin in the blood and the body breaks down body fat for energy." That's a true statement. But then they note that "high levels of ketones" can lead to "diabetic ketoacidosis and coma." They leave out the most important factor: that high levels of ketones alone can't result in ketoacidosis; it only occurs when very high blood sugar and very high levels of ketones happen simultaneously. And with no distinction about who exactly this would happen to (as we've already noted, mostly type 1 diabetics who have no insulin production), this kind of statement can only cause fear and panic about getting into a state of ketosis. In fact, in their definition of *ketosis*, the ADA describes it as "a ketone buildup in the body that may lead to diabetic ketoacidosis," with warning signs of "nausea, vomiting, and stomach pain."

Worse, the ADA's recommended treatment for diabetes is to eat carbs and just cover up their effects with insulin. There's nothing wrong with taking insulin if it's truly needed, of course, but even diabetics will experience all the problems that come from eating carbs that everyone else does (with far worse effects than those experienced by nondiabetics). And the ADA makes no mention of the therapeutic use of ketogenic diets in controlling blood sugar and improving health—including for the millions of people with type 2 diabetes who stand to benefit from a ketogenic diet (we'll tell you more about that in chapter 16). It's all just gloom and doom.

Given that their audience is composed of the people most at risk for ketoacidosis, the ADA's concern is understandable. But as long as their blood sugar stays low, diabetics have nothing to fear from ketosis—and since research shows that it can be hugely beneficial in controlling diabetes (again, more on that in chapter 16), they may actually have a lot to gain.

Source: Diabetes.org

MOMENT OF CLARITY Our studies suggest that the major protective effect of ketosis is a significant reduction in glucose metabolism. This is the opposite of diabetes.

— Dr. Charles Mobbs

Just as all these highly regarded organizations—each considered a major authority on health—have formed a united front on cholesterol as the cause of heart disease, (as we shared in *Cholesterol Clarity*), so too have they ganged up on ketosis, describing it as something that is both undesirable and dangerous. These messages from doctors, dietitians, and know-it-all gurus are totally bogus. That's why we decided to write this book: to present the arguments for ketosis that are nearly the exact opposite of what all these health groups are saying.

A ketogenic diet has been shown to produce certain therapeutic effects that have led many doctors and other health professionals to recognize it as even more beneficial than the most advanced medications on the market today. In the next chapter, we'll learn more about medical practitioners whose patients are following low-carb, high-fat, ketogenic diets, with some rather stunning results.

Key Keto Clarity Concepts

→ **Mainstream health organizations often use hyperbolic rhetoric to describe ketosis.**

→ **Most information we hear about ketosis is incorrect.**

→ **Confusion about the difference between ketosis and ketoacidosis is a major issue.**

→ **Major health authorities are united in their opposition to ketosis.**

Chapter 4

Doctors Are Using Ketogenic Diets with Great Success

> **MOMENT OF CLARITY** Humans went into ketosis every winter for thousands of generations. Being in a low level of ketosis is the more natural state for our metabolism. We do have metabolic flexibility and can operate on amino acids, glucose, or fat.
>
> — Dr. Terry Wahls

When you hear the leading health authorities say all those negative things about ketosis that we shared in the last chapter, it may lead you to the conclusion that no physician would ever want a patient to be put on a ketogenic diet. But the truth is that plenty of doctors are prescribing a low-carb, high-fat nutritional approach for patients who are dealing with a wide variety of chronic health problems, and they are seeing dramatic improvements on the diet. (I created a resource at LowCarbDoctors.blogspot.com to help connect patients to people in the medical profession who are willing to think outside the box to make them healthier.) In this chapter, we'll highlight a few of them and show how the low-carb, high-fat diet is working for their patients.

When Littleton, Colorado–based family physician Dr. Jeffry Gerber began teaching his patients about the connection between their illnesses and their diets of refined and processed foods, he got their attention fast. Unlike many of his medical colleagues, though, Dr. Gerber didn't pull out his prescription pad and advise his patients to take medications. Instead, he encouraged them to embrace a lifestyle change that included a significant reduction in carbohydrate consumption and a deliberate increase in natural dietary fats (including saturated fat). These changes, he explained, would help them control their hunger, promote weight loss, and ultimately heal the particular health calamity they were facing.

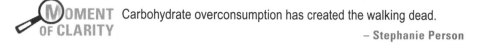

MOMENT OF CLARITY Carbohydrate overconsumption has created the walking dead.

– Stephanie Person

Dr. Gerber doesn't leave his patients to their own devices with this information. Instead, he tracks their changes in weight, cardio-metabolic markers, and other key health parameters to see how the shift to a ketogenic diet is working for them. Obesity and type 2 diabetes are two obvious signs of metabolic disease and inflammation brought on by a substandard diet. Dr. Gerber does not subscribe to the notion that we get fat and unhealthy by eating too much. He describes this as "shortsighted" and points instead to the *quality,* not *quantity,* of calories that come from a diet of whole, unprocessed, nutrient-dense foods, like those our early ancestors ate.

What's more, Dr. Gerber says, a large part of skyrocketing health-care costs stems from using ineffective therapies for chronic health problems, including the overuse of drugs, surgeries, and other treatments that never address the underlying issues. Making nutritional therapies, such as the ketogenic diet, the first step in treatment would save costs and perhaps even result in better patient outcomes than if we continued to do things the same way we always have. This may sound like a simple solution, but its advocates have had a difficult time spreading the message in the face of the federal government's nutritional guidelines and the heavy lobbying by the processed food industry, which stands to lose billions of dollars in annual revenue if people begin cleaning up their diets.

MOMENT OF CLARITY Unfortunately, conventional nutritional guidelines continue to support the concept that carbohydrates are required for life and health. The most recently updated American Diabetes Association dietary guidelines, for example, urge Americans, with or without diabetes, to get at least 130 grams of carbohydrates per day to provide sufficient nutrition for the brain. But this runs contrary to the science and real-life experiences in which humans have survived without dietary carbohydrates for months, even years.

– Dr. William Davis

Interestingly, Dr. Gerber notes that there have been many clinical trials in recent years showing that a low-carb, high-fat, ketogenic diet results in greater, more sustainable weight loss, improved cholesterol markers, and better blood sugar control than the standard low-fat, high-carb diet. It really comes down to understanding the role of insulin metabolism and that dietary carbohydrates, not saturated fat, drive the increase in insulin production and inflammation that are at the heart of virtually every chronic health problem people are dealing with today—including heart disease, which is the result of inflammation and oxidative stress, not high cholesterol. (Our book *Cholesterol Clarity* explores this idea in detail.) The scientific evidence is a major reason Dr. Gerber is so enthusiastic about using ketogenic diets with his sick patients. And having seen how much his patients improve on a ketogenic diet, he knows from experience that it's the therapy that will work best for them. He's not alone.

Dr. Sue Wolver, an internist based in Richmond, Virginia, has been practicing medicine for twenty-five years and once dished out the standard low-fat diet advice that has become so many doctors' default position on nutrition. When her patients failed to see the kind of health improvements she was expecting, she just assumed they weren't following her advice very well. But after watching patient after patient fail to lose weight or improve their health despite frequent conversations she had with them about diet and exercise, Dr. Wolver knew there had to be a better way.

MOMENT OF CLARITY Most of my clients are just amazed at how great they feel. And unlike with other diets, you aren't starving all day long and battling cravings. You get to eat tasty, full-fat foods and don't get any cravings. There is a sense of freedom for most people since they no longer think about food all day, as they used to on low-fat diets.

– Maria Emmerich

It wasn't until Dr. Wolver hit middle age herself that she realized why her patients were so unsuccessful on the low-fat diet. She suddenly found, she said, that "my own advice didn't even work for me!"

"Despite my adherence to a low-fat diet and exercise, every time I got on the scale I weighed more," Dr. Wolver explained. "That's when I first started thinking the advice I had been giving might actually be wrong."

She attempted to cut calories and reduce her fat intake, but it just didn't work. In fact, Dr. Wolver even decided to go on a low-carb diet, but she combined that with a low-fat diet, with predictable results. "I was hungry all of the time," she recalled. "That was no good because I couldn't stick with it."

MOMENT OF CLARITY Counting calories is likely not very helpful for most people. On a ketogenic diet you will be less hungry and your improved brain function will guide you in the amount of food you should be eating. Isn't it marvelous to have your brain back?

– Dr. Bill Wilson

But Dr. Wolver had an epiphany when she heard physician and researcher Dr. William S. Yancy, Jr., give a talk entitled "Taking the Fat Out of the Fire," in which he discussed the health benefits of a low-carb, high-fat, ketogenic approach to nutrition. She "was hooked." Dr. Wolver immediately began putting herself into a state of ketosis and the weight poured off and stayed off, and all without the intense hunger she had previously experienced. These days, she uses herself as a prime example for her patients of how ketogenic diets can help them with their weight and health issues.

"I now teach this to my patients and have had overwhelming success 'reversing' many of the conditions I spent years simply managing before," Dr. Wolver said. "I have taken patients off their insulin, blood pressure medications, and CPAP machines while watching their cholesterol, blood pressure, and blood sugar numbers improve."

MOMENT OF CLARITY I have seen mood stabilization, reduced or eliminated depression, reduced or eliminated anxiety, improved cognitive functioning, greatly enhanced and evened-out energy levels, cessation of seizures, improved overall neurological stability, cessation of migraines, improved sleep, improvement in autistic symptoms, improvements with PCOS (polycystic ovary syndrome), improved gastrointestinal functioning, healthy weight loss, cancer remissions and tumor shrinkage, much better management of underlying previous health issues, improved symptoms and quality of life in those struggling with various forms of autoimmunity (including many with type 1 and 1.5 diabetes), fewer colds and flus, total reversal of chronic fatigue, improved memory, sharpened cognitive functioning, and significantly stabilized temperament. And there is quality evidence to support the beneficial impact of a fat-based ketogenic approach in all these types of issues.

– Nora Gedgaudas

Dr. Wolver says these kind of results make using a ketogenic therapeutic approach worth it despite the general negativity about low-carb, high-fat diets.

"This is the most fun I have had in my career practicing medicine," she shared. "I just wish it hadn't taken me twenty-five years to figure this out."

The same could be said about Dr. Lowell Gerber, a cardiologist from Freeport, Maine, who went through a similar epiphany about nutrition in his own life that has revolutionized the way he looks at his patients.

When Dr. Gerber himself began packing on the pounds, he realized, just as Dr. Wolver did, that he was wrong when he pushed a low-fat diet on his patients all those years and then accused them of lying about following it because they were gaining weight and seeing worse cardiac risk factors. Dr. Gerber is now ashamed of the arrogance he displayed in shaming his patients.

"It was an unnerving realization that my patients were not ignoring my advice," he admitted. "When I [tried a low-fat diet] myself, the truth was facing me. The low-fat diet just did not work for them, or for me."

> **MOMENT OF CLARITY** [In Dr. Atkins' clinic, we] made it clear to our patients that this was not a low-fat diet. Natural fats were an important part of the plan.
> – Jackie Eberstein

This sent Dr. Gerber on a personal investigation into what went wrong. He started looking at all the evidence for a low-carb, high-fat, ketogenic diet and began implementing it into his own lifestyle in 2009. After seeing its positive effects on his own weight and health and that of members of his family who became keto-adapted, Dr. Gerber started recommending it to his patients with obesity, pre-diabetes, type 1 and type 2 diabetes, high blood pressure, abnormal cholesterol readings, polycystic ovary syndrome, and metabolic syndrome.

Even among those who are open-minded or even enthusiastic about ketosis, Dr. Gerber explains, ketones are usually seen only as an alternative fuel source when glucose availability is limited—most do not understand their broader therapeutic role. But the health benefits ketones provide is something that Dr. Gerber has seen many times in his patients.

"Ketones upregulate the NRf2 pathway, which modulates many genes involved with inflammation and cell function," he noted. "For example, the genes regulating pro-inflammatory cytokines are downregulated, resulting in less [inflammation], and the gene regulating IL-10, an anti-inflammatory cytokine, is upregulated. "

What this means is that eating a ketogenic diet lowers inflammation naturally, without the use of prescription medications such as statins. It's this inflammation that is the true culprit in heart disease, and the fact that ketosis reduces systemic inflammation is further evidence supporting the use of a low-carb, high-fat diet for improving heart health.

MOMENT OF CLARITY Ketosis reduces systemic inflammation as long as blood glucose is also lowered. Having higher levels of ketones with simultaneously higher levels of blood glucose would be unhealthy. Most of the side effects encountered on a ketogenic diet occur when blood glucose levels remain elevated. Indeed, insulin insensitivity, elevated blood glucose, and dyslipidemia will result from excessive consumption of the ketogenic diet.

– Dr. Thomas Seyfried

Dr. Gerber connected the dots when he began digging deeper into the role of ketosis. "So [a] low-carbohydrate, high-fat, ketogenic diet may have multiple beneficial effects, in addition to its role as an alternative fuel source, preferred by the heart, muscle, and brain," he concluded.

In fact, rather than immediately putting his cardiac patients with high cholesterol—including patients with the genetic form of heterozygous familial hypercholesterolemia (which simply means a predisposition for high cholesterol passed on by one parent)—on a statin drug, he instead prescribes a ketogenic diet to "stabilize and perhaps reverse existing plaque" in their arteries. He monitors this through regular checkups on their blood markers and CT scans of the heart. Dr. Gerber is "eliminating the need for statins" in even his most high-risk patients because of the anti-inflammatory effect of ketosis.

"The toxicity of statins, including myopathy, cognitive decline, sexual dysfunction, cataracts, skin cancer, and diabetes, are all avoided while improving the patient outcome," he reported. "The low-carbohydrate, high-fat, ketogenic diet is the foundation of it all."

MOMENT OF CLARITY It is not ketones that I generally follow when patients are on my diet. I prefer to follow those markers that also change during calorie restriction, even though my diet doesn't restrict calories. I wrote a paper that showed that patients on my low-carb, high-fat diet had changes in laboratory parameters that almost exactly simulated the changes seen in calorie restriction. These markers essentially indicate both a high affinity and ability to burn fatty acids and ketones, not glucose, as one's primary fuel. These markers include significant reductions in blood serum insulin, leptin, triglycerides, and free T3 from initial baseline. One would also see an increase in the size of LDL particles. However, historically, I've done this mostly to appease a person's cardiologist and keep them off of cholesterol-lowering drugs.

– Dr. Ron Rosedale

Dr. Gerber also is seeing improvement in patients with non-alcoholic fatty liver disease (NAFLD), psoriasis, and Crohn's disease, who all "have done very well" on a ketogenic diet. He plans to continue to educate himself further on all the benefits that this way of eating has to offer. The same could be said about the next traditionally trained physician who prefers to use nutritional therapies to help improve the health of his patients.

New York City–based family practitioner Dr. Fred Pescatore, author of several bestselling books, including *The Hampton's Diet* and *Thin For Good*, says using a low-carb, high-fat, ketogenic approach with his patients is "the only way I practice medicine."

"I don't know how every other doctor on the planet doesn't do this," Dr. Pescatore said. "I first learned about it twenty years ago working with the late, great Dr. Robert C. Atkins."

MOMENT OF CLARITY The Atkins Lifestyle saved my life by helping me avoid diabetes. I control my reactive hypoglycemia symptoms, which were never understood or explained to me until Dr. Atkins diagnosed me. I am on a 20- to 30-gram maintenance plan now because of my advancing age and postmenopausal hormone status. I have plenty of energy, low cardiovascular risk, and low to normal blood pressure. I have also been told I do not look my age. I wear a size 4 and can maintain that without hunger or cravings. And the inches lost while in ketosis are a plus.

– Jackie Eberstein

And all those years of being tutored by Dr. Atkins himself taught Dr. Pescatore that this isn't just some weight loss gimmick but rather "a way to unlock your body's healing energies."

"I have treated every condition from allergies to weight loss and everything in between using a ketogenic therapeutic approach to practicing medicine, and it has worked every time," he explained.

Dr. Pescatore has seen a ketogenic diet normalize cholesterol numbers, completely zap hunger, eliminate bloating, improve chronic fatigue, and much more. Dr. Pescatore sees the ketogenic diet as a way to "enjoy life to the fullest and eat really well along the way."

"This isn't a diet for rabbits," he concluded.

MOMENT OF CLARITY I followed a low-carbohydrate diet for over a year in an effort to lower my postprandial blood glucose levels, which frequently topped 180 at the one-hour mark. While I had some success with low-carb, it wasn't until I began consuming a ketogenic diet limited to 30 to 35 grams of carbohydrate per day that my postprandial blood sugar levels completely normalized. I've had several clients who struggled with extra weight for years and were finally able to successfully lose weight once they started a well-balanced ketogenic diet. Their satiety and energy levels increased, and several have reported improvements in the quality of their skin—a benefit I've personally experienced as well.

– Franziska Spritzler

Canadian physician Dr. Jay Wortman discovered the ketogenic diet through "pure serendipity" after he developed type 2 diabetes in November 2002. While he started to investigate what he could do about his illness, Dr. Wortman immediately removed all starch and sugar from his diet. Thinking he would be taking a drug to manage his diabetes for the rest of his life, as he had seen in his work as the resident doctor at a diabetic children's camp, he was astonished at how well removing carbs from his diet controlled his disease.

"Nowhere in my medical training or practice had I encountered carbo-hydrate restriction as a therapeutic option, yet I very quickly discovered that the elimination of carbs was dramatically reversing all the signs and symp-toms of my type 2 diabetes," Dr. Wortman said.

Within a few days of cutting carbs, he noticed that his blood sugar had normalized, he was feeling dramatically better, and he'd begun losing weight at about a pound a day. The "unexpected and seemingly miraculous" results he was seeing were perplexing to Dr. Wortman because he had never been exposed to information about the therapeutic effects that could come from a change in diet.

"Like most of my physician colleagues, I had only a passing familiarity with nutritional science and virtually no knowledge of ketogenic diets," he said. "But after my condition quickly improved on a low-carb, high-fat diet, I became quite curious and started looking into the scientific literature."

What Dr. Wortman found was confirmation that he was not an anomaly. Study after study showed the benefits of the way of eating that he had stumbled on almost by accident. Needless to say, he became "fully committed" to the low-carb lifestyle and has "made it [his] mission to understand this phenomenon and to explore the possibility that it could be a viable therapy for others."

Dr. Wortman was working with the First Nations and Inuit Health Branch of Health Canada, where type 2 diabetes was a significant problem, and he surmised that the modern diet full of sugar and refined carbohydrates was the primary driver of this epidemic. He became quite intrigued by the idea that returning to their traditional hunter-gatherer diet of meat, seafood, and fat would result in a turnaround in health for the First Nations people. He had the great fortune to meet several prominent American researchers and clinicians, who helped him design a dietary trial to test his theory.

"Dr. Stephen Phinney, Dr. Eric Westman, and Dr. Mary Vernon collaborated with me to launch the dietary trial in a small Canadian First Nations community known as Alert Bay," Dr. Wortman recalled. "I was approached by a documentary filmmaker named Mary Bissell who wanted to record the study in a film for the Canadian Broadcasting Corporation."

That documentary, *My Big Fat Diet,* was broadcast nationally on Canadian television several times. It followed several of the study participants and documented their weight loss and improved health markers. The success of the study captured the attention of Health Canada, Canada's federal health department, which agreed to fund a research position for Dr. Wortman so that he could continue to look into the health benefits of a ketogenic diet.

"I developed other study protocols, some of which led to clinical trials, others of which did not get funded," he said. "I learned during this period that it is very hard to challenge the conventional thinking in the area of nutritional science. I came to understand just how perfectly the system is designed to protect the status quo."

MOMENT OF CLARITY The ketogenic diet was likely the diet of hunter-gatherers for most of our existence on Earth, except possibly in tropical areas where fruit was available much of the year. It has been known since the early 1900s that nutritional ketosis occurred in many of the Inuit people living in the Arctic, in whom chronic disease was a rarity. Therefore, it is safe to presume that ketones have been part of a healthy human metabolism for millennia.

– Dr. Keith Runyan

Nevertheless, the popularity of *My Big Fat Diet* and other similar documentaries have helped to keep the momentum for examining ketosis going strong. When the funding from Health Canada eventually ended, Dr. Wortman said it's likely "the office that produced the Canadian Food Guide was relieved." He returned to clinical practice, where he offers his patients hope that ketosis can improve their health.

"One of the striking things I find in offering up the ketogenic diet to my patients is the incredibly positive feedback I get from the ones who have corrected their poor metabolic markers, lost weight, and greatly improved their general sense of well-being through this simple dietary approach," Dr. Wortman noted. "It is not uncommon to see tears of gratitude from my patients. I have yet to see that ever happen after prescribing a drug."

MOMENT OF CLARITY Many chronic symptoms and health conditions—such as fatigue, sleepiness, mood disorders, insomnia, gastroesophageal reflux disease, lipid disorders, high blood pressure, headaches (including migraines), gas, bloating, irritable bowel syndrome, joint inflammation, acne, and difficulty concentrating, to name a few—will improve on a ketogenic diet. Treating lifestyle conditions with lifestyle change such as this can make us a healthier and less drug-dependent country.

– Jackie Eberstein

These are just a few of the many medical professionals who understand the importance of ketogenic diets for their patients' health.

But to experience all the health benefits of ketosis, you need to follow certain guidelines—restricting carbs, moderating protein, increasing fat intake, and testing ketone levels. We'll explore each of these concepts much more extensively over the next few chapters.

Key Keto Clarity Concepts

→ **Plenty of doctors are prescribing ketogenic diets for their patients.**

→ **Lifestyle changes should be the first treatment option.**

→ **Low-carb, high-fat diets improve a variety of health markers.**

→ **Low-fat diets have failed patients who have tried it.**

→ **Ketogenic diets can reverse many chronic diseases.**

→ **Ketones provide therapeutic health benefits; they're not just an alternative fuel source.**

→ **The ketogenic diet can improve health without prescription drugs.**

→ **Doctors are not trained in using low-carb, high-fat diets with patients.**

→ **Returning to a traditional hunter-gatherer diet can improve health.**

→ **Nutritional research is intended to protect the status quo.**

Remember this acronym to help you get into and stay in ketosis!

Keep carbs low

Eat more fat

Test ketones often

Overdoing protein is bad

Chapter 5
Find Your Carbohydrate Tolerance Level

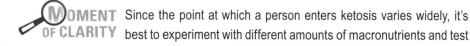 **MOMENT OF CLARITY** Everyone is different and has different carb-tolerance levels. Some people, especially athletes, can maintain ketosis with as much as 100 grams of carbs a day. But most people need to be at 50 grams or less, and those with metabolic syndrome typically need to stay below 30 grams of total carbs a day to produce adequate ketones.

– Maria Emmerich

If I had a dollar for every time someone asked me how many carbohydrates they should be eating to get into ketosis, I'd be a very rich man. The honest answer is, I have no earthly idea! We each have our own metabolic history and varying amounts of damage done to our bodies over the course of our lives. Attempting to undo the sins of our past is impossible, but you can make an assessment of where you are now and respond accordingly.

In an effort to simplify what it takes to get into nutritional ketosis and experience the benefits that come from being in that healthy metabolic state, some have suggested that all you need to do is lower your carbohydrate intake to less than 50 grams daily. I suppose if we were all identical robots and programmed in exactly the same way, then that formula would probably be applicable. But the reality is we are not all the same, and we all have varying levels of carbohydrate tolerance that we have to determine for ourselves. Because I used to weigh over 400 pounds and was severely addicted to refined, processed carbohydrates, my ability to tolerate carbs is going to be radically different from that of someone who has been thin their entire life with no blood sugar abnormalities.

MOMENT OF CLARITY Since the point at which a person enters ketosis varies widely, it's best to experiment with different amounts of macronutrients and test beta-hydroxybutyrate (blood ketone) levels using a blood ketone meter. For instance, one person might maintain serum beta-hydroxybutyrate levels above 1.0 millimolar consistently when consuming 60 grams of carbohydrate and 110 grams of protein daily, while another may need to limit carbohydrates and protein to 25 grams and 80 grams per day, respectively, in order to achieve the same blood ketone levels. At lower carbohydrate and protein intakes, the percentage of calories coming from fat increases even if the amount does not change. Most people in nutritional ketosis consume anywhere from 65 to 80 percent of their calories as fat.

– Franziska Spritzler

That is why it would be impossible for us to give you a specific amount of carbohydrates to consume in order to get into ketosis. You can only determine that figure through personal experimentation. But once you figure out your carb tolerance, you'll be well on your way to keto success.

Keep carbs low

Eat more fat

Test ketones often

Overdoing protein is bad

So when we say "Keep carbs low," the definition of "low" can vary. I think it's safe to say that almost everyone who wants to be in ketosis needs to keep total carbohydrate intake below 100 grams a day, and the vast majority need to keep it under 50 grams a day. If you are especially sensitive to carbohydrates (in general, that means most people who are overweight or obese, or who have metabolic syndrome or type 2 diabetes), then you might need to consume under 30 or even 20 grams a day. You can only know for sure by giving it a go and seeing where you stand in your carbohydrate tolerance.

MOMENT OF CLARITY The level of carbohydrate restriction prescribed at the beginning of therapy for each patient [in Dr. Atkins' clinic] was dependent on a variety of factors, such as the amount of weight to lose or gain and especially the tendency for insulin/blood sugar imbalances. Anyone with a personal or family history of diabetes, gestational diabetes, PCOS, metabolic syndrome, high triglycerides, high-carb diet, and carbohydrate cravings would be started on a ketogenic plan of less than 40 grams. Most often we began patients on a 20-gram-per-day induction phase. We also had the benefit of extensive blood sugar and insulin testing to determine the proper starting level.

– Jackie Eberstein

Here is a three-step plan to help you determine your carbohydrate tolerance.

1. Start at 20 grams total carbs daily and adjust from there.

If you want to get into ketosis and have no idea how many carbs you should be eating, a great starting point is 20 grams total carbohydrates daily. This is the level at which ketosis should definitely be happening, so try it for two weeks to see how you do. For the purposes of generating ketones, the popular low-carb notion of "net carbs" (calculated by taking total carbohydrates and subtracting the fiber) doesn't apply.

MOMENT OF CLARITY The culprit in the inability to create adequate ketone levels is still, overwhelmingly, eating too many non-fiber, sugar-forming carbohydrates. People may think carbs like starches are perfectly fine to eat and that they will not prevent ketosis. But that would be wrong. It takes a mere 100 grams of glucose-producing foods per day—which can easily come from starches—to prevent ketosis.

— Dr. Ron Rosedale

I spoke with Marylou Van Hintum, a bariatric nurse based in Manassas, Virginia, about this, and she noted that she has seen so many frustrated patients counting "net carbs" and wondering why they are not seeing results.

"When sugars are present in foods, even with comparable amounts of fiber, [it] can trigger a sugar response in many people," she explained. "After eating something like a 'low-carb tortilla,' you may find yourself craving either more of the tortilla or even things that have more carbohydrates than you have been eating, including fruits."

Unfortunately, as she noted, these foods are not conducive to producing adequate ketones to stave off hunger and cravings and make positive changes in your health. Far too many people fall for the "net carb" marketing gimmick or purchase products whose packaging advertises "no sugar added," "gluten-free," or "great for low-carb diets." Van Hintum says you need to be aware of how these food choices are impacting you if you want to be in ketosis.

"Learn to listen to your body if you are eating a low-carb, high-fat, ketogenic diet," she said. "And if you happen to find yourself suddenly craving foods, especially carbohydrates, that's your cue to reassess what you are eating to make sure [that] there aren't any hidden sugars in your diet [and that] you haven't consumed too many carbohydrates for your personal tolerance."

Van Hintum's best advice for ketogenic dieters: "Steer clear of sugars in any form (including starchy carbohydrates) because they can be disruptive to the way you process and metabolize foods."

MOMENT OF CLARITY When it comes to carbohydrates and simple sugars, follow my simple rule—when in doubt, throw it out! Carbohydrates should come mainly from non-starchy vegetables rather than starchy and refined carbohydrates. For people with any degree of insulin resistance (and that would be just about everyone these days), it will be a challenge to achieve and maintain ketosis if you consume more than 50 grams of carbohydrates per day. Those without insulin resistance can probably consume more carbohydrates and still maintain a state of ketosis.

– Dr. Bill Wilson

After two weeks, if you are producing ketones (we'll share how you can measure them in chapter 8), try slowly adding 5 to 10 grams of daily carbohydrates for one week, to see what that does to your ketone production. If ketones remain at the appropriate level of nutritional ketosis, then you're able to tolerate a little more carbohydrate in your diet. Keep repeating this weekly until ketone production begins to decline, then return to the level of carbohydrates that allows you to continue producing adequate ketones.

If you're not producing ketones after two weeks of consuming 20 grams of total carbohydrates daily, consider going down to 10 to 15 grams daily and restricting your protein consumption (a topic we'll explore more in the next chapter). Don't lose hope; it is possible to get into ketosis even if you are especially carbohydrate sensitive. Believe me, I understand this completely. I cannot consume more than about 30 grams of carbohydrates daily or I get out of ketosis. You have to remain committed and purposeful in your pursuit of this. It won't just happen by chance.

DOCTOR'S NOTE FROM DR. ERIC WESTMAN: Carbohydrate tolerance is an individual thing. In general, you can eat more carbs if you are younger and more active. But postmenopausal women tend to have to keep their carb consumption really low.

2. Test your triglyceride levels.

You're probably thinking, *Hey, I thought this book was about ketosis. Why in the world are we talking about a part of the cholesterol panel?* It's a good question. If you read our previous book, *Cholesterol Clarity*, then you already know that one of the best ways to lower your triglycerides (a key measurement of fat in the blood) is by slashing your carbohydrate intake. If your triglycerides are over 100, then you are most likely eating too many carbs for your personal tolerance level. The blood chemistry doesn't lie.

MOMENT OF CLARITY Heart disease is not caused during the fasting state; it is caused during the hours after eating. After a meal, there is a flood of digestive by-products of the meal that generally lasts six to eight hours. While fats make a modest contribution to after-meal lipoproteins, carbohydrates cause a much larger, though delayed, after-meal surge in lipoproteins. This delay occurs because the liver must convert sugars from carbohydrates to triglycerides . . . . Remove carbohydrates and the after-meal surge in lipoproteins is substantially diminished, thereby further reducing heart disease risk.

– Dr. William Davis

Let's say you got your triglycerides tested and they came back at 137. While that's not super-high and would fall within what your doctor thinks is "normal," it does indicate you are very likely eating a few more carbohydrates than your body can properly manage. Cut out all sugar, grains, and starchy foods for thirty days and then get tested again. What you'll probably discover is that your triglycerides drop like a rock below 100, and most likely even below the optimal goal of 70. This is a simple yet highly accurate way to figure out how many carbs are right for you.

After thirty days of cutting out all sugar, grains, and starches, you can slowly reintroduce small amounts of these foods one at a time to see what happens. The *New York Times* bestselling book *It Starts with Food,* by Dallas and Melissa Hartwig, is a great resource for exploring this kind of an elimination diet.

3. Get a glucometer and test your blood sugar levels.

MOMENT OF CLARITY It is helpful to measure fasting blood glucose and fasting beta-hydroxybutyrate levels and monitor progress by keeping a journal.

Testing can be done with glucose and ketone monitors and test strips that can easily be purchased over the counter.

— Dr. Mary Newport

One of the best ways to determine just how sensitive you are to carbohydrates is to get a blood glucose meter—also known as a *glucometer*—from your local pharmacy or drugstore. Test your blood sugar in a fasted state when you first wake up and then at thirty-minute intervals for at least two hours after consuming a specific food. This will show you exactly how your body is responding to that food. Ideally you will see your blood sugar rise only slightly one hour after eating and then return to baseline within two hours of your meal.

For example, let's say your blood sugar when you first wake up is 88 and it only rises to 105 an hour after eating a breakfast of bacon and eggs. Two hours after eating, it comes back down to 89. That's a perfect response. But let's say your fasting blood glucose is 88 and you eat a whole-wheat bagel with fat-free cream cheese or oatmeal topped with margarine. Don't be surprised if you see your blood sugar soar to 160 and not even come close to returning to baseline within two hours. (This is an extreme example, of course, because you're probably not eating grains and fat-free foods—or at least you shouldn't be after you read this book!)

MOMENT OF CLARITY Cutting carbs to the level of ketosis has numerous health benefits in addition to normalizing weight. Not only does a ketogenic diet tap into the excessive fat stores people are carrying around, but this level of carb restriction also improves blood sugar and insulin balance, making one less likely to develop type 2 diabetes. If one has diabetes, it allows for better blood sugar control with less or even no medication.

— Jackie Eberstein

Getting into ketosis is harder for some than others. Dr. William Wilson explains that people with type 2 diabetes or severe insulin resistance will very likely have trouble getting their blood sugar levels low enough. He suggests two shortcuts for circumventing this issue to help you produce ketones: first, have your doctor write a prescription for a medication called *metformin*, and second, get an over-the-counter supplement called CinSulin, a concentrated form of cinnamon. There is also a supplement called Glycosolve, made with berberine and banaba leaf, that helps to normalize blood sugar levels naturally.

Dr. Wilson says that these "work by improving insulin sensitivity and reducing glucose production, resulting in more stable blood glucose." If you need an additional boost in controlling your blood sugar, Dr. Wilson says 200 to 800 mcg daily of chromium picolinate (also available from any vitamin store) will "help push you into ketosis if you have insulin resistance." He describes these supplements to his patients as "mommy's little cheaters" for getting into ketosis!

MOMENT OF CLARITY I started measuring serum insulin nearly twenty years ago, when there was only one laboratory in the country doing it, and found out quite quickly that as a person's diabetes was rapidly improving, as indicated by lower, more stable glucose measurements, their serum insulin numbers would also greatly decrease. What was happening was that they were becoming more insulin sensitive. Their cells were able to listen to insulin much better; their ability to "hear" insulin was being much improved. They were getting much more bang for their insulin buck.

— Dr. Ron Rosedale

Watch out for carbs that you may not even realize you are consuming. A blog reader once wrote to me wondering why she wasn't seeing the ketone production she expected when she was eating what she thought was a good low-carb, high-fat, ketogenic diet. I asked her to share a sample of her menus with me, and she revealed that she ate "a lot of fruit." When I explained that fruit is high in carbohydrates, she retorted, "But I didn't think you had to count the carbs in fruit because it's natural!"

I hate to break it to you, but cutting carbs means cutting them from any source, no matter how natural. Yes, fruit has some great micronutrients, but the sugar content will make it next to impossible for many people to produce adequate ketones while eating fruit. As Dr. Westman prominently displays on the walls of his patient rooms, "Fruit Is Nature's Candy."

MOMENT OF CLARITY The most common criticisms I have heard of the ketogenic diet, none of which have any basis in science, include the question "Aren't you missing important nutrients by excluding or severely limiting 'healthy whole grains' and fruit?" My response is that all the nutrients found in grains and fruit can be obtained from meat, poultry, fish, eggs, non-starchy vegetables, nuts, and seeds, while avoiding the carbohydrates and gluten that accompany grains and fruit. That said, low-sugar fruits, including berries, could be a part of the ketogenic lifestyle.

— Dr. Keith Runyan

If your carbohydrate tolerance allows for a little bit of fruit, then go for it. But it's probably not a good idea for many. Again, pull out your glucometer and see what happens to your blood sugar when you eat fruit. If you see a large spike or sustained elevations in your blood sugar levels, then you know you probably can't have that many carbohydrates.

Here's something interesting you probably never thought about before. Do you know what it means if you experience intense cravings for sugary, carb-rich foods when you start eating a ketogenic diet? No, it's not permission for you to give in to that desire for pizza, chocolate chip cookies, or whatever else you think your body wants you to consume. But at the same time, you don't want to fight the signal your body is giving you.

Here's the secret—when this craving hits, it's not carbohydrates that your body really wants. It's—surprise, surprise! —dietary fat! Don't believe me? The next time you get a hankering for something carb-y, resist that urge and instead eat a high-fat snack. I like to roll up a slice of full-fat cheese with grass-fed butter in the middle. It may sound crazy, but don't be surprised when your desire for carbs relaxes. We'll talk more about why fat consumption is a critical element of ketosis in chapter 7.

MOMENT OF CLARITY There are three reasons why people fail to reach a ketogenic state: too many carbohydrates, too much protein, or not enough fat. Most people who attempt to follow this approach understand the importance of limiting carbohydrates. In my experience, when they fail to do so it's usually because of their strong cravings for sweet or starchy foods. We now believe that these cravings are the cardinal symptom of a form of food-induced brain dysfunction that I describe as Carbohydrate-Associated Reversible Brain syndrome (CARB syndrome). Unless you suppress these cravings, you're often doomed to failure in your pursuit of ketosis.

– Dr. Bill Wilson

Once you nail down your carbohydrate tolerance, the next important step in pursuing ketosis is determining your personal protein threshold. The idea of moderating your protein intake is probably going to be new to a lot of you because low-carb diets are often described as "high-protein." But the reality is that they should be high in fat, and protein needs to be monitored just as carbohydrates are. We'll explore this more in the next chapter.

DOCTOR'S NOTE FROM DR. ERIC WESTMAN: Adults have only about 1 teaspoon of sugar (5 grams) in their entire bloodstream! You can do this calculation with a little bit of high school math. First, you have to know that there are 100 milligrams of sugar in a deciliter of blood. A milligram is one thousandth of a gram; a deciliter is one tenth of a liter. Then you have to know that an adult has about 5 liters of blood. So multiply out these conversions—100 milligrams/deciliter x 1 gram/1000 milligrams x 10 deciliters/liter x 5 liters of blood—and you get 5 grams of sugar in the entire bloodstream. Half a bagel has approximately 10 grams of carbs, so from that one food you are consuming twice the amount of sugar present in your blood. It's no wonder that the blood glucose levels go up after eating carbs!

Key Keto Clarity Concepts

→ **Determining your carbohydrate tolerance level is key to getting into ketosis.**

→ **Each individual has a different level of carb tolerance.**

→ **It takes personal experimentation to find your carb tolerance.**

→ **Overweight and diabetic people tend to be more sensitive to carbs.**

→ **The idea of "net carbs" doesn't apply in pursuing ketosis.**

→ **Beware of "low-carb" food marketing claims.**

→ **Start your carbohydrate intake at 20 grams daily, then raise it by 5 to 10 grams daily for one week.**

→ **When ketones drop, return to the previous level of carb intake.**

→ **If there's no ketone production at 20 grams, drop carbs and protein intake.**

→ **Test triglycerides and aim for under 100 to determine carb tolerance.**

→ **Cut out sugar, grains, and starchy foods to drop triglycerides.**

→ Get a glucometer and test your blood sugar levels often.

→ Test blood sugar at thirty-minute intervals for two hours after meals.

→ Metformin and supplements can help lower blood sugar.

→ Be aware of which foods contain carbs and may be preventing ketosis.

→ "Fruit is nature's candy" for people who are struggling making ketones.

→ When carb cravings hit, your body is really screaming for fat.

→ Try a slice of full-fat cheese with grass-fed butter in the middle to satisfy cravings.

→ There is only about one teaspoon of sugar in your entire bloodstream.

Chapter 6
Determine Your Personal Protein Threshold

MOMENT OF CLARITY There is an important distinction that separates many low-carb diets from ketogenic diets. That would be the fact that a low-carb diet tends to be one that is high in protein. But since our bodies can't store excess protein, it has to be used. When we consume too much protein, our bodies convert much of it into glucose through a process called *gluconeogenesis*. This can increase blood glucose levels and keep you from achieving ketosis.

– Maria Emmerich

Once you've determined your carbohydrate tolerance level, it's time to move on to what is arguably one of the most important elements of ketosis. As much as carbohydrate restriction is an absolute must if you are going to produce adequate ketones to experience the health benefits they provide, it would be foolish to neglect the critical role that protein plays. That's why the O in the acronym "KETO" warns that "overdoing protein is bad."

I can guess what you're thinking right about now: *But I thought protein was a good thing. Now you're saying it's bad?* Don't misunderstand me; protein is indeed good for your body, and like dietary fat, it's an absolute must (unlike carbohydrate, which is not an absolute or "essential nutrient"). But the body is able to reuse the protein that it already has in its muscles, bones, and other tissues. Up to 300 grams of the protein in your body can be recycled every day! Many people think that we need to eat protein in order to get an adequate amount for our body, but actually, since our body can reuse protein it already has, the amount you need to consume in your diet probably isn't as much as you think. And

Keep carbs low

Eat more fat

Test ketones often

Overdoing protein is bad

keep in mind that eating protein in excess can be a problem, especially for those who are already sensitive to carbohydrate. It's time for me to get a little bit geeky on you, but I promise this will make the reasons for moderating protein much clearer.

> DOCTOR'S NOTE FROM DR. ERIC WESTMAN: *In nutrition, the term* essential nutrient *means a nutrient that cannot be made by the body and therefore must be consumed for the body to function properly. Essential nutrients for humans include water, vitamins, minerals, protein, and fat. Carbohydrate is not an essential nutrient!*

The first time I heard anything about the possible negative consequences of consuming too much protein was at the Nutritional and Metabolic Aspects of Carbohydrate Restriction conference in Brooklyn, New York, in January 2006. There I learned about a fascinating concept that forever changed the way I look at protein, because it holds the key to why some low-carb diets work well and others do not. Understanding this revolutionary concept will put you light years ahead of most doctors, dietitians, and all the other health gurus out there.

So what is it? *Gluconeogenesis* (pronounced GLUE-CO-NEE-OH-GEN-EH-SIS). Glucosaywhatsaywhat?! Get used to hearing and saying this word, because it is a fundamental principle that can determine whether or not you are successful on the ketogenic diet.

MOMENT OF CLARITY Gluconeogenesis provides all the glucose you need to restore thyroid function and heal the thyroid when you are in ketosis. Several of my keto clients have now thrown away their thyroid medications.

– Stephanie Person

Gluconeogenesis (sometimes abbreviated as *GNG*) is the body's way of creating glucose by breaking down proteins, and it occurs mainly in the liver. You may have heard that the body needs carbohydrates to function—and it does—but gluconeogenesis allows your body to make its own carbs from the protein you consume, so that you don't have to get carbs from dietary carbohydrates. Pretty nifty, huh? The body is incredibly efficient at making exactly what it needs from the raw materials we feed it. In this case, if glucose levels in the blood are low because there is little to no carbohydrate in the diet, then protein becomes the body's source of glucose.

The liver normalizes and maintains blood glucose levels in the body by creating glucose through gluconeogenesis. During those times when the body is not taking in any food (for instance, while you are sleeping), the liver goes to work on gluconeogenesis, using amino acids (the building blocks of protein), lactic acid, and glycerol (a molecule that comes from fat) to create the sugar the body needs. Hormones such as cortisol and insulin control this process to maintain steady levels of glucose. After about one day of fasting, the glycogen (stored glucose) in the liver is reduced enough that gluconeogenesis begins in earnest and the liver begins creating glucose for the body. Isn't this an incredible process?

MOMENT OF CLARITY Individuals having underlying issues with, say, abnormally depressed cortisol or possibly even adrenal autoimmunity leading to depressed cortisol may experience abnormal cravings for carbohydrates and unexpected low blood sugar symptoms in the face of impaired gluconeogenesis.

— Nora Gedgaudas

So what is the significance of gluconeogenesis in ketosis? If you are consuming a low-carb, high-fat diet and you're eating the right amount of carbohydrate for your personal tolerance level, but you're still struggling to see adequate ketone production, it's quite possible that you're eating too much protein. Consuming high amounts of protein and low amounts of carbs can force gluconeogenesis to begin, increasing your blood sugar and insulin levels and ultimately discouraging the production of ketones. To remedy this, it's necessary to reduce protein intake.

Here's an important thought to keep in mind when attempting to determine your protein threshold: if you are especially sensitive to carbohydrates (like me), then you will also be more sensitive to protein. It makes sense if you think about it: if increased quantities of carbohydrates raise your blood sugar levels, then gluconeogenesis from consuming excess protein, which results in more blood glucose, will have a similar effect.

MOMENT OF CLARITY I generally recommend that my patients eat any kind of meat, poultry, or seafood, but I make it clear that this is a high-fat diet, not a high-protein diet. Unless there is some unusual metabolic dysfunction, the main blocker of ketone production is insulin. Since insulin levels are determined by dietary carb intake and even protein, these components of the diet have to be managed so that ketosis is maximized.

— Dr. Jay Wortman

What can you do to determine your protein threshold? Ketogenic diet experts have varying opinions about what the ideal protein intake is. Many have guessed that 1 to 1.5 grams per kilogram of body weight is the right amount, but this could bring on gluconeogenesis in many people. Dr. Ron Rosedale, an expert in nutritional and metabolic medicine, advises that those who want to be in ketosis consume 1 gram of protein per kilogram of ideal body weight (based on your body mass index; a good calculator is available online at www.nhlbi.nih.gov/guidelines/obesity/BMI/bmicalc.htm) and then subtract 10 percent. Meanwhile, on my *Ask the Low-Carb Experts* podcast, renowned protein expert Dr. Donald Layman suggested limiting protein intake to no more than 30 grams per meal and no more than 140 grams per day. To figure out what amount of protein works best for you, though, there is no perfect formula. Just as with carbohydrates, it comes down to a process of trial and error.

I'm a pretty tall guy at six foot three, and I started out at around 120 grams of protein daily to see how I would do. When I wasn't seeing the ketone production and other health effects I was looking for, each week I dropped my daily protein intake by 10 grams, until I discovered that ketones started to increase to beneficial levels at about 80 grams of protein a day. Now that may not seem like very much protein—there are 6 grams of protein in just one egg, for example—but it is what I needed to do in order to produce ketones in my body. Moderating my protein intake turned out to be a critical factor in my success on a ketogenic diet.

MOMENT OF CLARITY Ketosis simply takes the concept of high-fat dieting to a more extreme level, and rather than implementing the 20 percent carbohydrate, 65 percent fat, 15 percent protein approach, a ketogenic diet actually brings carbohydrate calories down to 5 to 10 percent, protein calories to 10 to 15 percent, and fat calories up to 75 to 80 percent.

– Ben Greenfield

Coming up in the next chapter, we're going to talk about what you need to be eating *more* of if you want to be ketogenic. Since you're cutting carbs and moderating your protein consumption, you're going to be eating a lot more fat. This will no doubt be one of the most difficult things to wrap your head around because in America today, we have been conditioned to be scared half to death of eating fat, especially saturated fat. But you'll soon find out why this fear is totally unfounded and how eating more fat from natural, real foods can send your ketones skyrocketing.

MOMENT OF CLARITY The most reliable way to get into a state of ketosis is to take carbohydrates down to 30 grams or less per day and protein down to around 0.5 grams per pound of body weight, and to consume fat throughout the day from a combination of medium-chain triglycerides (MCTs) and animal sources like butter, heavy whipping cream, and fatty meats.

– John Kiefer

Key Keto Clarity Concepts

→ **A ketogenic diet is not high-protein but rather high-fat.**

→ **Carbohydrate restriction is a must, but protein moderation is critical as well.**

→ **Protein is an essential nutrient, but its consumption needs to be moderated.**

→ **If you are sensitive to carbohydrates, protein needs to be reduced.**

→ **Gluconeogenesis can be problematic for ketosis if too much protein is consumed.**

→ **You don't have to eat carbs; your body will make its own carbs.**

→ **Eating too much protein can prevent adequate ketone production.**

→ **Making ketones takes much less protein than you might think.**

Chapter 7

Consume Fat, Especially Saturated Fat, to Satiety

MOMENT OF CLARITY There is a big difference between a ketogenic diet in which the fats consumed are coming from soybean and canola oil and one in which they're coming from butter and coconut oil.

— Dr. Zeeshan Arain

If we were to eat at a restaurant together, you'd very quickly see how serious I am about getting quality fat in my meals. One of the first questions I ask the server before ordering any food is whether or not they have real butter. Sometimes the server will give me a funny look that reveals she has no idea what I'm talking about, and other times we're 100 percent on the same page. Butter in restaurants can be anything from real butter (cream and salt) to a blend of butter and vegetable oil (cream, salt, and soybean or canola oil) to margarine (soybean or canola oil).

Once I ascertain that they have genuine butter, my next statement tends to make the server's eyes completely bug out: *"Bring me more butter than you've ever brought any one human being in your life!"* Sometimes they think I'm joking, but my wife, Christine, will usually chime in, "He's not kidding." It's always an interesting experiment in human behavior and societal constructs to see how this request is interpreted by the servers. I've received as little as two pats of butter all the way up to sixteen pats of butter, at the famous locally sourced restaurant 24 Diner in Austin, Texas. (Yes, I ate it all with my food!) You should see the reaction I get when people watch me eat a bite of butter with nearly

Keep carbs low

Eat more fat

Test ketones often

Overdoing protein is bad

every bite of food. In fact, they should give me my own reality show with cameras following me around and showing how people react to my butter consumption!

DOCTOR'S NOTE FROM DR. ERIC WESTMAN: I can vouch for Jimmy's high-fat eating habits. On a visit to Durham, North Carolina, during the writing of this book, we went out to lunch at a restaurant called Dain's, where he ordered a menu item called the "Defibrillator" (another nod toward the mistaken notion that eating fat causes heart disease), a bunless bacon cheeseburger topped with a hot dog and chili. Jimmy ate a bit of butter with every bite.

Can someone please tell me why restaurants are so willing to accommodate their customers who want low-fat, vegetarian, and even gluten-free options, but they can't do the same thing for people on a low-carb, high-fat, ketogenic diet? Maybe someday an ambitious restaurant chain will create a keto menu full of delicious, full-fat dishes. Or maybe they will give you the ability to "cut the carbs and double the fat" in any given meal to help make it more ketogenic. This might sound crazy right now, but why not meet the needs of your customer base? It certainly wouldn't hurt if we all contacted our favorite restaurants and asked them to provide more low-carb, high-fat menu items.

MOMENT OF CLARITY Inadequate fat intake is an obvious way to thwart ketosis. Fat should make up at least 50 percent of your diet, but this percentage can go much higher for many people.

– Dr. Bill Wilson

Make no mistake about it—a ketogenic diet is a fatty diet! Why is consuming more fat, especially saturated fat (found in butter, meat, cheese, and similar whole foods, for example), such an important part of a ketogenic diet? While you may not need to eat a bite of butter with every morsel of food you put in your mouth, dietary fat is an integral part of a healthy diet and the final piece to the nutritional puzzle of what it takes to produce adequate ketones. When you cut down on your carbohydrate consumption and moderate your protein intake, you need to replace the carbohydrate and protein with something. And that something is the only thing that is left— dietary fat. Eat the amount of carbs and protein that you've determined through trial and error is right for you, and then eat fat until the hunger is gone—in other words, to satiety. Fat intake is the ultimate key to feeling full.

I can already hear some of you saying, "But isn't eating all that fat going to raise my cholesterol and clog my arteries, leading to a heart attack?" That is the prevailing message we have heard ad nauseum for most of our lives, and it doesn't help matters when pop culture reinforces the notion that there is something wrong with consuming fat. Take, for example, a couple of episodes of the hit CBS TV show *The Big Bang Theory*. In one, the character Bernadette orders a nonfat yogurt but gets the full-fat version instead. Her reaction? "This isn't a nonfat yogurt, this is fatty-fat-fat!"—implying that the fat in it is somehow bad. And in another episode, Bernadette, who is a waitress at The Cheesecake Factory, plots revenge against a friend's ex and his new girlfriend: "If she orders something low-fat, I'll totally give her the full-fat version." The very clear implication is that fat would harm her in some way. I can't help but roll my eyes whenever I see this kind of erroneous message in our mainstream culture, knowing that it just reinforces the lies and distortions regarding dietary fat and that viewers are like lemmings, nodding in agreement.

MOMENT OF CLARITY One of the most frequent roadblocks to ketosis is trying to do low-carb *and* low-fat. [In Dr. Atkins' clinic] it was sometimes difficult to get patients to eat natural fat because of their fear of it. Some expected to have a heart attack after the first serving of full-fat cheese. Once patients experience the ease with which they can lose weight with fewer cravings and manageable hunger and they see their cardiovascular lab values improve, they tend to relax.

– Jackie Eberstein

Let me encourage you to pick up a copy of our previous book, *Cholesterol Clarity*, to learn the truth about the connection between saturated fat, cholesterol, and heart disease. The prevailing wisdom on this subject is already beginning to change among medical and health professionals around the world. Cracks in the once-indomitable armor of the anti–saturated fat message are beginning to appear, and it's only a matter of time before it starts to crumble and fall. Learn more about why saturated fat is good for you in the blockbuster 2014 book *The Big Fat Surprise*, by Nina Teicholz.

DOCTOR'S NOTE FROM DR. ERIC WESTMAN: Richard Veech, one of the world's experts on ketones, said, "If I had a heart attack, I [would]

*want to be given intravenous ketones." Several animal studies have
shown that ketones improve heart function during periods of low blood
supply or during a heart attack.*

In October 2013, a cardiologist named Dr. Aseem Malhotra wrote an
earth-shattering commentary in the prestigious *British Medical Journal*
defending the consumption of foods containing saturated fat such as butter,
cheese, and red meat and putting the blame for chronic health problems
such as heart disease directly on the real culprits—sugar, fast food, baked
goods, and fake fats like margarine. He notes that a low-fat diet and food
products that use "low-fat" as a health claim on their packaging are generally loaded with sugar. Dr. Malhotra sounded the alarm about how deeply
misled we have been about the role of fat in the diet. But he's not alone.

In the May 1, 2013, issue of the journal *American Society for Nutrition*,
Long Island University biochemistry professor Dr. Glen Lawrence states
that blaming dietary fat for health calamities like obesity and heart disease
is completely unfounded. Dr. Lawrence says we need a "rational reevalua-
tion of existing dietary recommendations" regarding the role of saturated
fat in the diet, along with a closer examination of the highly inflammatory
properties of so-called healthy oils like the polyunsaturated fats (canola oil,
soybean oil, and so on). While many self-proclaimed health experts boldly
state that saturated fat is harmful to health, Dr. Lawrence contends that
there hasn't been any evidence that isolates the role saturated fat plays from
other factors. He concludes that we need "to use a more holistic approach to
dietary policy." Absolutely!

And finally, a story on National Public Radio's "Morning Edition" by
Allison Aubrey that aired February 12, 2014, entitled "The Full-Fat Para-
dox: Whole Milk May Keep Us Lean," revealed that the truth about dietary
fat isn't what we we've been told. Aubrey cites a study in the *Scandinavian
Journal of Primary Health Care* that found that men who ate a diet rich in
butter, cream, and other high-fat dairy had a significantly lower likelihood
of becoming obese compared to men who did not eat dairy. She also noted
that a meta-analysis (a detailed examination of multiple research papers that
looks for patterns in the data) published in the *European Journal of Nutrition* found that there is no evidence that high-fat dairy foods contribute to
a risk of obesity or heart disease, and in fact that eating high-fat dairy was
associated with a lower risk of obesity. This goes against everything we have
been told about the role fat plays in our diet. And yet stories like this one

indicate that the tide is beginning to turn when it comes to the perception of dietary fat's role in a healthy lifestyle.

MOMENT OF CLARITY Some fats are more apt to readily convert to ketones than others: short- and medium-chain fats, like those found in pastured butter, cultured ghee, coconut oil, and especially MCT oil (taken as a supplement), will readily convert to ketones. This can help improve the efficiency by which a person adapts to a healthy fat-based, ketone-fueled metabolism.

– Nora Gedgaudas

What is most astounding about this is the fact that the fat phobia that's rampant in American society is not supported at all by the scientific evidence. And yet if you asked the average person about their thoughts on dietary fat, the overwhelming response would be that it is unhealthy and should be avoided at all costs. Why is our culture vilifying whole-food sources of saturated fats like butter while at the same time promoting canola oil, a highly processed rancid rapeseed oil that's treated with deodorizers, as a "healthy" option? It doesn't make any sense at all, and yet that's the world we currently live in.

A Gallup poll conducted in July 2012 found that 63 percent of Americans believe that a diet low in fat is beneficial to their health, compared with just 30 percent who think the same about a diet low in carbohydrates—this despite the mountain of evidence that has been building in favor of low-carb eating in recent years. However, the same poll shows the tide is already beginning to shift ever-so-slightly in the public's thinking about low-fat and low-carb diets. Compared to the same poll conducted a decade prior, fewer Americans are now lending credence to cutting fat and more are starting to recognize the benefits of carbohydrate restriction. We still have a long way to go in what my *Low-Carb Conversations* podcast co-host Dietitian Cassie describes as "unbrainwashing" ourselves from the decades of nutritional propaganda.

MOMENT OF CLARITY We have been ingrained (pun intended) with a fear of fat, and most everything else, other than pure fiber, can interfere with ketosis.

– Dr. Ron Rosedale

This is one of the reasons why the book you are holding is so sorely needed now more than ever before—to break through the decades upon decades of indoctrination we have been subjected to on the subject of fat.

Here's the truth of the matter: when you cut the fat in your diet, it's replaced by carbohydrate, which is far more damaging to your health than fat will ever be. Saturated fats, like those in butter, coconut oil, and red meat, and monounsaturated fats, such as those found in avocados, olive oil, and macadamia nuts, are basically safe for consumption in terms of your health. They don't raise your blood sugar, and they don't cause any harm when eaten to satiety. In fact, they are quite beneficial: they are anti-inflammatory, raise HDL cholesterol, help you feel full, and—most important for our purposes—they help you create ketones. Compare this to the polyunsaturated fats found in vegetable oils, which increases systemic inflammation and are linked to multiple health problems, despite the fact that they are heavily touted as the healthy oils we should be consuming.

MOMENT OF CLARITY In the treatment of obesity, nutritional ketosis facilitates fat loss through a reduction in levels of insulin, the controlling hormone of fat storage. It does not guarantee fat loss if dietary fat intake meets or exceeds energy expenditure. This situation would be very unusual because most people become satiated prior to reaching that level of fat intake.

– Dr. Keith Runyan

Fat is not the enemy in your diet. Fat is your friend. So don't fear it. Fat makes you feel fuller for longer periods of time than anything else you could possibly consume. And don't forget, you need to eat fat in order to burn fat. And it only makes sense to eat fat when your body is a fat-burning machine, right?

One of the primary reasons for eating plenty of fat with your low-carb and moderate-protein intake is that it will prevent you from being hungry—without it, you'd quit a low-carb, high-protein diet in a very short amount of time due to frustration and exasperation because of the constant hunger! What many so-called health experts fail to realize is that people on low-carb diets *need* dietary fat to burn as an alternative fuel and to help them feel satisfied and energized between meals. When you switch from burning sugar to burning fat, you have more energy and better mental acuity, and you're more satisfied after a meal.

MOMENT OF CLARITY Once my clients get past the initial pitfalls of keto-adaptation, one of the first things they notice is a diminished sense of hunger where that annoying feeling of crankiness goes away. They also become more mentally clear, get their energy back like gangbusters, lose body fat, and get leaner. They often check their blood sugar and the numbers start to normalize. One of the most impressive reactions is noticing their sugar and carb cravings drop, and bad food starts to taste like *bad food.*

– Stephanie Person

Perhaps you've tried a low-carb diet before and thought that if low-carb is good, then low-carb *and* low-fat must be better. That would be a huge mistake. Mixing low-carb and low-fat diets is not a recipe for healthy living—especially if you are attempting to experience the benefits of being in ketosis. Think about it: If you cut your carbs and reduce the amount of fat you eat, then what's left? Protein. And as discussed in the previous chapter, eating too much protein can actually increase the amount of glucose in your body, making it next to impossible to create ketones.

Or perhaps you are currently overweight or obese and you're reading this chapter with a healthy bit of skepticism about consuming *more* fat in your diet. You may be thinking to yourself that you have plenty of fat on your body and therefore you don't need to be eating as much fat as everyone else. Please don't do that to yourself. Yes, you have a lot of body fat that will be used to fuel your body when you are in a ketogenic state. But think of eating fat as a way to prime your metabolic engine. The only way to access stored body fat and use it as fuel is by shifting your body from a sugar-burner to a fat-burner, and the only way to do that is to feed your body what it needs to commence fat-burning—dietary fat.

MOMENT OF CLARITY Effectively adapting to using fat and ketones as a primary source of fuel to form a very stable energy substrate, even in the absence of regular meals, is just like putting a big log on a fire burning in your wood stove.

– Nora Gedgaudas

In March 2013, there was a news story in RedEye Chicago, a website of the *Chicago Tribune*, about a thirty-six-year old Illinois man named John Huston who was embarking on a 72-day, 630-mile journey through the Canadian High Arctic in subzero temperatures. This was obviously going to be a very energy-demanding trek for Huston and his team, so how did he fuel himself? He consumed deep-fried bacon and at least a stick of butter a day! Here's how he said it: "It sounds disgusting, but when you're outside every day at forty below, butter is your best friend." Sounds like my kind of guy, because he knows dietary fat is an outstanding fuel source.

For most people, getting over the fear of eating fat is probably the most difficult aspect of being on a ketogenic diet. We're told by doctors, teachers, the government, and other health authorities that fat is bad, and somehow we've come to accept without a second thought that it will make us fat and eventually kill us. (But it won't.) I grew up watching my mom eat rice cakes and drink skim milk in her futile attempts to follow a low-fat diet. In the end, she never permanently lost the weight eating that way, and she ended up getting so frustrated that she resorted to gastric bypass surgery in her late fifties (though even that didn't keep her from gaining back the weight she lost). It's a sad reality that so many people still fear eating fat so much that they are unwilling to try a high-fat diet even though it could not only help them manage their weight but also prevent the onset of chronic diseases such as diabetes, Alzheimer's disease, and cancer. (More on that beginning in chapter 16.)

MOMENT OF CLARITY Insufficient fat intake is among the most common tripping points in trying to gain, then maintain, a ketogenic state. We need to rid ourselves of any residual fear that fat intake is somehow bad, causes us to get fat, or causes heart disease. Enjoy the fat on your T-bone steak or coconut oil used to sauté your vegetables.

– Dr. William Davis

Making people scared to death of eating fat, while saying nary a word about the negative health effects of carbohydrates, has had the unintended consequence of encouraging obesity and chronic disease. With the abysmal failure of the low-fat lie we've been fed, don't you think it's time to start looking at the role fat could play in making our health *better*? Lay your fears aside, eat more fat than you probably ever have before, and watch the remarkable things that happen in your health as a result. Dialing down the carbs and getting protein right are important, but eating the right amount of fat will take you over the top and make ketosis happen in earnest.

I realize that eating more fat may go against everything you've ever believed about healthy nutrition. Every fiber of your being will tell you not to do this. And that internal battle about whether this is the right thing to do for your health is something all of us who have chosen to pursue a low-carb, moderate-protein, high-fat, ketogenic diet have had to grapple with at some point. Once you are ready to take the plunge and go fullfledged keto, the remedy to fat phobia is to just embrace the fat and eat it in your diet confidently, knowing it is going to make you healthier than you've ever been before.

Occasionally people who are new to the ketogenic lifestyle may experience diarrhea and intestinal discomfort. Dr. Mary Newport, a neonatologist and authority on the therapeutic use of ketones, suggests that if you do experience discomfort right away, try increasing your carbohydrates slightly while decreasing your fat intake a bit. Then gradually decrease carbs and increase fat to help your body adjust.

MOMENT OF CLARITY I believe a lot of the side effects seen with ketogenic diets in past research studies have to do with poor design of the diets, mostly poor food quality, and the continued fear of saturated fat.

— Bryan Barksdale

Here's a handy acronym that will help you remember why fat is good:

Feel fuller

Alternative fuel

Triggers ketones

You may not need to eat a bit of butter with every bite of food like I do, but you'll be ramping up the amount of fat in your diet to levels you probably never thought you'd ever consume. For example, you can ask for heavy cream in your latte at Starbucks instead of milk. Your health will benefit as a result. Coming up in the next chapter, we'll put your new nutritional habits to the test to see how well they are working to start pumping ketones throughout your body.

MOMENT OF CLARITY A high-fat diet in the presence of carbohydrate is different than a high-fat diet in the presence of low carbohydrate.

— Dr. Richard Feinman

Key Keto Clarity Concepts

→ A low-carb, high-fat diet is a healthy diet.

→ If you want to produce ketones, you need to eat fat.

→ When you cut carbs and moderate protein, all that's left to eat is fat.

→ Fat is the key to being full and satisfied.

→ Our cultural perception about fat being harmful is wrong.

→ Leading experts are coming out in support of saturated fat.

→ The fat phobia that exists is not supported by the scientific data.

→ Americans are slowly realizing low-fat not as healthy as once thought.

→ It's time to break through decades of indoctrination against fat.

→ Fat is not the enemy in your diet. Fat is your friend.

→ Consuming fat is necessary so that you can burn it as an alternative fuel source.

→ Never, ever, ever eat a diet that's both low-carb and low-fat.

→ You may need to eat a lot more fat than you currently are.

→ An Arctic explorer realizes the benefits of eating fatty foods.

→ Every fiber of your being will fight you about eating more fat.

→ Fat leads to feeling fuller, acts an alternative fuel, and triggers ketone production.

Chapter 8

Using Technology to Measure for Ketosis

MOMENT OF CLARITY The ketone testing technology for the urine, blood, and breath are definitely interesting and a great direction for measuring for the specific level of ketosis.

– Dr. Dominic D'Agostino

At this point in the book, you've heard all about what ketones are, why you probably want to increase the amount of them in your body, and what it takes nutritionally to make this happen. But you may be wondering how in the world you are supposed to figure out if you are actually in a state of ketosis. That's what this chapter is all about, and it will cover some of the old, traditional ways of measuring, the current devices available on the market, and some really cool emerging technologies that could forever change the way we check for ketones in the future.

Keep carbs low

Eat more fat

Test ketones often

Overdoing protein is bad

Before we dive into the latest gizmos and gadgets that technology has to offer for measuring ketones, let's first identify the three types of ketone bodies that are found inside the body:

1. **Acetoacetate (AcAc),** the primary ketone body in the urine
2. **Beta-hydroxybutyrate (BHB),** the primary ketone body in the blood
3. **Acetone,** the primary ketone body in the breath

For decades, the traditional method for measuring the presence of ketones has been testing acetoacetate levels in the urine. The ketone test strips

in a bottle of fifty for around $12 to $15. (To
the strips in half lengthwise and just use
ips change color to signify the level of ace-
our pursuit of ketosis, you may see beige
), or purple (a lot of ketones).

ıe test strips as a measure of keto-adaptation.
... ıo looking for banana peels in your garbage to figure out
..ow many apples are in your refrigerator and how many of those you are eating.
Apart from only measuring ketones eliminated as a waste product, urinary ketone
test strips measure only one kind of ketone, acetoacetate, and fail altogether to measure the most critical and predominantly utilized ketone in a healthy state of ketosis:
beta-hydroxybutyrate. This is *always* better and more accurately measured with a
blood ketone meter.

– Nora Gedgaudas

But in recent years, newer and more precise devices that can measure the
ketone body primarily found in the blood (beta-hydroxybutyrate) have become popular among low-carb, high-fat dieters. There are two major blood
ketone monitors available on the market at the time of writing: the Precision
Xtra brand from Abbott (sold under the brand name FreeStyle Optium in
Europe and Australia) and Nova Max Plus from Nova. Since 78 percent of
the ketones present in the blood are beta-hydroxybutyrate, being able to test
for this is a really big deal. Precision Xtra is a better meter for accurate and
consistent readings (NovaMax displays "LO" instead of a number readout
when ketones fall below a certain level, even when you could be in ketosis).

Although blood ketone testing is considered the gold standard for
ketone testing, for reasons we'll explore later in the chapter, there are some
roadblocks that you need to be aware of. Blood ketone monitors can be
difficult to find in local stores and pharmacies, and the companies that make
them seem uninterested in widening their market beyond type 1 diabetics
and the few type 2 diabetics who no longer make insulin and need to test for
whether or not they are in ketoacidosis. While the monitors themselves are
usually affordable, the strips they require can cost as much as $5 each,
making daily testing extremely expensive. My argument to these companies
has been that they would do better to make their products cheaper and
more widely available because their current, narrow market of consumers is
minuscule compared with the number of people (like you and me) who

want to test our blood ketones to assess our progress in our health goals. Why wouldn't these companies want to broaden the appeal of their products by marketing to those desiring to test for nutritional ketosis? That makes good business sense, and you'd think these companies would be all over it.

MOMENT OF CLARITY Ideally, a state of ketosis is achieved and maintained with finger-stick blood ketone monitoring and by keeping beta-hydroxybutyrate levels at 1 to 3 millimolar per liter. My experience with urine dipsticks for ketones is that, because they are set up to assess for the much higher levels of ketones indicative of diabetic ketoacidosis, they are insufficiently sensitive to be of much assistance to monitor the more subtle levels of physiologic ketosis.

– Dr. William Davis

However, when I contacted these companies, both Abbott and Nova showed zero interest in what I was sharing with them about using their products to test for nutritional ketosis, stating that their focus was on helping diabetics test for ketoacidosis—nothing more. That's just silly if you ask me, and they're missing an opportunity to increase their bottom line. But something tells me that if enough people started demanding better access to their product, they'd find a way to make it more readily available at an affordable price. Contact Abbott at (888) 522-5226 and Nova at (800) 681-7390 and let them know you need access to their products to test for nutritional ketosis.

Even though blood ketone monitors are fairly new, the next generation of ketone testing devices is already on the way. One ketone monitor that measures for the presence and amount of acetone in the breath is already available to consumers, and others are in development and show great promise. Breath ketone monitors have been shown to be just as accurate as blood ketone monitors, and since they don't require strips, they're much more affordable. Plus, you get good results without the pain of a finger prick.

MOMENT OF CLARITY I'm a fan of breath ketone testing, as it's less invasive and painful than blood testing. For my personal experiments with ketosis, I used a breath test that detects levels of ketones (acetone) in breath condensate. Breath condensate and blood ketone levels are well correlated, and they're more reliable and readily detectable than urine ketone levels. Several studies indicate that breath ketones are a reliable measurement for ketosis compared to blood and urine samples.

– Ben Greenfield

In a July 2002 study published in the *American Journal of Clinical Nutrition,* researchers investigated which is more accurate, testing for ketones in the urine or breath. They found that breath acetone is "as good a predictor of ketosis" as ketones in the urine. Several breath ketone meters are currently in development and not yet available to the general public (most likely we'll be seeing them by 2015).

As of the writing of this book, only one breath ketone monitor is available commercially to consumers: the Ketonix, a USB-powered device that you can use thousands of times. Created by a forty-nine-year-old Swedish engineer named Michel Lundell, the Ketonix measures the ketones in the user's breath and responds with a sequence of colored lights that changes depending on the level of ketones detected. Inventing this device was a necessity for Michel when he was diagnosed with epilepsy in 2012.

After having little success in reducing his number of seizures even after doubling the recommended dose of epilepsy medications ten times in one year, Lundell began investigating the ketogenic diet, which has long been considered an excellent treatment option for epilepsy (we'll examine the evidence for this in chapter 16). He first attempted to measure his ketones using urine strips and then a blood ketone meter. But neither of these options worked for him, so he began to search for alternatives. He came across the idea of measuring acetone in the breath, and when he failed to find any devices for this, he put on his engineering hat and made the very first Ketonix for himself.

Lundell went on to market and sell his device online, making it the first breath ketone monitor to be commercially available, and he has been receiving orders around the world from people with epilepsy, people who are pursuing nutritional ketosis, and even athletes who are measuring their ability to use fat for fuel during sporting events. In June 2014, he was selected as one of only six people from around the world to give a presentation about his invention at the special Shark Tank Competition that was part of the 2014 Epilepsy Pipeline Conference in San Francisco, California.

MOMENT OF CLARITY Using nutritional ketosis to prevent and treat diseases other than epilepsy and obesity is a relatively new concept. So there are currently no large clinical trials in existence. Even most biochemistry textbooks hardly mention ketosis except in reference to starvation and diabetic ketoacidosis.

– Dr. Zeeshan Arain

Look for many more breath ketone meters and associated technologies to be developed in the coming years. According to the July 25, 2013, issue of the *Journal of Breath Research*, Japan's NTT Docomo is developing a breath ketone reader device and app for smartphones. And a Swedish engineer named Jens Clarholm posted detailed instructions on his JensLabs.com blog for making a homemade breath ketone meter he calls Ketosense (he made one for me to use, and its results are remarkably close to the readings I find on my blood ketone monitor). It would not surprise me if we'll be able to purchase breath ketone meters in stores by 2016! Now that would be cool.

I've said it before, but this point bears repeating: it's important to remember that when your blood sugar level is in the normal range, the presence of high levels of ketones in the urine, blood, or breath is not at all harmful, no matter how much weeping and gnashing of teeth you may hear from health gurus. Diabetic ketoacidosis, as we've already discussed, tends to occur mostly in type 1 diabetics who cannot produce insulin and some type 2 diabetics who are insulin-dependent, and only when blood sugar levels are in excess of 240 mg/dl and blood ketone readings well in excess of 10 millimolar per liter. For everyone else who can make even a little bit of insulin, there is no danger in seeing higher levels of ketones. But since it can be difficult to produce ketones without deliberate effort, being able to test and see where you stand can be reassuring as you pursue ketosis.

Let's list the pros and cons of each method for measuring ketones.

Urine testing

PROS

► It's the least expensive method for testing ketone levels.

► The test is completely painless, since you just pee on a stick.

► There is a clear color change within fifteen seconds when ketones are present.

► If you have ketones in the urine, then you are definitely in ketosis.

CONS

► It only measures the ketone body in the urine (acetoacetate).

► Once you become keto-adapted, ketones in the urine may disappear.

► Long-term ketosis cannot be measured using this testing method.

► If you do not have ketones in the urine, you still might be in ketosis.

Everybody likes urine ketone testing because the strips are readily available in stores, cheap, and easy to use, and they produce a color change if you are in a state of ketosis. But this mode of ketone testing is fool's gold for people who have become fully keto-adapted after a few weeks of low-carb, moderate-protein, high-fat eating and are now burning fat for fuel efficiently. After a period of transition as you shift from a sugar-burner to a fat-burner, ketones may stop spilling over into the urine, giving you the false test result that you are out of ketosis. What has actually happened is that your ketones are now showing up in the blood and you're experiencing the long-awaited benefits of nutritional ketosis. Thus, solely relying on urine ketone strips to see if you are in ketosis after successfully making the switch is futile. The bottom line is they are just not a reliable means for tracking your ketone production beyond the initial period of adaptation.

Blood testing

PROS

- ► It's the most precise measurement for detecting ketones (beta-hydroxybutyrate).
- ► There's no ambiguity about the results with a clear digital display.
- ► It tests for the most prevalent ketone your body is using for fuel.

CONS

- ► The testing strips are more expensive ($2 to $6 per strip).
- ► Blood ketone testing supplies are hard to find in stores, so you may have to purchase them over the Internet.
- ► The test requires a painful finger prick for a blood sample.

If you're not used to pricking your finger to test your blood, then blood ketone testing will likely be intimidating at first. But once you get over this mental roadblock and start testing your blood often, there's a certain confidence and assurance that comes from knowing your blood ketone levels. The blood ketone monitors (especially the Precision Xtra) give an incredibly accurate digital measurement of your level of ketone production. In the next chapter I'll share my experience testing blood ketones at least twice daily for an entire year to give you an idea of what to expect. But this is arguably the very best method right now for knowing how well you are doing on your ketogenic diet, and it's worth every penny it costs to test.

Breath testing

PROS

▸ It's an easy testing method that you can do practically anywhere.

▸ It's the only way to measure ketones (acetone) in the breath, which correlate well to the level of beta-hydroxybutyrate in the blood.

▸ Unlike blood ketone testing, there's no painful finger prick.

CONS

▸ These devices are not yet as commercially available as the other ketone tests.

▸ Different meters have different ways of showing results, and currently there's no standard for correlating breath ketones to blood ketones.

▸ Not everyone may be able to or want to blow into a device for the ten to thirty seconds required.

I had the privilege of personally using some of the new breath ketone devices in the midst of writing this book, and so far they're very promising. There are still some obstacles to overcome for breath ketone testing, such as the fact that the devices use different ways of displaying results and there's no exact, apples-to-apples comparison to the results you would get from a blood ketone monitor. But if the companies developing breath ketone meters can smooth out these problems, then this could be one of the biggest breakthroughs not just in ketone testing but in health in general. Ketones play a vital role in many chronic health issues, and having an easy-to-use, pain-free device for determining how well you are producing them would be invaluable.

DOCTOR'S NOTE FROM DR. ERIC WESTMAN: Dr. Lubna Ahmad, president of Invoy Technologies, which is developing a breath ketone analyzer, did a small study comparing breath ketones, blood ketones, and urine ketones in about forty people, some of whom were following a low-carb, high-fat, ketogenic diet and some of whom were not. Two important findings are clear: 1) occasionally the urine ketones are absent but the blood ketones are present; and 2) morning ketone levels are lower than evening ketone levels. What this means is that if you only check ketones in the morning urine, you might be in ketosis even if the tests are negative.

We are living in exciting times when patients like us have access to equipment that you used to see only in a doctor's office. And now that we have these at-home technologies to determine how well we are doing in our pursuit of health, the power is in our own hands. I envision ketone testing to be part of the wave of the future for those who are interested in being in a state of ketosis.

MOMENT OF CLARITY A ketogenic diet is a great opportunity for self-experimentation. Start with a set of simple generic guidelines, such as Atkins Induction, and manipulate the variables to see how your body responds by measuring blood or breath ketones. I think this is probably the best way to know what works for you.

– Bryan Barksdale

Self-testing is a powerful thing, and I highly encourage you to give it a go for yourself. If you cannot afford to do any of the ketone testing discussed in this chapter, then you might be interested to know that there is a fantastic free website, The Low Carb Flexi Diet (www.flexibleketogenic.com), that provides a ketogenic ratio calculator. All you do is plug in how many grams of carbohydrates, protein, and fat you are consuming, and it tells you how ketotic you are. Give it a try and see for yourself!

Coming up in the next chapter, I want to share with you what happened to me over the course of one year when I decided to put the idea of being in a constant state of nutritional ketosis to the test. The results and lessons of that experiment were what really propelled me to write this book. Get ready to be blown away by what I discovered!

Key Keto Clarity Concepts

→ **New technology is being invented to test for ketones in the urine, blood, and breath.**

→ **There are three types of ketones—acetoacetate, beta-hydroxybutyrate, and acetone.**

→ **Urine testing is the cheapest, easiest way to test for ketosis.**

→ **Blood ketone testing is much more accurate than urine ketone testing.**

→ **The high cost of blood ketone testing make it too expensive to test daily.**

→ **Blood ketone monitor companies are uninterested in marketing to people pursuing nutritional ketosis.**

→ **Breath ketones correlate very closely to blood ketone levels.**

→ **Several companies are working on breath ketone meters for consumers.**

→ **There are pros and cons for each way of testing the presence of ketones.**

→ **At-home ketone testing is the wave of the future for people seeking to be healthy.**

→ **Self-testing is the only way you can know for sure if you're in ketosis.**

Chapter 9

My One-Year N=1 Experiment in Nutritional Ketosis

MOMENT OF CLARITY Because each person is different, I think it pays to do a little experimenting. Measure your ketones and manipulate your ratio of fat to protein and carbohydrate to see what it takes to keep you in ketosis.

– Dr. Bill Wilson

What exactly does ketosis look and feel like in the real world? I wanted to know the answer, so I embarked on my own one-year ketosis experiment in May 2012. In the language of scientific research, it was an "n=1" experiment—"n" stands for the sample size, and in this case, it was just one: me. So let me be very clear up-front that this experiment only reflects my own experiences, no one else's, and it does not take the place of any objective scientific research that has or will take place on ketogenic diets. This is merely what happened to me during my year of testing the impact of nutritional ketosis on my body.

In the spring of 2012, I read *The Art and Science of Low Carbohydrate Performance,* a book by two fabulous low-carb and ketogenic diet researchers named Dr. Jeff Volek and Dr. Stephen Phinney. In it, they explained the science behind ketogenic diets for athletes who are keenly interested in optimizing their exercise performance and argued that burning fat and using ketones as the body's primary fuel source provides better, longer-lasting energy for exercise performance than carbohydrates.

It was in this book that I first learned about blood ketone testing and the concept they called "nutritional ketosis," which I'll refer to as "NK" from here on. While Volek and Phinney admit that blood ketone testing strips are "relatively expensive", they make a compelling case for giving it a go: "Is this (hassle/expense) worth . . . pricking your finger once per day for a month or two? Based upon our experience working with many people, we think that the answer is 'yes.'" On the annual Low-Carb Cruise I helped organize and lead in 2012, I announced to a crowd of over 250 people that I would be testing NK for ninety days to see what would happen. In fact, Dr. Volek himself was in attendance as one of the special guest speakers that year, and he presented an awesome lecture outlining the benefits of NK.

MOMENT OF CLARITY People need to do considerable self-experimentation to assess their response to the ketogenic diet, and in particular how much carbohydrate and protein they require to sustain ketosis.

– Dr. Dominic D'Agostino

At the time, I was struggling with a bit of weight regain, lackluster sleep, and constant fatigue, despite eating what I thought was a pretty good low-carb, high-fat diet. So when I decided to begin this n=1 test, I was hoping to figure out what I was doing wrong. During the experiment, I always checked my blood ketones using the Precision Xtra blood ketone meter in the morning after I woke up and while in a fasted state; at the same time, I also checked my weight and blood sugar levels. I repeated the blood ketone and blood sugar tests at night at least four hours after my last meal. This ritual became part of my daily routine for an entire year.

Keep in mind that I wanted to examine the results of NK as scientifically as possible, which explains why I did so much testing. But for the average person, testing blood ketones once in the morning and once at night during the week will allow you to track your progress without breaking the bank on blood ketone test strips by testing more often. However, since blood sugar testing is much more affordable than blood ketone testing, checking that daily in a fasted state as well as after meals is probably not a bad idea. In fact, Google announced in January 2014 that they are working on developing a contact lens that will be able to keep a constant check on your blood sugar levels. I've got to get me a pair when they come out with that!

MOMENT OF CLARITY When it comes to adapting to the ketogenic lifestyle, a lot depends upon exactly who is embarking on this path and what their underlying issues might happen to be. I generally find that jumping right in with both feet is the least painful and often the most effective and compliance-friendly way to go about it.

– Nora Gedgaudas

Remember, for the overwhelming majority of you who are reading this book, NK carries no known risks—it's not the same thing as diabetic keto-acidosis. If you are truly concerned about an elevated blood ketone reading, then the best thing you can do is to test your blood sugar at the same time. If that reading is below 240 mg/dl, then you're just fine. What you'll probably see is that your blood sugar drops significantly (a very good thing!) when blood ketones rise. For example, it is not uncommon for me to see a blood sugar reading in the 60s and blood ketones in excess of 2.0 millimolar when I test in the morning, and I feel perfectly fine. This is just one of the many benefits that come from being in nutritional ketosis.

During my yearlong testing of NK, I was looking for quantifiable changes in body weight, blood sugar levels, and blood ketone levels. Additionally, I wanted to keep an eye on how I was feeling, my sleeping patterns, what my energy levels were like during exercise, and anything else that was happening to my body while in a state of ketosis. If changes were happening, then I was taking notice. And boy, did the changes happen!

MOMENT OF CLARITY I encourage my patients to follow Jimmy Moore's example and do their own n=1 experiment. If eating in a certain way leads to health problems, then stop doing it! But if changing your diet leads to an improvement in your metabolic health and brain function, then you are on the right track. People vary somewhat in their response to any given type of diet, so you need to experiment to see what works best for you.

– Dr. Bill Wilson

I officially began my experiment on May 15, 2012, when I measured my blood ketones for the very first time. As someone who'd been eating a low-carb, high-fat diet for over eight years, I was utterly shocked by the results: 0.3 millimolar! According to Volek and Phinney, to get the benefits of being in a state of NK, ketones need to measure between 0.5 and 3.0 millimolar. I wasn't even close to being in ketosis. I realized I had stumbled across something fascinating that could help not only me but potentially many other would-be low-carb dieters who experience frustratingly lackluster results: *Just because you're eating low-carb doesn't mean you're ketogenic.*

Because I was already eating a low-carb, high-fat diet, it didn't take me long to enter into a state of NK once I slightly adjusted my intake of carbs, lowered my intake of protein considerably, and increased the amount of fat, especially saturated fat, in my diet. I was seeing blood ketones over 0.5 millimolar within four days, well over 1.0 millimolar by the end of one week, and as high as 5.0 millimolar within two weeks. It can take from two to six weeks to make the switch from being a sugar-burner to a fat-burner, so be patient with yourself during this transition period. Chapter 14 has some invaluable tips and strategies for improving ketone production if you are struggling.

MOMENT OF CLARITY The physiological acclimatization to a carbohydrate-restricted keto-genic diet, known as *keto-adaptation,* is not instantaneous, and this has led to a misunderstanding that it's not a normal state.

– Dr. Bill Lagakos

For me, it worked to start with a diet with that was 85 percent fat, 12 percent protein, and 3 percent carbohydrate. Over time that shifted closer to 80 percent fat, 15 percent protein, and 5 percent carbohydrate, which I still eat to this day. I didn't obsess about it being absolutely precise down to the percentage, but when I ran the numbers that's where I ended up. Of course, choosing the best-quality whole foods will maximize the benefits of ketosis on your health. Please note that I did not count calories doing this, but my intake was probably close to 2300 to 2500 calories per day. When you nour-ish your body well and get into ketosis, the calories take care of themselves. More on that in a moment.

Remember, this is not necessarily what *you* need to do in order to produce ketones. I realize people like to follow precise percentages, mac-ronutrient equations, and lists of foods to eat, but ketosis doesn't work that way. You need to figure that out on your own by using the diet guidelines we shared in chapters 5 to 7. My wife, Christine, was so impressed by my results that she decided to try a ketogenic diet for four weeks herself, and she got into ketosis with a fat/protein/carbohydrate ratio of 57/29/14 and about 1500 calories a day—her average morning blood ketone level was 0.7 millimolar and average nighttime blood ketone level was 1.8 millimolar.

MOMENT OF CLARITY Any condition in which there is decreased glucose uptake in the brain or nerves, or mitochondrial dysfunction, could possibly respond to a ketogenic diet. My feeling is, what do you have to lose by trying this strategy?

– Dr. Mary Newport

So what kind of results did I see in NK? One interesting thing that I noticed right away was my hunger simply dissipated. Zapped. Poof . . . gone!

There are some powerful prescription drugs out there that people pay good money for to curb their appetite. And yet ketosis did the exact same thing naturally, allowing me to spontaneously begin fasting for twelve, sixteen, even twenty-four hours at a time. I know it probably sounds absolutely crazy to think you could go that long without eating, but your body is designed to feast on ketones and stored body fat during fasts. We'll expand more on the subject of fasting in chapter 11, but for now, know that one of the biggest benefits you'll receive from ketosis is hunger control like you've never experienced before.

My blood sugar levels, which began in the upper 90s and low 100s at the start of the experiment, dropped down into the upper 70s and low 80s within just a few months. Although I took a blood sugar–stabilizing supplement called Glycosolve, I eventually stopped taking it when my blood sugar remained in the healthy range through ketosis alone. In fact, I tested my blood sugar levels hourly for a week just to see what happened to it after meals. What I discovered was that ketosis helped me maintain a pretty tight rein on blood sugar, keeping it within a twenty- to thirty-point range. There are no huge spikes in blood sugar when you are producing ketones through nutrition.

MOMENT OF CLARITY In my opinion, controlling both the quality and quantity of carbohydrate foods allows for a more normal insulin and blood sugar response and fluctuations in these values. This is what we saw in clinical practice at the Atkins Center. Since a disturbed insulin and blood sugar response has a negative impact on every cell in the body, maintaining normal function of this metabolic system is vital to long-term health.

– Jackie Eberstein

When I tested my HgA1c level (a key marker in blood sugar regulation that shows the average blood glucose over the previous three months) at the beginning of this experiment, it registered at 5.4. That's not horrible, but it could definitely have been better. When I retested after six months in nutritional ketosis, it had dropped to 4.7, or an average daily blood sugar reading of 88 mg/dl.

My heart health indicators changed as well: HDL cholesterol went up, triglycerides went down, LDL particles shifted to more of the healthier large, fluffy kind, my C-reactive protein (a key inflammatory marker) fell into the optimal range, and a CT scan of my heart revealed zero calcium plaque build-up in my coronary arteries. Remember, all these positive changes happened while eating a diet composed of more than 80 percent fat, mostly saturated fat. Although my LDL and total cholesterol levels remained elevated, as they had been before ketosis (indicating an increased risk factor for heart disease according to conventional medical standards), every other relevant marker on my cholesterol panel improved dramatically. More important, the CT scan found no sign of actual disease taking place in my arteries.

MOMENT OF CLARITY As a cardiologist, I often view life from the perspective of heart health since heart disease is the number-one cause of death in Americans. Achieving ketosis leads to dramatic improvements in lipoproteins, even in crude cholesterol values. Many doctors rely too much on LDL-C, which is calculated—yes, calculated, not measured directly. It's based on an outdated equation developed in the 1960s that makes crude assumptions about diet composition, not factoring in such things as carbohydrate reduction. Genuine risk is much more accurately revealed via advanced lipoprotein testing, which readily identifies carbohydrates as the culprit in creating the most common causes of heart disease, including excess small, oxidation-prone LDL particles, and exaggerations in postprandial lipoproteins. Fat makes little to no change in lipoproteins.

– Dr. William Davis

One of the more curious results of my n=1 NK experiment was its effect on my exercise performance. We haven't discussed the relationship between ketones and exercise much yet, but there are tremendous benefits in this realm. I held off on doing any intensive exercise program for the first few months of my experiment because I wanted to make sure I was fully keto-adapted first. I noticed that my energy began to increase within the first couple of months of the experiment, so that gave me a sneak peek at how I would do in the gym once the ketones were my primary fuel. But I was still skeptical, since all my other attempts at high-intensity training had led to bad bouts with hypoglycemia (in other words, significant drops in blood sugar).

If you've ever gone to the gym to work out and experienced dizziness, hunger, nausea, fatigue, and even blackouts, that's hypoglycemia. Going through these sorts of side effects just a couple of times will completely turn you off from the idea of working out ever again. Add to that the fact that it would take me seven to ten days to recover from the muscle soreness from lifting weights, and exercise for me was disastrous. Some people told me I needed to eat high-sugar fruits or starchy carbohydrates pre- and post-workout, but that never fully resolved the problems I was having.

So when I started exercising while in a ketogenic state, I committed to doing a full-body twenty-minute weight lifting session every three days. Yes, I was skeptical, but I wanted to see if all the hoopla about ketones and exercise performance detailed in *The Art and Science of Low Carbohydrate Performance* was actually true or not. And to really put this concept to the ultimate test, I decided that I'd precede every workout with an eighteen- to twenty-four-hour fast to see how I'd do. Am I crazy? Yeah, maybe a little bit.

MOMENT OF CLARITY I can go twelve hours without food and still power through a three-hour workout with energy to spare. My strength improved 50 percent in ketosis while my muscles became toned. One of the most amazing physical responses to ketosis is the 10 percent body fat I am able to maintain without any effort at all. My low body fat is consistent, and I suffer no ill health effects from eating a low-carbohydrate, high-fat diet.

— Stephanie Person

Here's what happened for me: no dizziness, no blackouts, no fatigue or weakness, robust energy, no hunger or cravings, surprisingly full strength, feeling of invigoration post-workout, quick muscle recovery, and amazing strength gains. This took me totally by surprise. My strength increased nearly threefold, and I saw noticeable increases in muscle definition. I never would have expected this from a diet so low in carbohydrate and protein.

Make sure you don't test your blood sugar or blood ketone levels immediately after a workout. Wait a few hours so that you don't get discouraged by the results. Your blood sugar will very likely be elevated because the liver releases glucose into the bloodstream during exercise. Additionally, with the rise in blood sugar levels, you'll likely see a temporary drop in blood ketones. This may lead you to believe the exercise made your pursuit of ketosis worse, not better. But be patient and wait a few hours after exercising, and you'll see normalized blood sugar levels and a rise in blood ketone levels.

MOMENT OF CLARITY I think a healthy diet and lifestyle tends to produce ketones (not necessarily the other way around). When a person eats seasonally, fasts intermittently, and exercises with intensity, there will be periods when they are producing higher levels of ketones, and this produces many beneficial and protective properties in the body.

— Bryan Barksdale

What about weight loss? My results were pretty stunning—seventy-eight pounds lost in that single year of being in a constant state of nutritional ketosis. People love to look at weight loss as the grand be-all, end-all signifier of a diet's efficacy, thanks in part to television shows like *The Biggest Loser* that glorify the number on the scale. But to me, it was probably the least interesting statistic from my n=1 experiment. When you are eating and living healthy (as you are while in ketosis), weight loss is merely a side effect, and one that's less important than the other health benefits. While so many people emphasize losing weight, it's much more important to be consistent in doing what makes you healthy. If you do that, then the weight loss will quickly follow.

But I did measure weight and fat loss, along with muscle growth, during this experiment. I had a dual-energy X-ray absorptiometry (DXA) scan, which measures body fat and lean muscle mass. It's also used to track bone density in people with osteoporosis, but it can be a powerful tool in tracking your progress toward your fat-loss goals. My first DXA scan done at Dr. Jeffrey Galvin's Vitality Medical Wellness Institute (VitalityMWI.com) in Concord, North Carolina, on September 13, 2012, and another was done two months later on November 12, 2012. This noninvasive test takes about ten to twenty minutes to conduct, and all you do is lie down and stay as still as possible.

The results of the tests showed that in just two months, I'd lost 9.7 pounds and 5 percent of my total body fat (a mindboggling 16 pounds of body fat shed—this was huge), and I'd gained a whopping 6 pounds of lean muscle mass. Remember, my protein intake at the time came in at just 12 percent of my total caloric intake, about 80 to 100 grams daily. I didn't consume any pre- or post-workout carbohydrates to help aid muscle growth, but I added muscle anyway pretty much across the board in every part of my body. The idea that low-carb, ketogenic diets cause muscle wasting is completely unfounded. In fact, it's best for preserving and increasing lean muscle, as Phinney and Volek have shown in their published research on this topic.

MOMENT OF CLARITY Nutritional ketosis allows my brain to be fueled with ketones and protects me from the symptoms of the occasional hypoglycemic episode. This neuroprotection allows me to enjoy scuba diving, swimming, and other sports without fear of hypoglycemia. Since starting my ketogenic lifestyle, I have enjoyed a reduction in my average blood sugar from 140 to 83 mg/dl, HbA1c from 6.5 percent to 5.0 percent, and hsCRP from 3.2 to 0.7 mg/L, while HDL-C increased from 61 to 91 mg/dL—all with half the insulin dose.

– Dr. Keith Runyan

As for the changes that are less quantifiable: I quickly went from struggling to get four to five hours of sleep each night to enjoying seven to nine hours of restful slumber. My mental acuity improved dramatically (no more foggy brain!). Acne breakouts were greatly reduced. Skin tags I had had for years began shriveling up and disappearing. And I realize this is TMI, but even my pooping pattern normalized after getting into ketosis. These are just a few of the many benefits I saw on a low-carb, high-fat, ketogenic diet.

As you can see, I think my one-year n=1 experiment of nutritional ketosis could be very easily described as a resounding success. If you want to dig a little deeper into the month-to-month details of my personal testing of NK, I updated my blog every thirty days to track my progress: livinlavidalowcarb.com/blog/n1.

The amazing health improvements I saw in nutritional ketosis would have been difficult to believe if I hadn't seen them for myself. Coming up in the next chapter, I'll share about the five major mistakes I had been making in my low-carb diet that were remedied when I began tracking my ketones.

MOMENT OF CLARITY The best ways to manipulate macronutrients to induce a state of ketosis, the role that ketone bodies play, and their potential side effects are all unknown. Individuals are doing the experiments that will provide us with valuable information. They will be criticized as anecdotal, but anecdotal data is valuable as long as it pertains to the question asked.

– Dr. Richard Feinman

Key Keto Clarity Concepts

→ I tested nutritional ketosis for one year on myself to see what would happen.

→ Testing for blood ketones was popularized by Dr. Jeff Volek and Dr. Stephen Phinney.

→ I tracked my blood ketones, blood sugar, and weight twice daily during my n=1 test.

→ When I began testing my blood ketones, I was not in a state of nutritional ketosis.

→ Just because you're eating low-carb doesn't mean you are ketogenic.

→ Blood ketones rise as you become keto-adapted within two to six weeks.

→ The composition of my diet was customized to help me create ketones.

→ My wife consumed a far different diet than I did while in nutritional ketosis.

→ I saw stunning results in hunger control, ability to fast, and blood sugar stabilization.

→ All the relevant cholesterol and inflammation markers got better while in ketosis.

→ Exercise improvements happened even while working out in a fasted state.

→ Don't test blood sugar or blood ketones right after a workout—wait a few hours.

→ Weight loss is perhaps the least significant statistic from my n=1 experiment.

→ Health, not weight loss, should be the focus of any diet change you make.

→ A DXA scan revealed both body fat loss and lean muscle mass gain during my n=1 experiment.

Chapter 10

Five Low-Carb Mistakes and How Nutritional Ketosis Rescued Me

MOMENT OF CLARITY The biggest challenge with a ketogenic diet is reducing the carbohydrate and protein intake sufficiently to get into and maintain ketosis. If you eat too much protein, your body will convert the amino acids into glucose. If you eat too many carbs, your blood sugar will be too high to have ketones. It takes fat to make the ketone bodies.

— Dr. Terry Wahls

Many people who switch to a low-carb, high-fat, ketogenic lifestyle lose weight and improve their health without ever needing to test for ketones. So can you just eat low-carb and high-fat and let that suffice?

The short answer: maybe. When I began following the Atkins diet in 2004 as a 410-pound man, any move away from the massive amounts of carbage (get it? carbs + garbage = carbage) I was consuming was going to improve my weight and health. But my recipe for success at thirty-two may not work for me now that I'm over the age of forty. Years of poor eating habits will catch up to you, and for those who have more metabolic damage or who may be experiencing hormonal challenges (especially postmenopause), it's crucial to pay strict attention to your diet and test for ketones.

Many people believe that they're following a ketogenic diet but are adding in foods that derail their progress toward ketosis. Maybe they're eating a banana with breakfast, throwing off their carb intake, or having a chicken breast at dinner, sending their protein consumption too high. This probably explains why some people believe ketosis failed them: their diets weren't strict enough to actually get them into ketosis, so they never got to experience its health benefits. Figuring out the amounts of carbohydrate, protein, and fat that are right for you and adhering precisely to those amounts makes all the difference in the world.

MOMENT OF CLARITY Increasing protein is not usually necessary and is generally self-limiting, meaning tolerance and appetite for protein will limit intake and it is therefore rarely, perhaps never, necessary to purposely increase or decrease protein intake. A substantial increase in protein may even impair the capacity to achieve a ketogenic state.

— Dr. William Davis

In chapter 2, I explained the difference between the low-carb Atkins diet, which many people have used for decades to lose weight and improve health, and the concept of nutritional ketosis. Now I want to share with you the five key mistakes that I was making in my own diet that prevented me from getting into a therapeutic state of nutritional ketosis. Correcting these major errors in my routine was absolutely necessary for me to experience the full benefits of a ketogenic diet. If you have been struggling with your weight and health goals while on a low-carb diet, these might be hampering your progress.

1. Consuming too much protein

MOMENT OF CLARITY Every individual will have somewhat different sensitivities to protein. The mice we used in my lab are highly sensitive to protein. Protein moderation at varying levels is perhaps necessary for humans as well.

— Dr. Charles Mobbs

This is discussed in detail in chapter 6, but it bears repeating, since it goes against what we've been told about a low-carb diet needing to be high in protein. The media and so-called health experts would have people believe that a grilled chicken breast on a bed of green leafy vegetables is a perfectly fine meal on a ketogenic diet. And while it is indeed low in carbohydrates, there's one really big problem with this meal: there's way too much protein in it if you want to get into ketosis. A low-carb, ketogenic diet needs to be high in *fat*, not protein, to produce adequate ketones.

It all goes back to gluconeogenesis. When you consume excess protein, your liver transforms it into glucose. If you are making lean meats like chicken breasts, turkey, and lower-fat cuts of beef and pork the central focus of your nutritional plan, then you might be defeating the purpose of going ketogenic to begin with. Consuming too much protein (and, therefore, getting more glucose in your bloodstream) can stoke hunger and cravings, and make you ravenous between meals. To keep this from happening, try to choose fattier cuts of meat and control the total amount of protein you are eating to see how that affects your blood ketone levels.

MOMENT OF CLARITY Low-carb dieting has been relatively easy for me over the last ten years, but the ketogenic diet presented challenges when I first attempted it. Restricting carbohydrates was not a problem for me, but eating high-fat was challenging at first. I also needed to significantly reduce my protein intake to achieve nutritional ketosis. It is nearly impossible for most people to maintain even moderate levels of ketosis if protein is greater than 2 grams per kilogram of body weight, unless there is very high energy expenditure through exercise.

– Dr. Dominic D'Agostino

While protein has been receiving quite a bit of attention in recent years in food marketing, if you consume more than the amount your body needs, you could be preventing yourself from being in ketosis. This is very likely the biggest mistake people make when they shift to a low-carb, high-fat diet. Yes, protein is a good thing for your body, but be aware that too much can give you problems no matter how low your carbohydrate intake.

2. Using urine ketone testing strips to measure ketosis

MOMENT OF CLARITY When patients are first beginning a ketogenic diet, I have them follow their urine ketones to confirm that they are in ketosis. However, since kidneys will adapt to and excrete fewer ketones after about a month of being in ketosis, I only expect to see a trace to small amount of ketones in the urine. If I am checking for blood ketones then I look for 0.5 millimolar or higher.

– Dr. Terry Wahls

Far too many people on a low-carb, high-fat diet are relying on urine ketone testing strips (the best-known brand is Ketostix) to measure their ketones. But, as we discussed in chapter 8, once you're fully keto-adapted within a few weeks of beginning a low-carb, high-fat diet, it would be an error of epic proportions to believe these strips will give you an accurate depiction of how you are doing at burning fat for fuel.

I understand the allure of urine ketone testing strips. It can be incredibly exciting and motivating, especially when you're new to this way of eating, to watch the strips magically turn from light pink to dark purple. They seem to validate our nutritional choices and prove that we're doing something constructive for our weight and health. In a way, seeing the change in color can feel like a reward for our nutritional efforts.

Unfortunately, urine ketone testing strips can curb your enthusiasm at the very point when you are on the verge of real success with ketosis. Their inherent flaw is that they don't measure the particular ketone body, beta-hydroxybutyrate, that your body uses as fuel once you've made the shift from sugar-burner to fat-burner. The ketone body measured in the urine is acetoacetate, and as ketones become your primary fuel source, acetoacetate is converted to beta-hydroxybutyrate—which must be measured through a blood test or correlated to the acetone measured by a breath test. The urine strips only detect the presence of acetoacetate, which dramatically decreases or disappears once the body is relying on beta-hydroxybutyrate for fuel, making keto-adapted dieters think they're doing something wrong.

MOMENT OF CLARITY When people are keto-adapted, they tend to have more beta-hydroxybutyrate in the blood and excrete less acetoacetate in the urine. Over time, as beta-hydroxybutyrate becomes a more important substrate for energy production, the body makes less acetoacetate and more beta-hydroxybutyrate. This is the reason that urinary ketone strips are unreliable when tracking nutritional ketosis.

– Dr. Zeeshan Arain

Once you realize that switching from burning sugar to burning fat means that acetoacetate may no longer show up on these urine ketone testing strips, then you can feel confident that every area of your body, from your brain to your blood, is being nourished by the ketone bodies they prefer as fuel—no matter what the urine test strips show. Keep your carbohydrate and protein intake at your personal tolerance levels and you'll stay in the glorious state of ketosis where beta-hydroxybutyrate reigns supreme. If you want to know how well you are doing at creating ketones in the blood, you can measure beta-hydroxybutyrate using the blood ketone meters we talked about in chapter 8.

3. Not eating enough saturated and monounsaturated fats

MOMENT OF CLARITY Healthy, natural dietary fat is tremendously beneficial to the immune system, especially in foods like pastured butter, grass-fed cultured ghee, and coconut oil. These, along with certain poultry fats, contain antiviral and antimicrobial substances that can help directly support your immune function. An effective state of ketosis also is profoundly anti-inflammatory, helps to curb free radical activity, and supports antioxidant activity.

– Nora Gedgaudas

In chapter 7, we underlined the critical importance of eating fat, especially saturated and monounsaturated fats. When you reduce your carbohydrate intake, the macronutrient that needs to go up in response is fat. One of the lingering arguments made by the low-fat propaganda machine that's been working for over three decades is the idea that dietary fat is harmful, that it will clog your arteries and make you fat. We believe these things because we've had them hammered into our heads again and again as the gospel truth for most of our lives. And if a lie is repeated often enough, people will begin to believe it. That's exactly what has happened with the vilification of dietary fat, most notably saturated fat.

MOMENT OF CLARITY I find it astounding that many of my immediate physician and cardiologist colleagues cling to the outdated belief that total and/or saturated fat intake are somehow related to heart disease risk. Reassessment of the data used to justify such arguments, as well as more recent clinical studies, demonstrates that total and saturated fat intake have nothing to do with heart-disease risk.

– Dr. William Davis

So it's probably not a huge surprise that many people who begin a low-carb diet simultaneously cut their fat intake as well. They erroneously think that if low-carb is good, then low-fat *and* low-carb must be better. That's a fatal error if your goal is to get into a state of nutritional ketosis and experience all the benefits it has to offer you. In fact, eating more fat is one of the best ways to stave off the hunger and cravings, especially for carbohydrates, that come when you begin a low-carb diet.

Even if you think you're already eating a pretty good amount of quality, whole-food sources of fat, you may need to ramp it up a bit more. Before my yearlong nutritional ketosis experiment, my diet was probably around 60 to 65 percent fat. By any definition, that's a high-fat diet. As it turned out, though, I needed to bump that up even more, until 80 to 85 percent of my calories came from dietary fat. Combined with keeping my carbs to my personal tolerance and protein to my individual threshold, this got my body to begin creating ketones at the right levels for weight and health benefits.

MOMENT OF CLARITY On a low-carb, high-fat, ketogenic diet, the presence of ketones in the body signals the metabolism of fatty acids as an energy source, either directly or indirectly, via the production and burning of ketones as fuel. This to me is essential for the best health you could possibly have.

– Dr. Ron Rosedale

We share recipes and a meal plan in chapters 20 and 21 to show you what a high-fat diet like this looks like, but overall it's pretty simple: consume more butter, coconut oil, sour cream, cream cheese, full-fat meats, full-fat cheese, avocados, full-fat Greek yogurt, and more! Get creative, and don't fear the fat. While you may not need to get 80 to 85 percent of your calories from fat, as I do, you'd be surprised how adding just a bit more fat to your diet can make all the difference in reaching therapeutic levels of nutritional ketosis, gaining the amazing health benefits that come with it, and shedding pounds.

DOCTOR'S NOTE FROM DR. ERIC WESTMAN: Low-carb, low-fat diets (like the South Beach Diet, for example) were a marketing maneuver to combine the low-carb diet with the low-fat diet—but it doesn't make physiological sense. The time-honored low-carb, ketogenic diet, like the one used by Dr. Atkins in his clinic for thirty-five years, was always a low-carb diet that was simultaneously high in fat.

4. Eating too often or too much

MOMENT OF CLARITY The biggest nutritional lie I see is that you need to eat six to seven meals a day for optimal strength and fat-burning. This pattern of eating is time-consuming, impractical, and not supported by the science. Personally, I have been able to maintain the same level of mental energy, physical energy, and strength after reducing my meal frequency from six to seven meals a day to two meals a day. Eating less often by eating satiating, ketogenic meals is liberating because it reduces preoccupation with food, preparation, cleaning up, carrying food around, and stressing out in situations where you can't eat every two to three hours. Shifting the macronutrient ratio of your diet to less carbohydrate and much more fat has a profound satiating and protein-sparing effect.

– Dr. Dominic D'Agostino

While calories are certainly a controversial subject when it comes to the ketogenic diet, it could be argued that being aware of how much and how often you are eating can make a difference when you are trying to get into ketosis. So do calories count?

Well, yes and no. Yes, it is indeed possible to eat beyond satiety and consume more food than you really need. When this happens, more than likely you are pushing your carbohydrate and protein intake well beyond the point where your body can use them properly, stoking hunger and cravings and making you unable to feel satisfied with the proper amount of food. We keep coming back to the idea of keeping carbohydrates and protein at the point of your personal tolerance and individual threshold because this is what will make you most successful on your ketogenic journey.

As I learned when I experimented with nutritional ketosis, some truly remarkable things begin to happen to your body once you become keto-adapted: hunger is completely zapped, you may forget to eat, and you feel energized and alert while going many hours between meals. Your body is quite literally "eating" stored body fat all day long while your brain is being fueled efficiently by the ketone bodies you are producing. So while we have become conditioned to think that we must eat at specified times throughout the day, maybe we don't.

MOMENT OF CLARITY We tend to underestimate portion sizes, and often there are "hidden carbs" in meals eaten outside the home. In some people, consuming too much protein can prevent ketosis as well, although this is highly individualized. Measuring foods accurately and tracking your macronutrient and ketone levels for a few days can give you great information to use in formulating your diet to include the right amount of carbohydrates and protein for your own specific needs.

– Franziska Spritzler

There's this idea promoted by our culture that we need to be eating in a pattern that goes something like this: breakfast, snack, lunch, snack, dinner, snack, midnight snack. Can I just tell you how utterly ridiculous and unnecessary this is when you are no longer addicted to carbohydrates? Was the Eleventh Commandment God gave to Moses on Mount Sinai, "Thou shalt eat at least three times a day?" You'd think it was, considering how many people believe there is such a thing as mealtimes.

When you start to burn fat for fuel and produce ketones, it's very possible to feel completely satisfied and energized on one, maybe two meals a day. Some people may argue that this promotes an eating disorder or some such nonsense. But why should you eat more food than you need or eat when you're not hungry and your body is doing perfectly well using ketones as an alternative fuel source? There's no need to eat between meals when you're in ketosis; just eat to satiety at each meal and don't eat again until you're hungry.

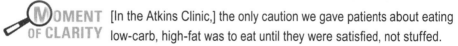 [In the Atkins Clinic,] the only caution we gave patients about eating low-carb, high-fat was to eat until they were satisfied, not stuffed.

– Jackie Eberstein

When you fall into a regular pattern of eating low-carb, moderate-protein, high-fat meals with a sufficient amount of calories from high-quality, nutrient-dense whole foods, you'll find that one meal can quite possibly keep your hunger satiated for twelve to twenty-four hours. I know it sounds preposterous to think you could (or would even want to) go that long between meals, but it happens naturally because you just don't get jittery and hangry (hungry and angry) when you are in ketosis. We all know people whose personality shifts dramatically when they haven't eaten in a while. My wife, Christine, will tell you I was one of those people before I started eating low-carb, high-fat. Now, believe it or not, she sometimes has to remind me to eat because I "forget."

As you can imagine, periods of spontaneous intermittent fasting (which we will explore even more in the next chapter) will help you lower your overall food and calorie consumption without feeling miserably hungry between meals. Too many people are habitually eating at appointed times during the day (breakfast before going to work or school, lunch during a break in the middle of the day, dinner at home in the evening with the family). But if you allow your cultural paradigms about food to shift from eating by the clock to eating when hunger kicks in, then you might be pleasantly surprised to see your blood ketone levels increase, leading to all the health benefits that will give you.

Think for a moment about who determines your meal's portion size. The restaurant bringing you a big plate of food? The food manufacturers who create the packaging? It should be your body that determines the amount that you eat. Also, were you raised with the idea that you had to eat everything on your plate "because there are starving children in Africa"? I think all of our moms pulled that trick on us a time or two growing up. You may have even been a member of the "Clean Plate Club" and were rewarded for eating everything placed in front of you. But these ideas from childhood no longer apply now that you are an adult.

> DOCTOR'S NOTE FROM DR. ERIC WESTMAN: *"Eat until you are 80 percent full" is the way most children in Japan are raised—letting their body's internal control mechanism determine the portion size. Is it a coincidence that Okinawa is well known for having the highest proportion of people living beyond the age of one hundred?*

5. Failing to stabilize blood sugar levels

MOMENT OF CLARITY To achieve a ketotic state, I ask people to begin with grain and sugar elimination. Grains are, by the way, the worst offenders for triggering high blood sugar, even worse than simple sugars, such as sucrose. So grain elimination—not reduction—is key for getting into ketosis.

– Dr. William Davis

Since we're focusing on ketosis, you might wonder why I'm bringing up the subject of blood sugar. Isn't that just something people with diabetes need to be concerned about? If only that were true. The reality is that everyone reading this book right now should be actively using a glucometer to test their blood sugar levels. It is arguably one of the most invaluable and yet underutilized tools at our disposal for assessing how we are doing metabolically. Blood glucose meters are widely available in any pharmacy or drugstore in the world.

What's the big deal about knowing your blood sugar? Plenty. Knowing exactly how your body is responding hormonally to food is empowering.

Keeping carbohydrate and protein intake to your personal tolerance and individual threshold and eating ample amounts of satiating, real food–based fats will lower your fasting blood sugar level to the 80s and even the 70s while simultaneously raising your level of blood ketones. There's almost an inverse relationship between the two numbers—when you're eating a low-carb, high-fat diet, as blood sugar goes down, blood ketones go up. Conversely, as blood sugar goes up (most likely when you consume carbohydrate and protein beyond your tolerance levels), then your blood ketones plummet.

MOMENT OF CLARITY On the whole, the more adherent you are to a ketogenic diet, the greater improvement you will see in the lowering of blood glucose.

– Dr. Charles Mobbs

Your blood sugar level could be the first sign of how well you are producing ketones. When I tested both my blood sugar and blood ketones day and night for a year, I noticed that blood sugar tends to normalize before blood ketone production increases. For example, if you see your morning fasting blood sugar drop from 99 to 85 within a week of starting on a low-carb, moderate-protein, high-fat diet, you may not see your blood ketones in the range of nutritional ketosis right away. But give it a few more days and the ketones will begin to rise precipitously, while your blood sugar may even drop some more. This is completely normal.

When you normalize your blood sugar, hunger pangs and cravings are controlled, your moods even out, and you experience a sense of well-being that can only come from getting off the roller coaster ride of alternating between hyperglycemia (elevated blood sugar) and hypoglycemia (sudden drops in blood sugar). Get your blood sugar well regulated, and nutritional ketosis will be easier to attain—and conversely, nutritional ketosis will help you regulate your blood sugar. They work together, hand in hand, to make you successful in your pursuit of ketosis.

MOMENT OF CLARITY Because ketones can supply up to 80 percent of the brain's energy needs in nutritional ketosis, when hypoglycemia does occur, the symptoms are minimal to nonexistent, because the brain is not starved by the lack of glucose.

– Dr. Keith Runyan

If you have been struggling with your low-carb, high-fat program and have fallen into some of the same mistakes I was making, don't be discouraged. You are not alone, and the low-carb, high-fat diet has not failed you at all. Even those of us who have been doing this for a very long time are susceptible to making these mistakes, and correcting them can make all the difference in your success.

Coming up in the next chapter, we'll talk more about intermittent fasting and the role it can play in making ketosis happen for you.

Key Keto Clarity Concepts

→ **Simply eating low-carb may not be enough to get into ketosis.**

→ **Consuming excess protein can derail production of adequate ketones.**

→ **Choose fattier cuts of meat and avoid the lean meats as much as possible.**

→ **Stop relying on urine ketones testing strips to determine if you are in ketosis.**

→ **Urine ketones may disappear as you become more keto-adapted.**

→ **Failing to eat enough saturated and monounsaturated fats is a huge mistake.**

→ **Never eat a low-carb, low-fat diet; your body needs the fat to thrive.**

→ **You may need to ramp up your fat intake substantially to experience benefits.**

→ **Calories count inasmuch as you shouldn't eat beyond satiety.**

→ **Counting calories is unnecessary if you pay attention to satiety signals.**

→ **Frequent meals are merely a cultural thing, not a physiological response to hunger.**

→ **Being in ketosis enables you to spontaneously fast for twelve to twenty-four hours.**

→ **Getting blood sugar levels under control is critical to nutritional ketosis.**

→ **Be encouraged that we all make mistakes in our pursuit of ketosis.**

Chapter 11
The Role of Intermittent Fasting in Ketosis

MOMENT OF CLARITY Ketones are normally only made in quantity during a prolonged fast, as probably occurred a lot during evolution and even now possibly during illness or dieting to lose weight. Ketones are somewhat elevated even after a normal overnight fast.

— Dr. Charles Mobbs

I know I've probably already lost at least half of you just by bringing up fasting (the other "f" word), but stick with me here because it could be another instrumental piece to the proverbial puzzle in maximizing the benefits you get from ketosis. Periods of fasting cause the body to react as if it is starving, increasing the production of ketones.

But just mention the word *fasting* to someone on the street and the reaction you'll get will probably fall somewhere between complete scorn to sheer terror at the idea of going without food for more than a few hours. Believe me, I understand, because I had the same reaction in 2006 when I first heard about intermittent fasting (IF) from a low-carb author, blogger, and physician named Dr. Michael Eades, author of the bestselling book *Protein Power*.

Dr. Eades wrote a blog post about IF that captured a lot of attention, generating the most comments that he had ever received on a blog post. The traditional method of fasting calls for alternating days of fasting and eating (eat Monday, fast Tuesday, eat Wednesday, fast Thursday, and so on). The IF plan that Dr. Eades was attempting, however, was a bit more practical. Here's what his sample IF eating schedule looked like:

- Day 1 – Eat anytime until 6:00 p.m. and then stop eating
- Day 2 – Don't eat until 6:00 p.m.

► Day 3 – Eat anytime until 6:00 p.m. and then stop eating

► Day 4 – Don't eat until 6:00 p.m.

And so on. Of course, you aren't constantly eating on the days you stop eating at 6:00 p.m.; you simply eat as you normally would, when you are hungry. And for the sake of his experiment with IF, Dr. Eades even said to feel free to eat whatever you want. However, he does advocate a low-carb diet and recommends sticking with low-carb foods while on IF to maximize its impact, especially for the purposes of weight loss.

Dr. Eades said it was very easy for him to skip breakfast and lunch. And if you think about what happens on the weekends, when your day is proba-bly not quite as regimented as it may be on a hectic work or school day, you likely end up eating fewer meals almost naturally—even spontaneously. Still, I was extremely skeptical of the whole idea of fasting, even on an intermit-tent basis. Why would you put yourself through the torture of going without food, bringing on ravenous hunger, and fool yourself into believing you'll enjoy it? Who in their right mind would ever do that?

That was then; this is now. The concept of fasting as part of a healthy lifestyle has become popular in recent years among people following a Paleo lifestyle (which hearkens back to the nutritional habits of our hunter-gather-er ancestors), many of whom are attempting to get into ketosis. Intermittent fasting can be a powerful strategy for optimizing weight and health, but it is still highly controversial and misunderstood by many people. Who should be fasting and who should not? How long should you fast to get the most benefits out of it? Can you produce adequate ketone levels without fasting? These are just a few of the questions we'll be answering in this chapter.

First, yes, it's possible to have beneficial levels of ketones without fasting, but it can be difficult for some. If you're eating the right amounts of carbs to your tolerance level, protein to your individual threshold, and fat to satiety and *still* aren't producing enough ketones, it could be that you're eating too much food, and perhaps too often, as we shared in chapter 10. Fasting will tend to bump up your ketone production.

MOMENT OF CLARITY The single largest problem for ketone production is excess calorie consumption. On the other hand, the ketogenic diet is therapeutic for a broad range of diseases when consumed in carefully measured and restricted amounts.

– Dr. Thomas Seyfried

When I started on my one-year nutritional ketosis experiment, I had no intention at all of fasting. But I quickly discovered that it just started happening spontaneously and naturally, especially when my blood ketone levels exceeded 1.0 millimolar. I remember early on, within the first few weeks of my experiment, my wife asked me when I last ate. After looking at the clock and then going back through my food logs, I realized it had been about twenty-eight hours. I had totally forgotten to eat. If you know me well, then you'll realize just how phenomenal this was! I was so satisfied by the ketones my body was producing that I couldn't remember that I needed to eat something. Those days of being "hangry" were long gone, and I was now experiencing the power of ketosis in action.

I realize this all probably seems a bit odd to those who still think they need three square meals a day, as we all grew up believing. But it's time to start looking outside the box of conventional wisdom and realize that fasting is probably a lot more normal than you think. If you're consuming a meal of whole foods that is low-carb, moderate-protein, and high-fat, with plenty of calories, then why would your body need to be fed again in just a few short hours? It wouldn't. As long as you didn't overdo it on the carbohydrates or protein and ate plenty of fat, you should be able to go twelve to twenty-four hours before your next meal rather easily.

Remember, this happens very naturally and shouldn't be associated with any hunger or discomfort at all. Try it and see what happens. You may be tempted to cut back on the amount of food you consume when you eat more fat in your diet, but don't. A meal should be pretty substantial, especially if it ends up being your only meal of the day. Maybe that breakfast of two eggs and two slices of bacon should become four eggs cooked in butter and topped with cheddar cheese and sour cream, three slices of bacon, and an avocado. The former meal will likely have you looking for more food in a few hours, whereas the latter meal might take your mind off of food for the rest of the day. What freedom you can experience by making IF a part of your life!

MOMENT OF CLARITY Each patient [in Dr. Atkins' clinic] was told to include a protein serving with each meal and snack. It was not necessary to trim the fat from meat or remove skin from poultry. We encouraged the liberal use of butter with vegetables and healthy oils like olive oil on salads. Sour cream and heavy cream were also allowed.

– Jackie Eberstein

Think of IF as a means for measuring your "keto fitness level." Once you become fully keto-adapted and begin spontaneously fasting for twelve to twenty-four hours at a time with ample hydration, there is a sense of freedom from no longer having to look for something to eat every three hours. Using ketones as fuel enables you to be mentally sharp and have total hunger control without consciously using your willpower to resist temptation to eat. Spontaneous intermittent fasting with no adverse side effects is a very clear indicator of optimal metabolic health.

MOMENT OF CLARITY In the context of commencing a high-fat diet, it indicates the metabolism is burning fatty acids and ketones and that is what is essential for optimal health.

— Dr. Ron Rosedale

But what do you do if you start to get hungry while intermittent fasting? The answer is pretty simple: *eat something!* When you feel hunger, your body is signaling that you need more food. But do keep in mind that not every gurgle and noise that comes from your digestive system is hunger.

DOCTOR'S NOTE FROM DR. ERIC WESTMAN: To drive home the point that you do not have to eat three meals a day, I created a sign for the wall of my clinic room that says "Eat When Hungry, Drink When Thirsty!" I want my patients to think of it as an ancient proverb! Many of my patients have told me that it helps remind them that they aren't "skipping meals" when they only eat once or twice a day.

I've seen Dr. Westman's "Eat When Hungry, Drink When Thirsty!" sign posted prominently on the wall of every single patient room in his Duke Lifestyle Medicine Clinic in Durham, North Carolina. It sounds so simple, doesn't it? But what makes it incredibly profound is the fact that very few people these days are actually listening for their bodies to tell them when they are genuinely hungry or thirsty. The fact is that eating carbohydrates makes you hungry. This is an important concept to figure out if you're going to attempt to engage in fasting.

When I weighed over 400 pounds, I was hungry virtually all the time. And it didn't seem to matter how much food I put in my mouth; I just kept eating and eating and eating. Getting my hunger under control and recognizing what true hunger was supposed to feel like was a huge part of my success. Of course, hunger is a subjective feeling that's different in each person, so I can't tell you exactly what true hunger will feel like for you. But I can tell you what hunger is *not*.

DOCTOR'S NOTE FROM DR. ERIC WESTMAN: For most people, hunger and cravings for carbohydrates will go away after one to three days of significantly reducing them in your diet. But as time goes on, other reasons for eating may become problems that interfere with your progress toward ketosis.

Sometimes what feels like hunger may actually stem from a nutrient deficiency. I once received an email from a blog reader who was new to ketosis. Despite eating a low-carb, high-fat diet, she was having trouble getting her hunger under control, as well as experiencing constant brain fog and the excruciating headaches that can accompany the switch to running on ketone bodies. I suggested that she boost her daily salt intake by adding extra salt to her food and drinking, for example, a bouillon cube mixed with some warm water. Within just a few days, she was seeing great results, as she wrote back to me:

Hey Jimmy,

Thanks so much for responding to my email! I took your advice and added the bouillon to my diet. Since then, my headaches have vanished and I can now tell when I'm truly hungry. I measured my blood ketones and blood glucose for the first time. I hit 1.2 millimolar in my blood ketones and my blood sugar was 93. Yesterday I ate bacon, spaghetti squash, and ground beef with marinara sauce along with some grass-fed butter, coconut oil, and 85% dark chocolate and felt completely satisfied. I should have been doing this a long time ago!

Simply by increasing the amount of salt in her diet, she was able to feel completely satisfied by the foods she was already eating. Her excitement about discovering what hunger and real satiation are supposed to feel like is something I wish I could bottle up and let you experience for yourself. Far too many people who attempt to go on a diet to lose weight think being hungry is a virtuous, even desirable, thing. Can I tell you how insane that is? If you are feeling hungry, your body screaming at you to feed it.

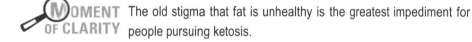

MOMENT OF CLARITY The initial stages of adopting a ketogenic approach can sometimes lead to significant sodium loss, which can produce hunger, short-term headaches, temporary fatigue, and weakness due to transitional issues related to fundamental energy substrate changes prior to becoming fully keto-adapted. This is easily remedied by adding more full-spectrum salts to the diet, preferably Himalayan sea salt.

— Nora Gedgaudas

When hunger pangs come on strong, the foods we crave tend to be processed carbohydrates. Instead of giving in and indulging in carbs, try feeding your body dietary fat instead. Nothing will zap hunger more quickly than fat (and maybe a little bit of protein, too)! One of my favorite ways to stop hunger is to eat a slice of full-fat cheddar cheese rolled up with a few pats of butter in the middle.

For people who are used to the dieting world, shifting to a low-carb, high-fat, ketogenic diet can be difficult. Most don't eat enough fat or food to completely satisfy their hunger. Skimping on fat will result in more hunger and cravings, and all the other side effects we've described already throughout this book. It's the perfect way to set yourself up for failure, so before you blame the diet, heed the advice in chapter 7 and eat more fat. You'll find that your hunger is completely satisfied, and of course you can't get into and sustain ketosis without eating enough fat. Ditch your fat phobia once and for all.

MOMENT OF CLARITY The old stigma that fat is unhealthy is the greatest impediment for people pursuing ketosis.

— John Kiefer

Failing to eat enough food when you are starting a ketogenic diet can also—unsurprisingly—bring on hunger pangs. So when hunger hits, it's time to eat up and enjoy the bounty of delicious and nutritious foods that are at your disposal on a low-carb, high-fat diet (a list of these satiating and mouthwatering foods is included in chapter 19). After you consume a meal like this, don't feel like you have to eat again the next time a "regular" meal-time rolls around just because of the time of day. If you're not hungry, then don't eat! It seems like a no-brainer, but far too many people succumb to the societal pull to eat by the clock and not by their need for food.

There are plenty of people like me who can comfortably eat one or two meals daily thanks to ketosis. Others may prefer to eat multiple times throughout the day. How much and when you eat is a personal decision; just monitor your progress and eat when you're hungry. Remember, carbs make you hungry while fat (with a little protein) fills you up and keeps you satisfied. Learn to listen to your body and eat accordingly.

There are many reasons for eating other than hunger: we often eat when we're bored, anxious, depressed, or worried; we eat with friends to be social; we eat as part of holiday celebrations; we eat because we're in a setting that we associate with eating (like eating popcorn at the movies or hot dogs at a ballgame). Some people may feel a stigma in social situations where everyone else is eating and they are not. For example, pastors, rabbis, and priests face an occupational hazard when they visit someone's home as a guest and are expected to eat whatever is prepared for them. The important thing to remember in these cases is that gathering together is about fellowship, not food. Simple phrases like "Thank you, but I just had something to eat" can keep feelings from being hurt, and in the worst-case scenario, eating "just a taste" may satisfy your host. Of course, be sure to say how wonderful the small taste was! And removing the eating aspect from socializing actually frees you up to engage more with others. You won't miss it if you are properly adapted to being fueled by fat and ketones.

MOMENT OF CLARITY Some roadblocks people encounter when attempting to follow a ketogenic diet include peer pressure to eat "normally" when they are with family and friends. But that is why I am so passionate about re-creating these favorite foods, such as protein noodle lasagna and healthy, sugar-free, extremely low-carb desserts—so clients don't feel the need to cheat.

– Maria Emmerich

Emotional eating is extremely common because carbohydrate-containing foods or beverages temporarily make us feel good. The good news is that bacon can become a comfort food just like macaroni and cheese, without the unintended consequences of weight gain and other health effects—but there is no question that most Americans have been raised to consider sweets and starches to be comfort foods. Fortunately, that changes over time when you embrace a low-carb, high-fat lifestyle.

Many people feel the urge to eat or hear their stomachs gurgling or growling at certain times of the day and assume that these feelings mean they're hungry. These feelings are not hunger; the brain simply draws that conclusion because we have eaten at that time of day for so long. It's a Pav-lovian response: just like Pavlov's dogs, who learned to associate the sound of a bell with feeding time and began salivating anytime they heard a bell, we also unconsciously become accustomed to eating at certain times, and our bodies generate stomach movements and secretions in response—but that's not true hunger. After you become keto-adapted, stomach noises and urges to eat that are associated with a certain time of day quickly fade away.

> *DOCTOR'S NOTE FROM DR. ERIC WESTMAN: I grew up celebrating holidays with the typical mountains of sweets: candy bars at Halloween, candy hearts on Valentine's Day, cookies at Christmas, and so on. The last sweet to go for me was jelly beans at Easter—it took me ten years to finally give them up!*

It's worth noting that some members of the online health community have questioned whether women should engage in intermittent fasting, citing concerns about hormonal dysregulation. But as long as fasting occurs in response to the natural satiating effects that come from being in a state of ketosis, there's no reason to avoid it. That said, it's definitely worth talking to your doctor if you have any specific concerns about this. And of course, pay attention to how you feel while fasting and make any needed adjustments. If you're hungry, that's your cue to eat!

With my affinity for doing tests on myself during my yearlong n=1 nutritional ketosis experiment, I was curious to see what would happen if I attempted a one-week fast, eating nothing and drinking only water. I had engaged in a one-week fast with water, diet soda, and chicken bouillon cubes in 2011, putting the words of cancer researcher Dr. Thomas Seyfried to the ultimate test. In my podcast interview with him on *The Livin' La Vida Low-Carb Show with Jimmy Moore* in November 2009, Dr. Seyfried noted that fasting for one week each year may be a great cancer prevention measure. The theory is that we can kill cancer cells by not feeding them sugar and carbs, and that the high amount of ketones generated during a weeklong fast may act as a protective measure against cancer. It took me a while to work up the gumption, but I tried it for the first time in April 2011. Dr. Seyfried even honored my willingness to give it a go in his 2012 book, *Cancer as a Metabolic Disease*.

Once my body had been running efficiently on ketone bodies (beta-hydroxybutyrate) for ten months in a row, I wanted to see if I could replicate that same one-week fast but with water only, forgoing the diet soda and boullion cubes I consumed last time as well as exercise and all my usual supplements. My goal was to make it for an entire week. With nutritional ketosis, regular eighteen- to twenty-four-hour fasts were already very natural and easy for me, but what would happen once I got beyond this time period? Of course, our hunter-gatherer ancestors went through regular, extended periods of deprivation when food was not readily available, but what would this feel like in the modern world? I wanted to find out for myself.

 **OMENT** The ketogenic diet has been effective in my practice in the treatment **OF CLARITY** of obesity and chronic disease without hunger or deprivation.

– Dr. Keith Runyan

Since I wanted to see what changes were happening to me during the entire week, I decided to test blood ketones and blood sugar every waking hour on the hour while observing everything that was happening in my normal routine. This would allow me to assess precisely how the fast was affecting all my numbers and state of health in real time. I promised myself and my wife that if at any point I started to feel bad beyond just simple hunger, or if my blood sugar dipped into the lower 50s for more than a couple of hours, I would end the experiment immediately.

During my first couple of days without food, my blood sugar began dropping slowly, until the bottom fell out in the early afternoon of the third day. That's when my blood sugar hit 59 for over two hours—and it was accompanied by a headache. Other than that, I felt pretty good. But even when my blood sugar rose back into the upper 60s again, my headache persisted.

My blood ketone levels followed a similar pattern but in the inverse. I saw normal readings of around 1.0 to 1.5 millimolar in the first couple of days, and then BOOM: it was 4.6 after forty-nine hours of fasting and slowly ticked up from there, to a high of 5.8 millimolar seventy-one hours into the fast. This coincided with my blood sugar dipping down to 59 for a couple of hours. As I've stated before, I wasn't at all worried about my blood ketones going that high because it coincided with a simultaneous drop in my blood sugar levels (I can't emphasize this point enough: diabetic ketoacidosis occurs only when *both* blood ketones and blood sugar are elevated to extremely high levels; nutritional ketosis produces higher blood ketones and lower blood sugar).

Because of the persistent headache, I decided to officially end the fast at 5:30 p.m. on the third day. Within an hour of eating a pretty sizable meal, the headache completely disappeared. I'm thinking now that my electrolyte balance was off; the bouillon cubes were a lot more effective in helping me sustain the fast in 2011 than I realized. It was a lesson learned for the next time I attempt to do a one-week fast. I can't help but wonder how much higher my blood ketones might have gone had I continued the fasting experience for the entire seven days. Incidentally, the night after I ended my three-day fast, I had difficulty sleeping, waking up after just a few hours.

Here are a few observations I made after my three-day fast was over:

- My first meal after fasting for seventy-two hours was pretty substantial.
- Despite eating a large amount of food, hunger persisted for a while, and I had to resist the urge to keep eating and eating.
- For a while after the fast, I felt hungry more often than I did before the fast began.
- Morning fasting blood sugar levels rose into the 90s in the days that followed the fast.
- Blood ketones dropped back down to normal within three days.
- When I went back to the gym, I still had full strength.
- My weight predictably rose several pounds after the fast ended.
- My sleep took a couple of days to become uninterrupted again.
- My mental clarity remained unchanged throughout.

You don't need to completely fast for days on end when you get into ketosis; I did it just to see what would happen. My conclusion is that you can get all the benefits of fasting by letting it happen naturally when you consume a low-carb, moderate-protein, high-fat diet with ample calories. Ketones give you the luxury of fasting that way, without even thinking about it.

Perhaps what you've read so far has spurred some questions in your mind about ketones that have not yet been addressed. Coming up in the next chapter, you'll get answers to some of the most frequently asked questions about keto.

Key Keto Clarity Concepts

→ Periods of fasting can help increase the production of ketones.

→ The idea of going without food over a period of hours seems crazy, but it's not.

→ Intermittent fasting (IF) is a popular strategy for weight loss and health.

→ Fasting is a natural, spontaneous response to higher levels of ketones.

→ There's no such thing as needing to eat three square meals a day.

→ Your meals should be substantial enough that you only eat once or twice daily.

→ Periods of fasting will help you determine your keto fitness level.

→ If you are hungry, eat something.

→ Eat when hungry, drink when thirsty.

→ Hunger is a subjective feeling and you need to determine what it is for you.

→ Not getting adequate salt on your ketogenic diet can make you feel hungry.

→ Glorifying hunger is insane.

→ When you are craving processed carbohydrates, eat fat and protein instead.

→ How much and when you eat is a personal decision.

→ Pay attention to the non-hunger cues that you associate with eating.

→ Comfort food doesn't have to be full of carbs; bacon can be your *new* comfort food.

→ Gurgling or growling noises in your stomach are not signs of true hunger.

→ **Closely observe how you feel while fasting and adjust mealtimes accordingly.**

→ **Prolonged periods of fasting raise blood ketones and lower blood sugar levels.**

→ **You don't need to completely fast for days to get the benefits of fasting.**

Chapter 12
Keto FAQ

MOMENT OF CLARITY There is a lot of misinformation and disinformation—if not outright, unwarranted hysteria—concerning the potential risks of a low-carbohydrate, fat-based, ketogenic diet. Some of this popularized hysteria borders on the absurd.

– Nora Gedgaudas

We're at right about the halfway point, and I'm sure you have a lot of questions swirling around the back of your mind about ketosis and ketogenic diets. Before we continue sharing about the tremendous health benefits of going keto, let's take a moment to answer a few of the most common questions.

Is ketosis a natural state for humans to be in?

MOMENT OF CLARITY The human body will naturally and wonderfully create ketones when carbohydrates are restricted, as long as there isn't an overabundance of dietary protein.

– Dr. David Perlmutter

Absolutely. Ketosis is simply the state of burning fat for fuel. Ketones are produced in the body as an alternative fuel source when there is a lack of glucose. Once you're on a ketogenic diet—one with substantially lower carbohydrates, a moderate amount of protein, and high fat—ketone production can begin in just a few days, but it may take a few weeks or more in some people. Our hunter-gatherer ancestors survived and thrived on ketones between their big animal kills. It was most certainly a natural state for them.

Modern-day humans have basically the same genetic makeup as our Paleolithic forefathers, so we can do perfectly fine in a state of ketosis.

What role does fiber play in ketosis?

MOMENT OF CLARITY I encourage the consumption of vegetable carbohydrates from mostly dark, leafy greens for their high fiber and nutrient content.

– Stephanie Person

When people think of fiber, the first thing that usually comes to mind is whole grains. After all, we've been told they are healthy by all the dietitians and health experts who are supposed to be in the know about this stuff. But grains, processed or whole, are not a part of a healthy ketogenic diet and will kill your ketone production very quickly. So is consuming fiber impossible in ketosis? Not at all.

Non-starchy and green, leafy vegetables, like broccoli and spinach, are a rich source of fiber that should not decrease your ketone production. The best thing you can do is try them and see how your body responds. Keep in mind that we've suggested counting all carbohydrates, including fiber, when you are determining your carbohydrate tolerance. This is the only way to be honest with yourself about how your body responds to certain foods and whether or not higher quantities of fiber are good for you.

I'm constipated on my ketogenic diet. What can I do about that?

MOMENT OF CLARITY Getting adequate sodium, potassium, magnesium, and water will help you avoid many of the short-term side effects of being in ketosis, including lightheadedness, headaches, muscle cramps, and constipation.

– Dr. Keith Runyan

This one is related to the last question in the minds of most people because they think they need fiber in order to prevent constipation. If you are constipated on your ketogenic diet, try adding more of the green, leafy vegetables we described above. It will also help to eat more saturated and monounsaturated fats; drink more water; get adequate levels of sodium, potassium, and magnesium; and even consume a piece or two of sugar-free chocolate, candy, or gum with sugar alcohols like erythritol, sorbitol, or xylitol (which can induce a bowel movement). Staying well-hydrated and eating plenty of fat tends to take care of this problem as well.

Is there any health advantage to cycling in and out of ketosis periodically?

MOMENT OF CLARITY I believe a well-designed ketogenic diet can overcome a lot of the negative effects people experience while eating a low-carb, high-fat diet. One such strategy some people may want to use is cycling in and out the various macronutrients, just as would have happened naturally in an ancestral diet.

– Bryan Barksdale

Physicist and researcher John Kiefer, author of *The Carb Nite Solution*, suggests eating one "cheat" meal every seven to fourteen days (less often for people who are especially metabolically damaged). Kiefer has found that people can shed more fat, get leaner, create more muscle mass, and enjoy some of their favorite foods time and again using this approach—which is sometimes called "carb cycling" —to go in and out of ketosis. However, although this idea has become more and more popular in recent years, it may not be an appropriate strategy for people who are looking for the therapeutic effects that ketosis has to offer.

Again, test it for yourself to see how it works for you. Eating a ketogenic diet during the week and then raising your carbohydrate and protein intake on the weekends may be desirable for some people, but it may be counterproductive, since getting back into ketosis can take anywhere from a few days to a few weeks. Figure out what works for you to keep you optimally healthy and do that. If cycling in and out of ketosis periodically gives you the results you desire, then go for it. If not, then there is certainly no downside to staying in a constant state of ketosis.

Why do my muscles cramp when I eat a ketogenic diet?

Often when people begin a low-carb, moderate-protein, high-fat, ketogenic diet, they forget to take care of the electrolytes in their body and drink enough water, and an electrolyte imbalance can cause, among other problems, muscle cramps. (I used to get bad charley horses in my calves when I first started eating a low-carb, high-fat diet.) Especially early on, when you are making the transition from using glucose as your primary fuel source to using ketones, you need to be replenishing your body with salt and fluids. No, this doesn't mean you have a Gatorade deficiency! (There's way too much sugar in it anyway.) Instead, there are three very easy strategies you can use to avoid those painful and annoying cramps.

First, you need to get more potassium and magnesium. While you can certainly use supplements for both of these, there are ketosis-friendly foods that are rich sources of both potassium and magnesium. Unfortunately, if you ask most people how to increase the potassium in their diet, they'll suggest eating bananas. But bananas are very high in carbohydrates (27 grams) and are not conducive for ketosis. A better option is avocados. One whole avocado contains twice the amount of potassium (975 milligrams) in a large banana (487 milligrams). As for magnesium, raw spinach, Brazil nuts, almonds, fish, and dark chocolate can provide you with this key nutrient.

Second, replenish your body's salt stores by making a warm cup of broth out of beef or chicken bouillon cubes a few times a day. Unless you have high blood pressure and are salt-sensitive, or you have experienced heart failure, doing this should work well to eliminate cramps. It should even boost your energy enough to prevent the "keto flu" symptoms that can accompany the early days of ketogenic eating. Concerns about salt raising blood pressure levels is a non-issue in those who are not sensitive to salt.

Third, drink, drink, and drink some more. Water is a crucially important factor in preventing cramps, since it helps muscles relax and contract. Staying well-hydrated is especially important if you are exercising regularly. Keep a water bottle with you at all times and take a sip now and then throughout the day. Don't be surprised if those cramps suddenly disappear. And the longer you do keto, the fewer cramps you'll experience.

Although it's unlikely, it is possible to drink too much water, which can deplete sodium and other mineral levels, so keep your water consumption under 800 milliliters per hour. But you're far more likely to not be getting enough water than to be getting too much.

Can any supplements help me get into ketosis?

You should be able to produce ketones simply by manipulating the macronutrients (carbohydrate, protein, and fat) in your diet to your individual specifications, as we outlined in chapters 5, 6, and 7. That said, there are a few supplements that may help boost your ketone production.

MOMENT OF CLARITY To facilitate beta-hydroxybutyrate (blood ketone) production, we add either MCT oil or coconut oil.

– Dr. David Perlmutter

Medium-chain triglycerides (MCT) oil, found in smaller amounts in coconut oil and sold as a supplement in vitamin and health stores, will raise your ketone levels very quickly over a two- to three-hour period. Be careful using it, though, because it can cause gastric distress, stomachache, and diarrhea if consumed in excess. Introduce it slowly over a period of time until you're able to consume higher quantities. Remember, MCT oil should not be a substitute for making the nutritional changes necessary to become ketogenic. But it could give someone who is struggling to produce ketones a much-needed psychological and physiological boost.

MOMENT OF CLARITY The major issue is whether the ketogenic diet provides the micronutrients from vitamins, minerals, essential fats, and antioxidants that are necessary to conduct the biology of life properly.

– Dr. Terry Wahls

In general, a ketogenic diet is incredibly nutritious and should provide you with most of the nutrients you need to be optimally healthy. Taking an iron-free multivitamin (unless you have low iron levels or are a premenopausal woman, in which case an iron supplement may be helpful) can help fill in the gaps here and there. Other supplements to consider include alpha lipoic acid, coenzyme Q10, L-carnitine, vitamin D, vitamin C, potassium bicarbonate, and magnesium. And if you still have strong carb cravings, try 1,000 mg of L-glutamine three times daily, taken on an empty stomach.

Do the ketones produced with MCT oil offer the same benefits as those produced through cutting carbs, moderating protein, and eating more fat?

Science has not yet settled this question. Many people enjoy using MCT oil because its effect on ketones shows up quickly on a blood ketone meter.

But why not induce ketosis nutritionally and naturally by consuming a high level of dietary fat (it doesn't necessarily have to be from coconut oil or MCT oil), reducing carbohydrates to your personal tolerance level, and moderating protein to your individual threshold? If you do this, then there's really no reason why you can't have all the ketones you'll need to experience their health benefits. If consuming MCT oil helps you feel good about the changes you are making in your diet, then go for it. But it's certainly better if you try to induce ketones naturally through diet and the strategic use of spontaneous intermittent fasting.

MOMENT OF CLARITY Don't forget to include some MCTs from fats like coconut oil—what I like to refer to as the cheater's way to stay in ketosis! When you do this, it allows you to liberalize your carbohydrate intake without necessarily throwing you out of ketosis.

— Dr. Bill Wilson

What happens to my gut microbiota when I eat a ketogenic diet?

This is one of great controversies in the online health community. I asked nutrition researcher Dr. William Lagakos for some insight about this one. He notes that the composition of the gut microbiome is primarily regulated by diet, especially the types and quality of dietary fibers, but there is currently a lack of research studies on ketosis's impact on gut microbiota. However, a study published in the January 23, 2014, issue of the scientific journal *Nature* found that ketogenic dieting increased microbes of the genus *Bacteroides* and decreased *Firmicutes*. This may be of clinical relevance for many reasons. For example, the opposite pattern—an increase in *Firmicutes* and decrease in *Bacteroides*—has been associated with obesity and an increased ability to harvest energy from food in animal and human studies. Furthermore, the microbial alterations induced by the ketogenic diet were associated with reduced levels of inflammation in a human study.

Cardiologist and *New York Times* bestselling author of *Wheat Belly* Dr. William Davis notes the critical importance of adding indigestible fibers to the diet for optimal gut health. He said that "they cause proliferation of healthy bacterial bowel flora species, such as *Lactobacillus* and *Bifidobacteria* . . . while also allowing [the] conversion of such fibers to fatty acids, such as butyrate, that nourish intestinal cells, thereby reducing colon cancer risk and even triggering a cascade of metabolic events that result in reduced blood sugars, reduced triglycerides, higher HDL, reduced blood pressure, and reduced visceral fat." Enriching the gut flora with more *Lactobacillus* is critical for preventing bile acid from being reabsorbed, causing it to instead be discarded into the stool.

Here's what Dr. Davis says is the key to obtaining all the benefits of ketosis while consuming the indigestible fibers that provide a prebiotic function: limit carbohydrate-rich legumes and tubers to no more than 15 grams net carbohydrates (total carbohydrates minus grams of fiber) per six-hour digestive window, while increasing your consumption of indigestible fibers that do not convert to blood sugar. This translates to half of a raw sweet potato daily, an unripe banana or plantain, or even a product like a Quest bar, all of which provide the fructooligosaccharides that feed your gut flora.

Unfortunately, this is far from settled science, and so much about it remains unknown. It is possible that eating certain foods on a ketogenic diet may feed gut flora. One study has also shown that body type and genetic predisposition seem to exert a bigger influence than diet. Regulation of the gut microbiome is complex and involves both dietary and nondietary components. There is no reason why gut health should not flourish on a ketogenic diet, and preliminary data suggest the gut microbiome may actually be improved by this way of eating.

Will drinking caffeine prevent me from getting into ketosis?

This is a question I have heard for many years from people who are struggling to get into ketosis. Dr. Atkins mentioned in his book *Dr. Atkins' New Diet Revolution* that "excessive caffeine has been shown to cause a hypoglycemic reaction" in some people—in other words, that it can cause blood sugar to drop. That may lead in turn to food cravings (usually for carbohydrates) and then to the consumption of excess carbs or protein, which would kick you out of ketosis. He recommended that people who experience hypoglycemia from consuming caffeine give it up or "consume caffeine only in moderation."

Jackie Eberstein, a registered nurse who worked with Dr. Atkins in his medical clinic in New York City for nearly three decades, says that there have been no scientific studies looking at caffeine and ketosis, but that the negative effects of caffeine on blood sugar could impact ketone levels.

"Some people are more sensitive than others, and of course the amount of exposure matters," Eberstein explained. "Other factors [also] matter, such as having caffeine when the blood sugar is more stable after eating a low-carb meal, [when caffeine] may have no or only limited negative effects. For some of us, [consuming] caffeine when we are stressed for other reasons can provoke [carb cravings]."

That's why she encourages people to "determine their tolerance," and if their blood sugar is unstable, to avoid caffeine altogether. For everyone else, limiting consumption to, at most, three servings daily is probably a good idea. I have personally never had any problems from consuming caffeine, and neither has my wife, Christine, who drinks a latte made with heavy whipping cream almost every day. It's something you'll need to tinker around with to see how it affects your body. Self-experiment and see what happens.

Can I eat dairy on a ketogenic diet?

This is another one of those "your mileage may vary" issues. Everyone is different, but personally, my ketogenic diet includes lots of dairy products, including heavy cream, sour cream, cream cheese, and hard cheeses. These are a big part of my personal low-carb, high-fat diet, and they have never given me any issues with producing adequate ketones. However, others are very sensitive to dairy and need to cut it out of their diet because of digestive and metabolic side effects. If you are concerned that full-fat dairy might be an issue for you, try cutting it out for thirty days and see how you feel. (By the way, never consume low-fat milk or yogurt; not only does the absence of fat reduce satiety and lower ketone production, the fat that's removed is replaced with a lot of sugar.)

> *DOCTOR'S NOTE FROM DR. ERIC WESTMAN: Many proponents of a Paleo lifestyle think dairy should be avoided. Dr. Loren Cordain, author of* The Paleo Diet, *once showed a slide of an intimidating moose with huge antlers and asked, "Are you going to milk that?" But while milk products should be avoided because they contain lactose (sugar), most people can remain ketogenic very well while consuming full-fat dairy like cream and cheese.*

How long will it take for me to see improvements in my weight and health after getting into ketosis?

MOMENT OF CLARITY Many people on a ketogenic diet have tried many different diets in the past. They may begin to doubt what they are doing is correct if they don't see the desired results quickly. This often turns into an obsession, and they spend a lot of time reading about what they're doing wrong in their diet and looking for loopholes. They seek out anecdotes for permission to stop pursuing ketosis. This anxiety and doubt manifests itself in many physical symptoms until the person finally gives up, eats more carbs, and feels better psychologically that they've done something good for themselves. But they never got to truly experience the full benefits that a ketogenic diet could offer them.

— Dr. Zeeshan Arain

This is a tricky question because the answer depends on individual factors: how long it takes you to become keto-adapted, what your state of health was like prior to beginning the ketogenic diet, and how well you adhere to your personalized strategy for getting into ketosis (sticking with your carbohydrate tolerance and protein threshold levels is key). But most people begin to lose both weight on the scale and inches around the waist within a few days. Once you reach nutritional ketosis, you should have more energy, complete appetite control, more even moods, and much clearer thinking.

Certain health issues—elevated blood sugar, high blood pressure, problematic cholesterol markers (namely higher triglycerides and lower HDL)—should begin to normalize within a matter of weeks. But even if you don't see results that quickly, be patient. Persistence pays off, and if you're showing good ketone levels in your testing, then you should see these effects soon. Don't doubt yourself just when you're on the verge of experiencing what keto can do for you.

Is being in ketosis safe over the long term? If not, then who should avoid doing it?

MOMENT OF CLARITY Sustained, long-term ketosis can have side effects in some individuals, but these are usually easily managed and are most common during the first few months, when the individual is gradually becoming keto-adapted.

Most of the problems people have with the ketogenic diet are experienced early on and can usually be remedied by proper hydration and mineral supplementation.

– Dr. Dominic D'Agostino

Because of the common confusion about ketosis, primarily from those who mistake it for ketoacidosis, questions about the long-term safety of a ketogenic diet have arisen. But a study by researcher Dr. Hussein Dashti that was published in the Fall 2004 issue of the medical journal *Experimental and Clinical Cardiology* found that a ketogenic diet produced "a significant decrease in the level of triglycerides, total cholesterol, LDL cholesterol and glucose, and a significant increase in the level of HDL cholesterol in the patients" and that "the administration of a ketogenic diet for a relatively long period of time is safe." I've been eating this way for over a decade, and I know plenty of others who have been keto-adapted for much longer. There is no evidence of problems related to following a ketogenic diet as a permanent lifestyle choice.

So is there anyone who should avoid getting into ketosis? While the vast majority of people will find tremendous health benefits from being on a ketogenic diet, it may not be right for everyone. As we'll cover in more detail in a moment, type 1 diabetics should approach it with caution because of the risk of ketoacidosis (as discussed in chapter 1). Also, if you have any problems with your gall bladder, you may need to address them before beginning a ketogenic diet (more on that later).

For everyone else, if you've been following a well-formulated ketogenic diet that keeps carbohydrates and protein at your personal limits and that includes large amounts of whole-food sources of dietary fats for a period of six to twelve months, you have ample amounts of ketones when you test your blood or breath, and you are not seeing any improvements in your weight and health markers, then perhaps you should move on to something else. But I've never heard of anyone who ate a ketogenic diet and produced plenty of ketones and did *not* experience all the amazing benefits we've been talking about.

If you are concerned about your long-term health on a ketogenic diet, find a medical professional who is willing to work with you in a positive manner and monitor your progress. (A list of ketogenic-friendly doctors is available at lowcarbdoctors.blogspot.com.) Here's a list of lab tests you can have run periodically to check your overall health:

- ▸ Fasting insulin

- ▸ Fasting blood glucose

- ▸ Homocysteine

- ▸ hsCRP

- ▸ NMR LipoProfile test

- ▸ Standard lipid profile

- ▸ Uric acid

- ▸ Full thyroid panel

DOCTOR'S NOTE FROM DR. ERIC WESTMAN: There are a few very rare hereditary conditions in which the body is unable to use fat for fuel—commonly referred to as "inborn errors of metabolism." These conditions are discovered very early in infancy, so adolescents and adults who haven't already been diagnosed don't need to worry.

Should a type 1 diabetic be on a ketogenic diet?

MOMENT OF CLARITY Obviously ketosis may not be appropriate for some type 1 diabetics. Otherwise, we have not observed any complications with this dietary approach.

– Dr. David Perlmutter

This is a fair question, especially since type 1 diabetics need to be concerned about ketoacidosis. But as long as your blood sugar levels are well controlled (which, coincidentally, a ketogenic diet will help with), then the level of ketones in the body will not rise to dangerous levels. And that holds true for everyone, including people with type 1 diabetes.

Keep in mind that a type 1 diabetic cannot make insulin, the hormone that pushes glucose into cells. But according to a May 2012 study published in the medical journal *Diabetology & Metabolic Syndrome*, type 1 diabetics who consumed a carbohydrate-restricted diet over a four-year period found that their requirement for insulin was greatly reduced. In other words, their condition became better as a result of a low-carb diet. If you have any specific questions or concerns about this, please consult with a physician who understands the biochemistry of low-carb, high-fat, ketogenic diets. You can find a medical professional in your area at lowcarbdoctors.blogspot.com.

Registered dietitian Franziska Spritzler says that people with diabetes, including type 1 diabetes, "often experience dramatic improvement in blood glucose control" while in a state of ketosis. Spritzler notes that there is research showing that if a type 1 diabetic is producing ketone bodies through a low-carb, moderate-protein, high-fat diet, they can continue to be just fine even if their blood sugar dips below 70 mg/dl—even though that level of blood sugar will cause hypoglycemia in anyone who uses glucose as their primary fuel source. This is why full keto-adaptation is so helpful for type 1 diabetics.

Do I have to count calories to make ketosis happen for me?

MOMENT OF CLARITY The major benefit of nutritional ketosis is that it helps regulate appetite in a way that prevents the consumption of surplus calories that would ultimately lead to weight gain and metabolic dysregulation.

– Dr. Dominic D'Agostino

This is one of the most freeing parts of a ketogenic diet—you don't have to count calories. When your carb and protein consumption is dialed in to your personal specifications and you consume enough fat in your diet, then something pretty amazing tends to happen: you are able to feel completely satisfied, with no cravings, no hunger, and no stressing about every little morsel of food you put in your mouth. That's what I call dieting, and it's time to break free from the bondage of calorie-counting forever. (If you're interested in learning why calories really aren't what you think they are, check out *The Calorie Myth* by Jonathan Bailor.)

Does this mean you have free rein to gorge yourself on as much food as you want within your low-carb, moderate-protein, high-fat diet, without consequences for your weight and health? Not at all. But if you are not stoking hunger by consuming too much carbohydrate or protein and are eating delicious and filling whole-food sources of fat, then you won't want to eat until you're stuffed, and calories naturally fall into line exactly where they need to be.

Ketosis changes the way you think about food; you start to see it more as a means for fueling your body than as a physical pleasure. That's not to say you don't enjoy food on a ketogenic diet—you do!— but it takes away any urge to binge.

What side effects can I expect to experience when I begin getting into ketosis?

MOMENT OF CLARITY When you think about it, the potential side effects from eating low-carb or ketogenic are really no big deal. If you want to see truly serious side effects from eating a diet, try eating the Standard American Diet (SAD). It's like a lesion that makes the practice of medicine extremely profitable for physicians while keeping your life utterly miserable. The choice is yours—a very short period of annoying symptoms as you become keto-adapted versus a lifetime of poor health and less than optimal functioning. To me the best choice is pretty obvious.

– Dr. Bill Wilson

During the transition from burning sugar to burning fat, some people experience a temporary feeling of discomfort that's referred to affectionately as the "keto flu." This can manifest in any number of ways, including bad breath, frequent urination, feelings of fatigue, lightheadedness, blood sugar dips, constipation, carb cravings, muscle aches, headaches, diarrhea and gas, and disrupted sleep. The thing to remember is that you may or may not experience these side effects, but even if you do, they won't last for more than a few weeks. If they do continue beyond a few weeks, it may signal a failure to become fully keto-adapted; you may be staying in "no man's land" between being a sugar-burner and a fat-burner. Get into ketosis and stay there to make these conditions go away.

DOCTOR'S NOTE FROM DR. ERIC WESTMAN: "Fat-burning" involves the use of fatty acids and ketones for fuel while "sugar-burning" involves glucose. Technically, the body always has some fat-burning and sugar-burning going on at the same time. If you are burning sugar, though, it is difficult to burn much fat because sugar-burning turns off fat-burning. The body only stores a few days' worth of energy as sugar (glycogen), so if the sugar storage capacity has been reached, additional sugar must be either burned or turned to fat. That means that burning excess sugar becomes the body's priority, while fat stays in storage.

Why am I getting up to go the bathroom several times a night when I start eating a ketogenic diet?

Excellent question. Ketogenic diet coach Maria Emmerich explains that because a low-carb, moderate-protein, high-fat, ketogenic diet improves your insulin sensitivity, your insulin levels will drop rather quickly. In response to this, your kidneys begin to dump any excess fluid in the body. And the way it gets rid of it is by making you pee it out.

So don't be alarmed if you have to get up a few times a night when you begin to pursue keto-adaptation. It's only temporary. Just make sure you consume enough salt, water, and potassium during the transition to replace what your body is losing and ward off side effects such as headaches, low energy, dizziness, and cramping.

Why does my breath stink when I am in ketosis and how do I fix this?

You may notice a funny, metallic taste in your mouth or have a thick feeling on your tongue after eating low-carb, high-fat for a few days. It sometimes means your loved ones will notice your breath stinks. This is enough reason for some people to never want to be in a state of ketosis. But it's foolish to rob yourself of the opportunity to experience what ketosis can do for your health. So what the heck is going on here?

In chapter 8 we mentioned that there are three types of ketones in the body. The one in the breath is called *acetone,* and that could be the source of foul breath. Additionally, eating too much protein can also give you bad breath because it produces ammonia (yet another reason to moderate your protein intake). Here's the good news: the bad breath is temporary and will go away when you become adapted to using ketones as your primary source of fuel.

Drink plenty of water, chew on some mint leaves or cinnamon bark, or even pop a piece of sugar-free mint or gum to deal with this. The key point to remember is it won't last forever and it's a sign that you'll soon be reaping the benefits of ketosis.

My ketones suddenly disappeared during my period. What happened?

Jacqueline Eberstein, a registered nurse who worked with Dr. Atkins, says that hormone changes that take place prior to menstruation could decrease ketones or make them disappear completely; during this time, the body primarily uses glucose created from dietary protein as fuel. However, she's quick to say that this isn't a reason to worry, since it is only temporary. Once your period ends, ketones will reappear.

What happens if I mess up and get out of ketosis?

MOMENT OF CLARITY Clients encounter a big motivator to stay on the ketogenic lifestyle when they cheat. They have the "carb flu" for the twenty-four to forty-eight hours afterwards and can't believe how bad they feel. That is a fantastic reminder for them not only to continue eating a healthy keto diet, but that it is right for their body.

– Maria Emmerich

Hey, we are all prone to mess up from time to time. We can be our own worst critics, but it's good to learn to be kind and forgiving to yourself. If you go off-plan and get out of ketosis, it's definitely not the end of the world. Just pick yourself up, dust yourself off, and start all over again. Be patient, and you'll be right where you need to be in no time. Whenever my ketones have fallen out of the range of nutritional ketosis, I almost always get back into ketosis within two or three days.

You can't receive the full benefits of a ketogenic diet unless you adhere to it strictly most of the time. Even one meal that goes beyond your carbohydrate tolerance or protein threshold can zap your ketones for several days. Fortunately, a ketogenic diet is so satisfying and delicious that you're motivated to stay on it virtually all the time (unlike low-fat diets, which make you hungry, cause you to constantly crave the foods you love, and leave you depressed and discouraged).

Can I exercise while I'm on a ketogenic diet?

MOMENT OF CLARITY Keto-adapted athletes or people engaging in long-duration physical activity will experience a modest increase in their performance, such as faster swimming or running times, or an improvement in their endurance.

– Dr. William Davis

Absolutely! One thing you'll experience when you become fully keto-adapted is a sudden desire to move your body. While television shows like *The Biggest Loser* and anti-obesity initiatives like First Lady Michelle Obama's "Let's Move" campaign place a heavy emphasis on exercise as a means for losing weight and getting healthy, the reality is that fixing your nutrition first leads to a spontaneous increase in physical activity.

And there's more good news: nutritional biochemist Dr. Bill Lagakos says that engaging in your favorite kind of exercise can actually "promote higher ketones [by] manipulating energy balance." When you reduce the energy surplus in your body, that directly "enhances fat oxidation by suppressing insulin and activating the sympathetic nervous system." And the net result of all that is an elevation in your ketone production. Awesome stuff!

The increase in physical activity leads to even more benefits for your health, including reduced stress, lower appetite levels (due to increased ketone production during exercise), muscle growth, and improved bone density. You'll have so much energy while in ketosis that you won't know what to do with it all. Play some basketball, go for a run, do some household chores, play with your kids—anything to put that energy to good use in a productive way. Your health will thank you for it!

Will consuming artificial sweeteners negatively impact my ketone levels?

This is an interesting question and one that can be easily answered—no, they do not have a negative impact on ketone production. That said, there are some things you need to be aware of regarding sweeteners such as Splenda (sucralose), Nutrasweet (aspartame), Truvia (stevia/erythritol blend), Sweet & Low (saccharin), and sugar alcohols (erythritol, sorbitol, maltitol, and more). Many of these come in powdered packets that use a bulking agent called *maltodextrin* that is basically sugar. Granted, it's only about 1 gram per packet, but that can add up if you use several packets in your morning coffee. This is why the liquid forms of sweetener are always going to be your best option—we recommend liquid stevia, the most natural of all the sugar substitutes.

While artificial sweeteners are certainly a good alternative to sugary foods and beverages, keep in mind that they can stoke hunger and cravings for sweets in a lot of people. What you'll find is that the longer you are in ketosis, the less you want to eat something sweet. You may wake up one day and suddenly realize that the sweet food you thought you could never live without no longer tempts you.

Can I drink alcohol on my ketogenic diet?

MOMENT OF CLARITY Alcohol consumption can turn off ketosis. While some people can tolerate a single serving of a low-carbohydrate beverage, such as one glass of red wine or a single shot of vodka, any more than a single serving, or indulging in higher-carbohydrate beverages, such as microbrew beers, will turn off ketosis.

— Dr. William Davis

It depends. It's best to avoid drinking alcohol until you are fully keto-adapted. Once that happens, you can begin to consume moderate amounts of certain alcoholic beverages to see how you do.

Some kinds of alcohol may be counterproductive to your goal of producing more ketones. The best choices are hard liquors such as tequila, vodka, and whiskey because they contain very few carbohydrates. Obviously, make sure you do not consume these in excess, since your body still has to metabolize the alcohol.

There's a popular mixed drink called the "NorCal Margarita" that was created by Robb Wolf, one of the leaders in the Paleo community. The ingredients for this drink are simple: two shots of tequila, some lime juice, and club soda. You can get even more adult beverage ideas from the book *Paleo Happy Hour* by Kelly Milton.

If you are sensitive to carbohydrates, be aware that drinking wine may not be a good idea. Otherwise, if you can tolerate the carbs, a glass of red or white wine may be an appropriate choice. You'll need to determine what alcoholic beverage is right for you. Beer, of course, including the "low-carb" ones, should not be consumed on a ketogenic diet.

My gall bladder has been removed, so how can I eat a high-fat, ketogenic diet?

The gall bladder stores digestive enzymes from the liver that break down fat and releases them after a meal that contains fat. Even so, most people who have had their gall bladder removed have no problems eating fat. My wife, Christine, had her gallbladder removed in 2008, and she had trouble consuming higher amounts of fat for about a year. But over time she has been able to slowly increase her fat intake to 60 percent of the calories she consumes. Some people who have had their gall bladder removed have found benefit in taking digestive enzymes or bile salts to replace the enzymes your gallbladder would be supplying.

Incidentally, Nora Gedgaudas, an expert on low-carb, high-fat, ketogenic diets, says that an underlying or preexisting issue with your gall bladder function can be a stumbling block towards keto-adaptation because of the role it plays in fat digestion. Addressing these issues is imperative to experiencing the maximum potential from being in nutritional ketosis. It may be possible to work with a health-care provider to restore your gall bladder's function rather than resort to having it removed.

Removing the gall bladder doesn't necessarily take away the underlying problem, Gedgaudas explains. "Getting your gall bladder out didn't 'cure' you—it merely masked the symptom," she says. Underlying thyroid issues and various digestive disorders are common causes of gall bladder problems. Plus, if you have been on a very low-fat, vegetarian, or vegan diet, you can be especially vulnerable to problems with your gall bladder. As Gedgaudas puts it, "If you don't use it, you might just lose it." Address any gall bladder issues before attempting a high-fat, ketogenic diet.

I'm a vegetarian. How can I eat a ketogenic diet without consuming meat?

While it is certainly easier to follow a ketogenic diet if you eat meat, it's not impossible for a vegetarian to experience the benefits of ketosis. If you allow yourself to consume eggs as part of your lacto-ovo vegetarian diet, they are an excellent source of fat and moderate protein, especially when cooked in delicious coconut oil. Green, leafy salads with avocado, a squeeze of lemon juice, and olive oil can be an excellent lunch or dinner. And there are plenty of low-carb, high-fat nut options for you, including macadamia nuts, almonds, and walnuts. Yes, it can be more challenging trying to get into ketosis if you are a vegetarian (and even more so if you are a vegan). But it's not impossible if you're eating plenty of healthy, plant-based fats and not too many carbohydrates or protein.

> *DOCTOR'S NOTE FROM DR. ERIC WESTMAN: Are humans herbivores, carnivores, or omnivores? There is much debate about whether humans are "supposed to be" mostly vegetarian or meatatarian, or if we should just "eat food, not too much, mostly plants," as Michael Pollan suggests. I think this is the wrong question to ask. A better question is, "What are the health consequences of eating a certain way? If I am a vegetarian or meatatarian, what is my health now, and what will my health likely be in the future?" (If ketosis is your goal, however, you probably need to consider being a meatatarian—it's difficult to get into ketosis on a vegetarian diet.)*

What if I only want the health benefits of ketosis, not the weight loss?

The human body is an extraordinary machine that operates pretty efficiently despite the demands we place on it. Yes, a ketogenic diet is extremely effective at bringing about weight loss in people who are carrying around some extra body fat. But what about people who are thin and only want to experience the health benefits of ketosis? How can they do this without wasting away to nothing?

Nutrition expert Nora Gedgaudas says that "your weight may normalize" when you start eating a low-carb, moderate-protein, high-fat, ketogenic diet. Since it's not a nutritional plan for weight loss but rather for vastly improved health, there should be no concerns about giving this way of eating a go for yourself. However, Gedgaudas warns that if you're underweight or experiencing unwanted weight loss while in ketosis, you may have some tendency towards malabsorption or endocrine dysfunction (such as autoimmune thyroid issues), and if that's the case, you'll need to address the underlying issue before you can start putting on healthy weight. Start by finding a health-care professional who's knowledgeable about ketosis.

When you're on a ketogenic diet, if your body needs to shed some weight, then it will. But if you are perfectly lean and begin eating a low-carb, moderate-protein, high-fat, ketogenic diet, don't assume you are going to lose weight— you don't have any to lose. However, if you are concerned about weight loss, then consider adding in small amounts of sweet potatoes or white rice, so long as they don't raise your blood sugar or lower your ketone levels.

A ketogenic diet isn't like the curse in the classic Stephen King horror story *Thinner*— you won't just waste away on it.

DOCTOR'S NOTE FROM DR. ERIC WESTMAN: The ketogenic diet is not a weight-loss diet—it's a fat-burning diet. If you have excess fat stores, the body will use them up. If you don't have excess fat stores, your body will use the fat you eat for fuel, and it will let you know when you need to eat more fat by making you hungry.

Every time I go on a ketogenic diet, I feel like crap. Why doesn't this work for me?

MOMENT OF CLARITY Most of my clients come to me with some kind of health issue that is blocking their progress. They are typically dealing with low energy, metabolic damage, high body fat, stress, gut issues, poor sleep quality, food issues, exercise frustrations, and whacked out hormones, and the dreaded doctor visits with looming test results scare the poo out of them. As a result, these poor people struggle to enter into a state of ketosis. The body won't work unless you fix these underlying issues!

– Stephanie Person

It sounds like you never fully got keto-adapted. As we stated earlier, the "keto flu" symptoms shouldn't last for more than a few weeks. Test your ketone levels and make sure you are producing enough to receive the therapeutic effects they have to offer you. Then be patient as your body adjusts from being a sugar-burner to becoming a lean, mean, fat-burning machine.

It is also possible that you aren't getting enough salt in your diet. Low-carb researchers Dr. Stephen Phinney and Dr. Jeff Volek estimate that most people need 5 to 7 grams of salt every day when they are following a ketogenic diet.

I'm showing great blood ketone levels, but I'm not losing weight. Why?

MOMENT OF CLARITY The level of ketones in circulation does not accurately reflect the degree or speed of weight loss. The mere presence of ketosis and an energy deficit, but not the depth of ketosis, per se, seem to be the primary mediator of weight loss.

– Dr. Bill Lagakos

This common question gets to the heart of an important lesson about ketosis. Yes, one of the great side effects of a ketogenic diet is indeed weight loss. But producing adequate blood ketones does not automatically mean you will lose weight quickly. I realize this can be discouraging for people who are using keto for that purpose, but there are plenty of other reasons to keep at it despite the slow or stalled numbers on the scale: reduced hunger and cravings, stabilized blood sugar, lower blood pressure, better sleep, more energy, mental clarity, and much more.

Perhaps you need to tweak your diet by adding in more fat and making sure your carbs and protein are where they need to be. But beyond that, know that weight loss (and, more accurately, fat loss) is an extremely complex issue. Yes, a ketogenic diet gives you a fighting chance in the battle against the bulge. For some people it can be a slog, but it's a fight worth getting into if you're willing to go the distance.

Dr. Zeeshan Arain, a general practitioner from South Yarra, Victoria, in Australia, follows a ketogenic diet himself and recommends it for his patients. He notes that it is a common misconception that higher levels of blood ketones (beta-hydroxybutyrate) automatically result in weight loss.

It is possible, he explains, for ketones to be produced in one of three ways: by burning dietary fat alone, by burning stored body fat alone, or by burning a combination of the two. The trick to weight loss is to burn at least some of the fat stores in your body. The best way to monitor that is by testing your ketone levels as often as possible to make sure you are on the right track with your ketogenic diet, especially if something has changed in your routine, such as food intake, exercise, or stress levels. But remember, higher ketone levels don't mean more weight loss will automatically happen.

As Dr. Arain says, "Being too fixated on the numbers can be counterproductive to weight loss [because of the] anxiety generated." Focus instead on doing the things you need to do to lose weight, including feeling good about your efforts, maintaining high energy levels, and keeping stress in your life to the bare minimum. These things will all serve you much better than if you are constantly worrying about whatever your ketone level happens to be.

Be encouraged that sooner or later you will find success. And don't forget that while you may not be losing weight on the scale, your clothes may very well begin to start fitting better. And that's always a good thing.

Why do others get to eat more carbohydrates and protein in their diet than I do? This just doesn't seem fair.

MOMENT OF CLARITY Ketosis, like most things in nutritional science, has an incredible degree of individual variability. Is the person overweight with insulin resistance or diabetes? What is the age and sex of the ketogenic dieter? Is the person suffering from epilepsy or a chronic neurological disorder? Perhaps the patient is an endurance athlete simply looking for a more efficient fueling strategy. Armed with this information, it is easier to determine the levels of macronutrients that are appropriate for helping them get into a state of nutritional ketosis.

– Dr. Zeeshan Arain

We like to compare ourselves to our friends, family, and coworkers, don't we? I suppose it's human nature, but we're only setting ourselves up for disappointment and discouragement if we expect to be able to eat what others eat and have it work exactly the same way for us. If there's one message we want to communicate loud and clear, it's this: we are all different and have unique metabolic needs based on our genetics, our environment, and other factors.

We're not all robots with a built-in program that produces identical results in everyone. We are unique snowflakes, and there is an incredibly wide range of variables involved in making our bodies operate the way they should. Some people need to consume less carbohydrate and protein than others. That's okay. It's how our bodies have developed, and we must accept the situation we are currently in.

The good news is that you are still in a fantastic position to optimize your health and run your body quite efficiently on ketone bodies, no matter how metabolically damaged you may be. Although I cannot consume more than 30 grams of carbohydrate and 100 grams of protein daily, that doesn't deter me from doing the things I have to do to be healthy. Who knows? Over time I may be able to add in more carbohydrate and protein as my body heals from the decades of damage I did to it eating the Standard American Diet. That's true for you, too.

> *DOCTOR'S NOTE FROM DR. ERIC WESTMAN: Sometimes the number on the scale can be misleading. Our total weight is a combination of body fat, lean muscle mass, and water. In our clinic, a special scale separates out the fat weight from the water weight, and when the total weight hasn't changed, we often we see that the fat weight has gone down (which is good) while the water weight has gone up (not so good). If the water weight builds up a lot, an obesity medicine doctor like myself might recommend a diuretic to assist in removing the excess water weight.*

Why do I have to eat more dietary fat on a ketogenic diet if I have plenty of fat on my body to burn as fuel?

MOMENT OF CLARITY Insulin resistance increases glucose and insulin levels, trapping fat within fat cells so it can't be released for energy. People with insulin resistance already have excessive body fat, and because of their high insulin levels, this fat isn't readily available for energy production. This pushes the body and brain to rely almost solely on glucose for energy, and this is clearly not a healthy metabolic state. Think of this as your body and brain on a Twinkie—not a pretty metabolic picture!

– Dr. Bill Wilson

It may sound strange that you need to eat fat to burn fat, especially for those who are overweight or obese.

It comes down to the purpose of consuming fat. Dietary fats fill in the gaps left when you cut down on carbohydrates and proteins. These fats help to fill you up and begin the process of creating ketones. Once you're in ketosis, you'll use not only the dietary fat for fuel but also stored body fat.

Some people erroneously think they can cut way down on their fat intake to try to burn more of their body fat. But doing this would be perilous to what you are trying to accomplish in your ketogenic lifestyle. You'd be hungrier and more irritable, you'd experience intense cravings (mostly for carbohydrates), and you'd probably get so frustrated by all of this that you'd simply give up. It's not worth going through all of that when all you really need to do is embrace consuming more fat in your diet so you can lose the fat on your body.

Remember, it makes sense to eat fat when your body is a fat-burning machine!

I'm a woman who's approaching menopause. Can ketosis bring back balance to my hormones without the need for medications?

Ladies who are dealing with the frustration of hormones that have gone all whackadoodle, be of good cheer. A ketogenic diet is an incredibly effective way to balance your hormones and bring them back in line. It may not happen overnight, and complete healing may take some time depending on the severity of your personal situation—you may need to consult with a physician who can help you work through these issues. But consuming a low-carb, moderate-protein, high-fat diet can certainly be a powerful modality for helping you deal with menopause without medications like hormone replacement therapy.

Atkins nurse Jacqueline Eberstein has herself gone through the struggle of trying to manage her weight and stabilize her hormones through the inevitable changes of menopause. Describing it as "an eye-opener," Eberstein realized she had to cut way back on her carbohydrate intake, to around 20 grams a day, and even that kept her just "barely in ketosis." Staying ketogenic is more of a challenge after menopause, and you may see the return of hunger, cravings, and other hormone-induced symptoms.

Eberstein says all of this can be discouraging for older women who desperately want to feel "normal" again, but staying within your personal carbohydrate tolerance and protein threshold while eating plenty of healthy saturated and monounsaturated fats to satiety will put you in the best position possible with your health. For her, it took several years of "hard work and establishing a bioidentical hormone regimen" along with a ketogenic diet to get back to where she was before menopause. Staying low-carb and high-fat helped Eberstein keep from gaining more weight, and eventually she got her weight back under control. These days, she consumes 20 to 30 grams of carbohydrates daily because that's all she can tolerate. "But the alternative is unacceptable," Eberstein says. "I can live happily with this."

This is by no means a comprehensive list of questions you may have about ketogenic diets, but we've done our best to share some of the more common ones. If you have a specific question about keto that isn't addressed here, please feel free to email us at livinlowcarbman@charter.net and we'll try to find out the answer for you.

Coming up in the next chapter are eight inspiring success stories of people who have turned their life around as a result of being on a ketogenic diet. If you need a swift kick in the pants to get you going, this is the chapter to make that happen.

Key Keto Clarity Concepts

→ **Ketosis is simply the state of burning fat for fuel.**

→ **You can get all the fiber you need from non-starchy and green, leafy vegetables.**

→ **Constipation is not an issue on a ketogenic diet using proper strategies.**

→ **Some people may do better cycling in and out of ketosis; others, not so much.**

→ **Balancing electrolytes will prevent muscle cramping early on in ketosis.**

→ **Supplements can help ensure maximum nutrition on a ketogenic diet.**

→ **MCT oil will temporarily raise blood ketones, but it's better to raise them through diet.**

→ **A ketogenic diet does not have to negatively impact your gut microbiota.**

→ **Caffeine can ultimately raise blood sugar levels, which can deplete your ketones.**

→ **Consuming dairy may be an issue for some people, but others can have it liberally.**

→ **Changes from a ketogenic diet should begin to happen within just a few days.**

→ **There is no evidence contraindicating the long-term safety of nutritional ketosis.**

→ **Most type 1 diabetics do just fine in ketosis, but some should be leery of ketoacidosis.**

→ **Calories are not a concern on a ketogenic diet as long as you are eating to satiety.**

→ **Any side effects from ketosis are temporary and go away within a few weeks.**

→ **Your kidneys will release fluid when you go keto, making bathroom visits frequent.**

→ Keto breath can occur when you first go low-carb and high-fat, but it dissipates.

→ Menstruation can temporarily make ketone levels go down.

→ If you get out of ketosis, just go back to doing what it took to get you into ketosis.

→ Exercise is not only possible but enhanced while eating a ketogenic diet.

→ Watch out for maltodextrin in artificial sweeteners; choose liquid stevia instead.

→ Certain kinds of alcohol in limited quantities can be consumed while on a ketogenic diet.

→ Even if you've had your gall bladder removed, you can still eat high-fat.

→ Eating ketogenic as a vegetarian is difficult unless you eat enough fat.

→ Lean people don't need to worry about losing weight on a ketogenic diet.

→ Overcoming the "keto flu" symptoms of the early days of keto is the key to success.

→ The purpose of ketosis isn't weight loss; other health benefits are much more important.

→ Individual variation means your ketogenic diet will be different from others'.

→ Eating fat helps stoke the flame of burning stored body fat.

→ A ketogenic diet combined with hormone replacement strategies can balance your hormones during and after menopause.

Chapter 13
Eight Keto Success Stories

MOMENT OF CLARITY When you start a ketogenic diet, I recommend writing down your goals and keeping a daily log of your progress. This will help keep you motivated and accountable. The key to success with any change is consistency and persistence.

– Dr. Bill Wilson

Perhaps you've been reading this book with an open yet skeptical mind so far and you're wondering how ketosis works in the lives of real people. In chapter 16, we'll begin revealing what the scientific literature says regarding being in a state of ketosis. But there's nothing like the inspiring testimonial of a life that has been changed forever for the better.

I've already shared my own weight and health transformation story, and now I want to introduce you to eight more people whose lives have been radically altered since they began following a low-carb, moderate-protein, high-fat, ketogenic nutritional plan. Let their stories inspire you to give it a go for yourself.

Lynne Daniel Ivey
Durham, North Carolina – Age 53

Lynne started her dieting efforts at the tender age of ten when she attended her first Weight Watchers meeting. In the decades that followed, she continued to struggle with managing her weight despite going on diet after diet, feeling hungrier and hungrier each time. She desperately wanted to get thin, stay thin, and never feel the agony of being constantly hungry ever again.

After attempting so many "gimmicks," as she describes them, to lose weight over nearly four decades—calorie-counting, low-fat diets, weight loss pills, diet shakes, protein bars, and those rah-rah support meetings that left her more broke than healthy—Lynne decided enough was enough when the reality that she carried 344 pounds on her five-foot-four-inch frame had her "very afraid" in September 2009.

"I was beyond discouraged," Lynne told me. "I was exhausted from extremely stressful situations in my work environment and at home. And I was struggling to balance the challenges that life was throwing at me."

One of those challenges was taking care of her ailing mother, who suffered from type 2 diabetes until she succumbed to the disease at the age of seventy-four. It was at that point that Lynne vowed to do something to prevent herself from experiencing the same fate, because that was "not the way to die." But all of the conventional dietary and lifestyle advice she had been given by doctors—namely, eating a low-fat diet and exercising more—were making her "hungrier, sicker, and fatter" than ever before.

"I was exhausted all the time. I felt like a complete failure," Lynne admitted.

In November 2009, Lynne went to see Dr. Eric Westman, who she had heard was having great success using a low-carb, high-fat ketogenic diet to manage his patients' obesity, type 2 diabetes, and other chronic diseases.

Dr. Westman opened Lynne's eyes to the stark reality that the low-fat diet she had been following in an attempt to lose weight and get healthy, was in fact the exact reason why she was having so much trouble getting her weight under control, and, ironically, it was putting her on the path to the same health problems that she had watched her mom go through. That was all it took to motivate her to give a ketogenic diet a try. By eating a 1600-calorie diet of 90 percent dietary fat, 8 percent protein, and just 2 percent carbohydrates, Lynne lost a total of 200 pounds. More importantly, she has kept that weight off for more than four years.

"I have lived—thrived!—in a steady state of optimal ketosis," she shared. "Thanks to Dr. Westman, I have learned to eat a well-formulated ketogenic diet enjoying delicious, fresh foods high in good dietary fats, moderate in protein, and very, very low in carbohydrates."

After years of fighting constant hunger on every eating plan she tried, hunger is no longer an issue for Lynne: now she eats only one meal a day and has "embraced intermittent fasting." This has brought her fasting blood sugar levels down into the 70s, with regular blood ketone readings between

1.8 and 4.0 millimolar. Her energy levels are through the roof and every measurable sign of her health is spectacular, including normal blood pressure and outstanding cholesterol ratios.

"These kind of improvements in my health are hard to believe for those who don't understand the science behind a ketogenic diet and nutritional ketosis. But it is true," Lynne stated.

Lynne eats lots of coconut oil, olive oil, butter, heavy cream, cream cheese, hard cheeses, whole eggs, and sometimes a few macadamia nuts. Protein is limited to small portions; she says she treats it like a condiment for her high-fat meals. As for vegetables, from time to time she consumes a few non-starchy ones, such as lettuce, kale, spinach, onions, tomatoes, green beans, squash, zucchini, broccoli, and bell peppers.

"I have the best health of my life and my healthiest years are still ahead of me," said Lynne. "Healing is indeed possible when you find the right diet for you."

And from the results she has seen, obviously a low-carb, moderate-protein, high-fat, ketogenic diet is what's right for Lynne.

MOMENT OF CLARITY As my grandmother used to say, when the you-know-what hits the fan, for heaven's sake change what you are doing and see if things get better. If you keep doing the same thing, don't expect different results. In my opinion a ketogenic diet would be a good choice for many people facing common chronic health problems.

– Dr. Bill Wilson

Freda Mooncotch
Chicago, Illinois – Age 40

Freda says the ketogenic diet "gave me back my life" after she struggled with adrenal burnout that had her sleeping most of the time for a period of eighteen months. In late 2012, she was still experiencing low energy and fatigue when she stumbled across the ketogenic diet. She immediately began adding in more fat to her diet in the form of raw cream and milk. When Freda noticed that her energy began returning and she was experiencing greater mental clarity and better memory than ever before, she knew she had found something special that could potentially get her out of her health rut.

In June 2013, Freda officially began a low-carb, moderate-protein, high-fat, ketogenic diet. Within a month, she was registering blood ketone levels in excess of 5.0 millimolar. What started off as a simple experiment to see what would happen has now become "a way of life" for Freda. Because of the increased energy from being in a state of nutritional ketosis, she was able to go back to school to obtain her undergraduate degree in nutrition and exercise science.

"Going back to school again was only a dream before I started on nutritional ketosis," Freda shared. "Now it's a reality and I will never go back to eating any other way."

While she admits there are times when she goes out of ketosis, when that happens she can "feel the change."

"It's like day and night," Freda said. "I go from Bradley Cooper in *Limitless* to Leonard in *Awakenings,* when the promised cure is starting to wear off and he realizes there is no chance for him to live his life. That scares the crap out of me."

Now, Freda says, being in a ketogenic state makes her more aware of the difficulties so many people have in getting their health under control.

"They are living on the brink of Leonard and just want their energy back," she noted. "Nutritional ketosis has given me an edge on life and has really helped me become the best version of me with ease."

More energized and motivated than ever before, Freda now helps others get their life back with ketogenic coaching sessions.

Peggy Holloway
Omaha, Nebraska – Age 61

Peggy says she is "living proof that a ketogenic diet works" and has seen nearly everyone in her family "reverse health problems" using this nutritional approach. Peggy herself was on the verge of diabetes in 1999 after years of following a low-calorie, low-fat diet, and she watched her sister gain weight and develop type 2 diabetes despite doing what she thought were all the right things.

"I spent my adult life dieting according to the prevailing wisdom in order to avoid the horror of the fate that befell my grandfather and father in their later years, when they eventually died from complications from severe insulin resistance," she said.

After watching her sister suffer with digestive issues, energy swings, brain fog, and an inability to lose weight without starving, Peggy began researching an alternative to the diet advice she had been given her entire life. She came across the work of Dr. Robert Atkins and considers him a hero for "leading me to an understanding that the crux of all of my family health problems was insulin resistance and carbohydrate intolerance." Interestingly, her brother also discovered the low-carb, high-fat diet at the same time, and it helped him overcome chronic fatigue syndrome.

Switching to a whole foods–based ketogenic diet helped Peggy resolve gastrointestinal issues, brain fog, and blood sugar dysregulation while maintaining a healthy weight for well over a decade. Her partner, a seventy-two-year-old retired family physician named Dr. Ken Peters, supported Peggy's efforts but continued to eat the Standard American Diet up until 2011, when he noticed he couldn't get rid of some "stubborn belly fat" that no longer responded to cutting calories and exercising more. He shed about thirty pounds in three months by eating low-carb, but he tried going back to carb-loading prior to the Bicycle Ride Across Nebraska. He "hit the wall" and had no energy, and he realized he needed to do more.

That's when he started listening to what Peggy was sharing about the exercise performance benefits that come from being in ketosis, which she learned about from Dr. Stephen Phinney and Dr. Jeff Volek's book, *The Art and Science of Low Carbohydrate Performance*. He started eating a ketogenic diet and "is now a total convert."

"The best side effect of our ketogenic lifestyle is the enhancement we have seen in our athletic pursuits, which we consider almost miraculous," Peggy said.

Consuming more fat in the form of egg yolks and pork belly, as well as putting butter and coconut oil in their coffee (a concept known as "Bulletproof Coffee" that was popularized by online health entrepreneur and Paleo podcaster Dave Asprey), both Peggy and her partner have been able to enjoy multiple long-distance bicycle rides with plenty of energy and without any carbohydrate-based snacks to fuel their exercise. In fact, she was amazed by how much energy they had after the rides and the lack of muscle soreness that would typically follow a long-distance ride. And they're no spring chickens, either, which makes this accomplishment all the more astonishing.

"We are sixty-one and seventy-two, respectively; neither of us has seen a physician for a medical problem in years; and we take no medications for chronic disease," Peggy explained. "We are naturally so excited to share this with everyone we can because we want everyone who is suffering from following the conventional advice to eat low-fat, low-calorie diets to experience what we have. And we have the science to back it up!"

MOMENT OF CLARITY I don't understand why cutting out foods with added sugars and refined and heavily processed foods and replacing them with natural fats, a variety of proteins, low glycemic load vegetables, and fruit is bad or can have negative metabolic effects. I haven't seen evidence to that effect. It makes no sense. This is what humans have been eating forever.

– Jackie Eberstein

Dane DeValcourt
Lafayette, Louisiana – Age 40

Dane's ketogenic success story involves a tremendous triple-digit weight loss but also, perhaps more important, an incredible turnaround in a rare disease he has been living with his entire life. In January 2013, at the age of thirty-nine, he weighed in at 293 pounds, and he knew that something needed to be done so he would be around for his little girl. At the same time, he was dealing with McArdle disease, an extremely rare metabolic condition. Also known as glycogen storage disease type V, this condition prevents the muscles from tapping into glycogen stores for energy. This leads to severe fatigue, muscle cramping, and the onset of muscle soreness with virtually any activity. It's a very painful condition, and in Dane it also led to degeneration in his vertebrae that required neck surgery.

In February 2013, Dane set a goal for himself to get down to 250 pounds. After failing to see any success after one month of eating healthier by conventional nutritional standards (a low-fat, high-carb, calorie-restricted diet), a friend in the medical field suggested that he try a low-carb, high-fat, ketogenic approach. The results were nearly instantaneous: as he switched from rice and bread to steak and bacon, the weight began pouring off of him. Plus, Dane's energy started to increase, and he even began exercising, even though McArdle disease used to make it too excruciating. After just ten months, he had lost a total of 110 pounds. But, more importantly, Dane was able to partially resolve the muscle pain and weakness from McArdle disease.

"Being ketogenic has helped me deal with McArdle disease because now my muscles are fueled through the fat I am eating in my diet," he explained.

These days, Dane eats what he describes as a very low-carb, high-fat, Paleo diet filled with real foods like those our hunter-gatherer ancestors ate. The radical changes he's seen in his life simply by implementing the principles of ketosis into his diet have made his story compelling to everyone he meets.

"Ketosis has had a tremendous impact on my life, and everyone I know asks me about it and listens intently to what I have to say," Dane said. "My friends and family all say what a great example I am [of] how to do things the right way and have been extremely impressed by my results."

As the crowning achievement in this ketogenic diet success story, Dane ran a half marathon in January 2014. This is the same guy who not that long ago couldn't run fifty feet, who had major neck surgery and the pain associated with it, and who has a chronic disease that for years caused muscle pain no matter how many muscle relaxers and pain medications he took. For Dane, running a half marathon was a bona fide miracle.

"To think that I am able to run in half marathons now when most other people with McArdle disease can't even fathom running [at all] is just mind-blowing to me," Dane remarked.

Adam Farmer
Indianapolis, Indiana – Age 19

As a sixteen-year-old, Adam first learned about low-carb, high-fat, ketogenic diets from a renegade health teacher who shared that saturated fat is not harmful to your health. That is what got Adam interested in looking at a ketogenic diet as a way to become optimally healthy.

"A lot of the information my health teacher was sharing with me was shocking and hard to believe," he said. "So I ended up doing my own investigation into what he was saying to see if there was any truth to it."

Adam researched low-carb, high-fat, ketogenic diets and "became convinced" enough to try it for himself beginning in February 2012. Interestingly, his family was less than enthusiastic about his foray into ketosis.

"They thought I was nuts," he shared. "My parents would take me to see doctors and complain about all the butter and animal fats I was eating in my diet. The doctors would try to tell me not to go too extreme and to find balance in my diet."

Refusing to get sucked in by the negative energy from his family and doctor, Adam stuck with his ketogenic diet and began seeing some incredible changes in his life. He lost weight, was able to stop taking Adderall for his ADHD, had steady energy all day long, was no longer dealing with bouts of depression, and had a much better general state of well being. Even after experiencing these remarkable improvements in his health, Adam said he continued to be "ridiculed" by his family for being on a low-carb, high-fat, ketogenic diet.

"My brother calls me a sissy because I refuse to eat grains or sugars," Adam said. "It doesn't happen as much anymore, but I still hear my family talk about how my diet is artery-clogging and heart-stopping whenever I add butter to whatever I'm eating or eat the fat my family cuts off their meat."

The phenomenal results he has seen from being on a ketogenic diet have motivated Adam to study to become a registered dietitian and perhaps a medical doctor to help spread the word about low-carb, high-fat diets to the people with heart disease, diabetes, and obesity who need them the most.

MOMENT OF CLARITY On the clinical and laboratory experimental end, we still do not know whether the demonstrably positive effects of dietary carbohydrate restriction are continuous with ketogenic effects, or even how they relate to calorie restriction. The effectiveness of a low-carbohydrate diet and, especially, the ability of a high-carbohydrate diet to exacerbate rather than help metabolic disease, suggest that there is little risk in experimenting with a ketogenic diet.

– Dr. Richard Feinman

Lawrence Petruzzelli
Melbourne, Australia – Age 21

Like most of the other people in this chapter, Lawrence found himself overweight despite restricting calories, cutting the amount of fat he was eating, and engaging in hours of cardiovascular exercise each week. He said this routine "never worked" for him, no matter how hard he tried. Then he heard about the Paleo diet, which "worked well for while" to make him feel better.

But when his weight loss stalled, he began lifting weights at the gym and started consuming more protein. Because of the gluconeogenesis effect discussed in chapter 6, in which excess protein is converted to glucose, this made Lawrence hungry and he began to binge eat, which packed on the pounds again. Attempting to get to the bottom of why this happened to him on what was supposed to be a healthy diet, he learned about the ketogenic diet and began following it immediately. The results were swift and stunning.

"Within two weeks I had lost the seven pounds I had put on, and I continued to lose weight as well as build muscle," Lawrence said.

He said the ketogenic diet gave him the best results he's ever seen with his strength training and he has never felt better in his life. The best part about ketosis, Lawrence says, is that he's not hungry even while he's losing weight and it's easy to engage in regular bouts of intermittent fasting.

"Over the Christmas holidays I didn't fast and I overate on many foods, but I didn't put on weight," Lawrence noted. "I just stayed the same, which is crazy since I was eating at least 1,000 calories per day more than usual."

Most of the time, though, Lawrence sticks with the highest-quality low-carb, high-fat foods he can find, such as organ meats, which nourish his body, control his hunger, and help his body run the way it was intended to.

Alice Russell
Cumberland, British Columbia – Age 52

Alice was not doing very well as 2012 began. She was feeling bloated, achy, moody, and anxious pretty much all the time. There were moments when she felt dizzy, nauseated, and on the verge of passing out. At forty-nine, she had noticed her weight going steadily up while she dealt with sleep apnea, nightmares, and waking up feeling tired every single day. It was a living hell. Needless to say she was quite scared and desperate to figure out what was wrong with her.

One of the first things she tried to turn her health around was quitting smoking, which she did successfully in February 2012. But when she passed out one day and went to see the doctor, her fasting blood sugar level came back at 126 mg/dl. Alice knew she needed to shift away from her high-sugar, grain-based, low-fat diet because it obviously wasn't helping her get healthy.

In May 2012, she visited her local library to search for books on nutrition and health, and the librarian suggested she read *Protein Power* by Dr. Michael Eades and Dr. Mary Dan Eades. Alice recalled learning about the low-carb, high-fat Atkins diet many years before, but this time the message seemed to click for her.

"I had worked as a cook in a hospital for a long time and I could see that the food pyramid wasn't working," Alice noted. "I was sick and so were lots of other people. We were becoming a fat and unhealthy society."

When she spoke with her husband about going on a low-carb diet with fresh meats and vegetables, they both decided to commit to it as a genuine lifestyle change. The impact was immediate as Alice lost weight, started exercising, and ate much more fat than she had ever consumed before.

"I did not let the fat scare me," she said. "I enjoyed consuming butter, coconut oil, cheese, eggs, meat, and cream in my coffee."

Like most people who are just finding out about low-carb and ketogenic diets, Alice continued to educate herself. She watched lectures on YouTube, listened to nutritional health podcasts, and soaked up all the wisdom of the doctors and authors who share online about the benefits of healthy low-carb, high-fat living.

In December 2012, she got serious about getting into a state of nutritional ketosis to help her deal with the lingering dizziness, lack of energy, and unstable moods brought on by erratic blood sugar levels. She cut her carbs down to just 20 grams a day while continuing to consume all the delicious, healthy fats she had grown accustomed to eating. The effect on her health could not be ignored.

"I felt the high," Alice said. "I had an edge that wasn't there before that gave me steady energy, robust strength, and a very natural ability to go about sixteen hours between meals."

When she attempted to add some fruit and root vegetables back into her diet in the summer of 2013, the positive effects she was seeing from being in ketosis stopped and the familiar issues with dizziness, anxiety, and mood swings returned with a vengeance.

"I was feeling dizzy even before I was hungry," Alice recalled regarding her bouts with hypoglycemia. "I was feeling my blood sugar levels drop and would have to consume an apple to feel well enough to eat my meal."

Alice realized she was super sensitive to carbohydrates and needed to get them back down to much lower levels to put herself into a ketogenic state. In November 2013, she dropped her carbohydrate intake back down to 20 grams a day, and the problems she was having with dizziness, anxiety, and mood swings all cleared up as she entered ketosis again.

"My moods are more stable now," Alice remarked. "I am no longer dizzy or anxious, I don't suffer from bloating or gas, I sleep very well with very few dreams, and my sleep apnea is completely gone."

Plus, the weight loss has remained, giving her confidence that the ketogenic lifestyle is the right path for her.

"I don't know if everyone would be willing to live in a keto-adapted state. But I do know that this is my preferred fueling mode," Alice concluded.

She added that while "not everyone is as carbohydrate intolerant as I am," it is important for people to be aware of the amount of sugar and starch they are consuming.

"People, sugar is bad for you," she warned. "It is not a secret."

MOMENT OF CLARITY By far, the greatest criticism of ketogenic diets is that ketosis is unhealthy, dangerous, and can even cause death. But where are the bodies? If it's so dangerous, why aren't the casualties piling up? More to the point, why does it keep saving so many lives?

– John Kiefer

Jim Small
Denver, Colorado – Age 60

Throughout his life, Jim has always been the "active guy." In high school and college, he was on the swim team, rode his bicycle everywhere, taught karate to kids, and more. He stayed active as an adult, and with a medical degree and PhD from Duke University, he knew that eating well and being healthy meant cutting fat and calories. Nevertheless, the weight gradually piled on over the years.

When he moved back home to Denver, Colorado, after completing his residency, Jim began getting serious about his bike riding again and participated in many races over a hundred miles long. With the added weight he had put on, he figured all this exercise would take off the pounds, but it didn't—in fact, his weight continued to climb. After his father had a heart attack and his grandchildren were born, Jim knew it was "time for a change."

Jim started searching online for more information about a diet that had worked well for him and his wife many years before—the Atkins diet. He started researching low-carb, high-fat diets and was pleased to learn that foods such as avocados, bacon, cheese, duck, eggs, and fish were all on the menu. This was the motivation he needed to give a ketogenic diet another go.

"We eat every day like most people eat when they are on vacation," Jim shared.

He lost about twenty pounds and his waist dropped from thirty-seven inches to thirty-three. His cholesterol numbers all improved dramatically, and the heartburn Jim had not been able to treat successfully for years simply vanished. Additionally, his snoring ended after a week on a ketogenic diet, and during a mission trip he was easily able to fast as part of the spiritual preparation. Jim explained to me that getting these kind of results in his health really didn't take as much effort as people might think.

"I don't weigh food portions," he said. "But I do weigh myself every day to keep myself in check."

People are amazed by the changes Jim has seen in his weight and health, and he's confident as a physician that this is something literally anyone could do to improve their health.

"This ketogenic diet is really good stuff," Jim concluded. "The science seems solid to me as a pathologist and physician."

Are you feeling inspired yet to try a low-carb, moderate-protein, high-fat, ketogenic diet for yourself? These eight individuals are only a few of the many whose lives have been changed by the power of ketones.

Perhaps you've tried to get into ketosis but have had problems producing adequate ketone levels. Coming up in the next chapter, we'll help you identify ten reasons why that may be happening and what you can do about it. Don't lose hope, and be encouraged by these success stories that good things are in store for you.

 **MOMENT OF CLARITY** People who seek out keto are hungry for change. Once they're adapted to ketosis, their quality of life improves exponentially.

– Stephanie Person

Key Keto Clarity Concepts

→ **Real lives are being changed by a ketogenic diet.**

→ **Giving up the gimmicks and embracing a low-carb, high-fat diet works.**

→ **Increasing your blood ketones results in incredible energy and steady mood.**

→ **It is possible to find benefits with ketosis at virtually any age.**

→ **There are many rare medical conditions that could be improved with ketosis.**

→ **Stay the course with your low-carb, high-fat diet despite any ridicule.**

→ **Sometimes low-carb or Paleo isn't enough, so give keto a go.**

→ **Knowing the difference between how you feel in and out of ketosis is key.**

→ **Even medical professionals are recognizing the benefits of ketogenic diets.**

Chapter 14

Ten Reasons You May Not Be Producing Adequate Ketones

MOMENT OF CLARITY Some people are in a big rush to begin producing ketones. If you try to hurry this process, don't be surprised if you struggle. The "I want it now" attitude leads to an increase in stress, and that's a surefire way to kill your ketones.

– Stephanie Person

Ever since I started writing on my blog about my nutritional ketosis n=1 experiment, I've received quite a few emails from people who are frustrated and concerned about their inability to produce adequate ketones while eating what they think is a good low-carb, moderate-protein, high-fat diet. Here's just one example of the comments I've received:

I'm using the blood ketone meter you recommended to check for ketosis. I eat under 50 grams of carbs most days and I'd be quite surprised if I went over 100 grams of carbs on a "bad" day. I've been eating this way for about six to eight months. Whenever I test my ketones at night, around 7 p.m. or so, I only get readings of 0.2 to 0.4 millimolar, below the level of being in nutritional ketosis. I desperately want to experience all the great benefits that ketones have to offer me, but I suspect I need to be tweaking something in my routine to make more progress. Can you help me figure this out?

I absolutely can, and that's exactly what this chapter is all about.

Perhaps, like this blog reader, your attempt to get into a state of nutritional ketosis has been unsuccessful. How exasperating is that? It can seem like no matter how hard you try to increase your ketone levels, they're just not budging one bit. What in the world is going on, and what can be done to fix this?

Below are ten reasons why you may not be producing adequate ketones, along with some practical solutions to help you reap all the great health benefits of a low-carb, high-fat diet.

1. You're automatically assuming your low-carb diet is ketogenic.

(M)OMENT OF CLARITY Most of the concerns I see with low-carb, high-fat, ketogenic diets are based on flawed scientific studies that claim to show low-carb diets are harmful. These studies are generally either done for a very short period of time or have the "low-carb" group consuming upwards of 150 grams of carbs a day along with lean meats—this is perhaps lower-carb, but nowhere near ketogenic.

– Maria Emmerich

In the example above, my reader said that he eats under 50 grams of carbohydrates most of the time, though occasionally he eats more. That's a low-carb diet, but perhaps he is one of those people who is so sensitive to carbohydrates that he needs to lower them even more. And because he is already sensitive to carbohydrates, it stands to reason protein in excess could be an issue for him because of gluconeogenesis.

This is why it's so important to find your personal carb tolerance level and your individual protein threshold and to eat saturated and monounsaturated fats to satiety. That really is the key to producing ketones and enjoying the benefits they can provide to you.

Interestingly, my blog reader from the example above would never have known he wasn't in ketosis if he hadn't been testing his ketones—which brings me to my next point.

2. You're not testing for ketones.

(M)OMENT OF CLARITY When someone tells me that they have tried the ketogenic diet and "it didn't work," they usually haven't attempted to measure their ketones and aren't really in ketosis. It's important to follow this diet for at least four to six weeks to evaluate it fairly.

– Dr. Dominic D'Agostino

This is perhaps the number-one mistake made by people starting a low-carb, high-fat diet. Whenever I receive an email from a blog reader who is flabbergasted that they're not experiencing the benefits of ketosis, one of the first things I ask is whether or not they are testing for the presence of ketones in their body. Many of them respond, "I just thought eating low-carb would put me in ketosis." If that were true, then nobody would ever struggle with switching over to a low-carb, high-fat lifestyle. As we shared in chapter 8, the only way to know absolutely sure that you are producing ketones is to test, test, test. Otherwise, it's merely a guessing game.

3. You're still measuring for ketones in the urine, not blood or breath.

We've talked about this before a few times, but it's such a critical point that bears repeating. Urine ketone testing can be helpful in the very beginning of your foray into nutritional ketosis. But here's what happens: The testing strip turns pink the first couple days, then it may even turn purple for a few days, indicating increased levels of the ketone body acetoacetate. However, after about a week or two of being very faithful to your low-carb, high-fat diet, your urine ketones may all but disappear, making you wonder what happened and what you did wrong.

Actually, you've done something very right: you've become fully keto-adapted. Congratulations! But then why did the testing strips stop showing the presence of ketones?

The ketone body acetoacetate, which was causing your urine ketone testing strips to change color for a little while, eventually was converted into the ketone body beta-hydroxybutyrate, which is present in the blood and is your brain's and body's preferred fuel source when it is running on ketones. This makes it look like your ketones are disappearing when in fact you are running quite efficiently on ketones. You've reached low-carb nirvana!

Switching from urine ketone testing to blood or breath (which contains the ketone body acetone, whose levels correlate quite well with the levels of the ketone body beta-hydroxybutyrate in the blood) will prevent you from becoming needlessly concerned about why you're not in ketosis.

4. You haven't given yourself enough time to become fully keto-adapted.

MOMENT OF CLARITY Studies suggest that keto-adaptation, in which the impact of glycogen depletion is no longer relevant as the body is capable of running on ketones, appears to take approximately three to four weeks in most people.

– Dr. Bill Lagakos

They say that "patience is a virtue," but whoever said that must not have tried to get into ketosis! After all, if I'm doing what I'm supposed to do, then I should see the results that come from those efforts, right?

That's right, you absolutely should. But keep in mind that everyone is different, and it could be that you just haven't given your body enough time to make the switch from being fueled by glucose (sugar and carbohydrates) to being fueled by ketones and fatty acids. Becoming keto-adapted can take as little as a couple of days (if you already eat pretty low-carb, it doesn't take long) to as much as four to six weeks (especially if you are coming off of the Standard American Diet, which is very high in carbohydrates). You know how they say "time heals all wounds"? That definitely applies when you are courting ketosis.

In your pursuit of ketosis, letting a little bit more time pass may be just what you need to find success. But there's one more thing about the passage of time you need to be aware of: as your body becomes more efficient at using blood ketones as fuel, they may eventually show up less and less when you test. Don't let this upset you unless your ketone level dips below 0.5 millimolar. It's just your body running like a well-oiled, ketogenic, fat-burning machine!

> *DOCTOR'S NOTE FROM DR. ERIC WESTMAN: Much of what I do in my clinic is what I call "recalibrating expectations." Not everyone will lose ten pounds in a week, as the gimmicky marketing for so many diet programs and products boldly proclaim. Remember how long it took to gain the weight, and then realize that one to two pounds of weight loss each week is a very healthy pace.*

5. You're exceeding your carb tolerance and protein threshold.

MOMENT OF CLARITY As a general guide based on anecdotal evidence, restrict carbohydrates to approximately 50 grams per day and protein to 1 to 1.5

grams per kilogram of lean body mass, and consume fat to satiety. For most individuals this will result in serum BHB levels between 0.5 and 3.0 millimolar per liter. Those who are severely metabolically damaged may need to restrict carbs and protein even further.

— Dr. Zeeshan Arain

This one is so important that we have already dedicated two entire chapters (chapters 5 and 6) to it. But the underlying lesson here cannot be emphasized enough—you should not expect to be able to create adequate ketones until you know how many carbohydrates and how much protein is right for you. If there were a one-size-fits-all equation to get everyone into ketosis, I'd share that with you. Unfortunately, there is not. So if you're not seeing results on your ketogenic diet, try tinkering around with your carbohydrate and protein intake to find your personal sweet spot for success.

Watch out for hidden ways you may be consuming too many carbohydrates and protein and be mindful of everything that goes into your mouth. If you are consuming low-carb products such as protein bars and shakes, trusting that the "net carbs" will stay below your threshold, then you're probably getting a double whammy—extra carbohydrates that you didn't think you needed to count as well as an increased amount of protein. Remember, you can't eat high-protein on your low-carb diet if you want to be creating ketones.

DOCTOR'S NOTE FROM DR. ERIC WESTMAN: There is often confusion between counting "net carbs" and "total carbs." "Net carbs," determined by subtracting the fiber grams from the total grams of carbs, works well for those who are not very metabolically sick or who don't have much weight to lose. But because some of the fiber is absorbed as glucose and your goal now is to become ketogenic, the more prudent approach is to not subtract even the fiber grams from the total grams of carbs.

6. You're not eating enough dietary fat.

MOMENT OF CLARITY One way to ensure adequate ketone levels on a daily basis is to maintain a relatively high intake of dietary fat—as much as 75 percent of calories or more. Fat is the metabolic precursor for the production of ketones, and it doesn't matter if the fat is provided by the diet or adipose tissue.

— Dr. Bill Lagakos

As I shared in chapter 9, when I talked about my one-year n=1 experiment in nutritional ketosis, one of the biggest mistakes I realized I was making in my low-carb diet was failing to eat enough fat. Although I was consuming over 60 percent of my calories in the form of fat, it wasn't until I bumped it up to over 80 percent that I was able to experience genuine ketosis. Eating fat to satiety, as discussed in chapter 7, is extremely important for getting into ketosis and staying there.

When you consume more fat, it satisfies your hunger and does not raise your blood sugar. Additionally, eating more fat keeps you from taking in more carbohydrate and protein, which could knock your ketone production down. You're looking to get the biggest nutritional bang for your buck, and whole-food sources of fat provide that in spades.

> **MOMENT OF CLARITY** The biggest criticism I hear the most about ketogenic diets are concerns about the high fat intake causing heart disease and heart attacks.
>
> – Dr. William Davis

I know we've long been told to stay away from dietary fat because of a misguided notion that it will clog your arteries and lead to heart disease (it's just not true) and that fat has 9 calories per gram, compared with 4 calories per gram in carbohydrate and protein. But nutrition is so much more complex than the simple mathematical equation that health experts have attempted to make it. The fat phobia that has dominated our culture for several decades will be coming to an end very soon.

So why not get a jump-start on everyone else and eat more whole-food sources of dietary fat? Don't be surprised when you see your ketones soar.

7. A medication or combination of medications is taxing your liver.

> **MOMENT OF CLARITY** Medications can "manage" chronic illnesses like diabetes and obesity, but they cannot prevent or reverse them. But following a ketogenic diet is a potent way to prevent or reverse these common chronic diseases. As a clinician, I like having safe approaches that work with my patients. If you start by focusing on your diet, then the rest will be merely window dressing.
>
> – Dr. Bill Wilson

Both prescription and over-the-counter medications can be hard on your body. Yes, sometimes drugs are necessary, but they can add more toxins that your liver needs to flush out of your body. This is very important, since most medications, including common over-the-counter ones, can be damaging if taken long-term. They may help manage symptoms in the short-term, but that comes with a price if it becomes a maintenance drug you take for the rest of your life.

What does this have to do with ketosis? Well, the liver is involved in regulating insulin levels, and when it's under strain from dealing with medications, your insulin can remain elevated. (This doesn't mean you should necessarily stop taking your medications. If you're concerned, please consult with your physician about the risks and side effects of the specific medication you are taking.) When insulin levels are high, this can knock down your body's ability to create ketones.

If you are able to come off of your prescription medication or forgo taking an over-the-counter drug, you may see your ketones begin to rise. It's certainly something you should be aware of if you are struggling to see results in your ketone testing.

DOCTOR'S NOTE FROM DR. ERIC WESTMAN: In diet and metabolism studies conducted in the early twentieth century, carbohydrates were called "the anti-ketogenic factor." Eating carbohydrates raises insulin levels, and it's the increase in insulin that turns off the production of ketones.

8. You're consuming too few or too many calories.

MOMENT OF CLARITY Following a well-formulated ketogenic diet with adequate calories to support your needs is unlikely to cause problems over the long term.
— Franziska Spritzler

We haven't discussed calories very much in this book, and for good reason. When you are eating a diet that is low in carbohydrates and moderate in protein, and you're consuming real, whole sources of dietary fats to satiety, calories take care of themselves, without any need for you to become obsessed with counting them. But in the pursuit of ketosis, some people can run into trouble with consuming calories either well below or beyond satiety.

In chapter 12, we discussed ways to distinguish true hunger from other factors that prompt you to eat, because with the abundance of food in our society, we're used to consuming a lot of food and eating for reasons other than hunger—making it difficult for us to know when to stop eating. And on the flip side, our society glorifies hunger as a good thing in the realm of dieting, which puts pressure on us to eat fewer calories than our bodies probably need. Both of these extremes can play a major role in your ability to produce therapeutic levels of ketones.

Encourage the production of ketones by paying attention to your hunger, eating enough food that you don't feel the need to eat again in two hours, and being careful not to eat until you are so stuffed that it hurts. This doesn't mean you obsess about calories; that would also be counterproductive. Just as you have to find your carb tolerance and protein threshold, experiment to find the amount of calories that makes you feel satisfied and lets you produce ketones at a beneficial level. You can do this!

Mindful eating is never a bad thing, and making sure you don't lowball yourself or overdo it on the calories could help the ketones start pouring through your veins very quickly.

9. You're eating food too often throughout the day.

We are living in an age when eating is not just about sustenance, it's also about fellowship and enjoying life. That's part of the reason there is a stigma attached to anyone who chooses not to eat with everyone else in a social gathering. There's immense peer pressure at work, your church or synagogue, or even at home to put food in your mouth simply because it's that time of day. But could eating too often hinder your ability to make ketones? You bet it could.

In chapter 11 we discussed the role of intermittent fasting in ketosis, and the two work in tandem—consume a low-carb, moderate-protein, high-fat diet with enough calories to completely satisfy your nutritional needs, and you should be able to very easily go twelve to twenty-four hours between meals without any problems at all. The proper composition of the core components of that meal (carbohydrate, protein, and fat) along with the extended period of spontaneous fasting will do so much to help your body get into ketosis. There's no need to partake in another meal if you are still satisfied by your previous one.

When someone asks you why you're not eating, you can respond, "I am eating . . . ketones!" The look on their face when you say this to them will be priceless.

10. Chronic stress and lack of sleep are raising your cortisol and blood sugar levels too high.

MOMENT OF CLARITY Chronic lack of sleep, leading to circadian rhythm imbalances and/or chronic levels of significant stress, can drive up cortisol levels in a way that can make getting into a state of ketosis essentially impossible.

— Nora Gedgaudas

Why are we so stressed all the time? Most of us don't fully realize the intense negative impact that chronic stress has on virtually every part of our health. Furthermore, stress takes a toll on our bodies when it prevents us from getting the restful sleep we so desperately need. This double whammy of stress and sleep deprivation is a ruthless cycle that can wreak havoc on your ability to be in ketosis.

If you want to completely kill your ability to ever produce a therapeutic level of ketones, then keep on worrying and stressing out about everything so that you only sleep for a few hours each night. Over time, that will undercut any nutritional lifestyle change you have implemented, no matter how strict you have been. For the rest of us, let's take a closer look at why being stressed out all the time is not such a good idea when you want to be in ketosis.

Stress increases levels of cortisol, a hormone that in turn raises your hunger and blood sugar levels as the body goes into self-preservation mode. This is one reason you can have problems losing weight no matter how strictly you adhere to a low-carb, moderate-protein, high-fat diet. Go out in your backyard and play, take a yoga class, do some fun activity with your kids—anything you can do to reduce stress in your life. Once you take proactive steps to lower stress, you'll find that your body is able to rest better at night. Take a chill pill, people!

Remember, stressed is just "desserts" spelled backwards—and it can have the same negative effect on your efforts to get into ketosis as the sugar contained in most desserts. Give your ketones a fighting chance and do something about what's worrying you sooner rather than later.

These are just ten of the many reasons you may not be seeing adequate ketone levels on your ketogenic diet. Other intangible factors could be involved, such as a lack of support from your friends, family, and doctor; mental barriers, such as a lack of confidence in your ability to follow the diet or the belief that you need carbs in your diet for brain health, for example; the failure to plan your meals well; and more. But don't worry about being perfect. Your goal is to continually pursue what it takes to get into ketosis. Be kind to yourself as you work through this process. You'll get there with persistence.

It's worth noting that substances like ketone salts, ketone esters, and various MCT oil products can be used to increase the level of ketones in the blood. However, there is still debate amongst the experts about whether increasing ketones through these means is as effective therapeutically as producing ketones through macronutrient manipulation alone. This question has yet to be answered by research. Until those studies happen, the best thing you can do is remain committed to your low-carb, moderate-protein, high-fat diet and, if you like, use these products as aids to help you reach your goal of higher ketone levels.

As you can see, there are so many elements involved in the process of making ketones. But not everyone is a fan of very low-carb, high-fat, ketogenic diets. In the next chapter, we'll take on the ten biggest criticisms about this way of eating and explain why they are probably much ado about nothing.

MOMENT OF CLARITY I think the obvious temptations that are all around us are the biggest problem with maintaining adequate ketones. One slip with too much carbohydrate will interfere with ketosis, and it can take several days to get back into it. Old habits die hard.

– Dr. Mary Newport

Key Keto Clarity Concepts

→ When you're just not producing ketones, there is a reason.

→ Assuming that eating low-carb is ketogenic is a very common error.

→ You can't know for sure you are in ketosis unless you are testing for it often.

→ Urine ketone testing alone is unreliable and can be discouraging.

→ Be patient; it takes as much as four to six weeks for full keto-adaptation to happen.

→ Tinker around to determine your carb tolerance and protein threshold.

→ Neglecting to eat enough dietary fat will result in poor ketone production.

→ Medications can tax the liver and slow the creation of ketones.

→ Consuming too few or too many calories can make ketosis difficult to attain.

→ If you are having to eat frequently throughout the day, it's hard to make ketones.

→ Chronic stress and lack of sleep will undo the benefits of your low-carb, high-fat diet.

→ There are many intangible factors that could hamstring your pursuit of ketosis.

→ If you're discouraged by your lack of ketones, use ketone-boosting products to help.

Chapter 15

Ten Criticisms of Very Low-Carb, Ketogenic Diets

(M)OMENT OF CLARITY The major criticisms of a ketogenic diet are for the most part theo-retical. We do not observe any of these commonly touted issues in our patients.

— Dr. David Perlmutter

You may have heard some of the lingering arguments opposing the use of ketosis and are concerned about whether or not they are true. In this chapter, we'll take on—and take down—ten of the biggest criticisms of very low-carb, ketogenic diets.

1. There's nothing special about ketosis; it simply reduces calories.

(M)OMENT OF CLARITY In many clinical studies, the spontaneous reduction in calorie intake experienced by low-carbohydrate dieters is similar in magnitude to that experienced by people advised to restrict calories by cutting down on dietary fat. One study compared two different low-carbohydrate diets, one with higher protein and another with higher fat, to a calorie-restricted, low-fat diet. The results showed that the spontaneous reduction in calorie intake in the two low-carbohydrate diets was modestly greater than what the low-fat dieters were able to accomplish and pro-vided more weight and body-fat loss. Another study found the spontaneous calorie intake reduction in those assigned to a low-carbohydrate diet didn't surpass that of those instructed to reduce calorie intake by reducing fat intake. And yet those as-signed to the low-carb group lost over twice as much body fat.

— Dr. Bill Lagakos

This one has always been especially amusing to me. The argument goes a little something like this: the only reason people succeed on a ketogenic diet is that their appetites are suppressed to the point that they don't eat as many calories as they otherwise would. Does anyone else notice the irony in this? While ketogenic opponents think this is a "gotcha" moment, it actually strengthens the case for ketosis even more. Pharmaceutical companies have spent hundreds of millions of dollars attempting to create effective drugs for reducing appetite levels. And yet here we have a natural way to do just that, without any risky side effects.

There's a huge difference between counting calories without regard to the *quality* of those calories and being mindful in selecting the kind of foods that will fill you up and satisfy you. The fact is, calories are naturally managed on a ketogenic diet when you eat to satiety because your hunger is completely controlled; you never have to pull out your calculator to make sure you've stayed within some arbitrary calorie goal. Have you ever wondered how animals in the wild stay so lean and healthy without counting their calories? This is a question we humans should be asking ourselves.

The idea that the kind of calories you eat matters immensely is something Temple University School of Medicine researcher Dr. Guenther Boden observed in a study published in the March 15, 2005, issue of *Annals of Internal Medicine*. Dr. Boden concluded that "excessive overeating had been fueled by carbohydrates." Carbohydrates increase insulin levels, which leads to the desire to eat more and more calories. But ketogenic dieters make fat and protein their primary food intake, and hunger is well under control. This doesn't occur by accident.

When most people begin a ketogenic diet, eating becomes just a normal response to appetite, sometimes for the first time in their lives. I'd say that makes ketosis very special and desirable for anyone who wants to be free from the bondage of calorie-counting forever.

DOCTOR'S NOTE FROM DR. ERIC WESTMAN: Eating carbohydrates makes you hungry. If you don't eat carbohydrates, there is no hunger. Of course, you'll never know this until you stop eating carbohydrates. Most Americans have eaten carbohydrates every single day of their lives!

2. Weight loss during ketosis comes mostly from a loss of water weight and the breakdown of organs and muscle.

It's always humorous to hear people criticize the weight loss that happens during ketosis by mockingly stating that "it's only water weight." But the fact is, when we start to lose weight through *any* method, it's mostly water weight we lose at first. This is partly due to the release of glycogen stores in the muscles. Glycogen, the stored sugar in the body, is filled with water. And since low-carb diets shift the body from sugar-burner to fat-burner, when glycogen is used up, it isn't completely replaced, and when the glycogen weight is lost, water weight is also lost.

It's also partly due to lowered insulin levels. Insulin signals the kidneys to hold on to water and salt, so when you are eating carbohydrates and generating more insulin, you are also retaining more water and salt. Reducing carbohydrate consumption lowers insulin levels, resulting in less retention of salt and water. These certainly aren't bad things, and they explain why some people who are overweight or obese lose a lot of weight when they first begin a low-carb, high-fat, ketogenic diet.

But the interesting aspect of ketosis is that once the water weight is lost, bona fide fat loss begins in earnest. Yes, the amount of weight lost is significantly lower at this point. However, your body is using stored body fat as fuel and is happily burning ketones. So the notion of breaking down organs and muscles on a ketogenic diet is pretty ridiculous, especially when you look at the published research.

Nutrition researcher Anssi Manninen from the University of Kuopio Medical School in Finland published a study in the January 2006 issue of the journal *Nutrition & Metabolism* that examined the effects of a very low-carb diet (defined as 10 grams of carbs per day) on muscle mass. He concluded that the ketones produced by the liver act as a restraining influence on the breakdown of muscle protein. Additionally, the presence of fatty acids and ketones can actually suppress the oxidation of the amino acids that can cause damage to muscles. In other words, rather than seeing muscle wasting on a very low-carb, ketogenic diet, Manninen says this way of eating is actually *protective* of your lean muscle mass.

DOCTOR'S NOTE FROM DR. ERIC WESTMAN: There is a brainstorming technique in which you "turn everything upside down" in order to see things differently, and often new solutions to problems will emerge. Muscle cells have glucose receptors (gateways) that require insulin to open. We typically think of these receptors as allowing glucose in, but what if we think of them keeping glucose out? With that shift in perspective, we can think of muscle cells as fat-burning cells that only need sugar when faced with sprinting or other activity that requires bursts of energy.

3. Very low-carb, ketogenic diets induce hypothyroidism and adrenal fatigue.

MOMENT OF CLARITY Is someone suffering from hypothyroidism because of ketosis, or is it caused by chronic low-calorie intake, stress, or something else—or even a combination of all of this? Without isolating variables, it cannot be said for certain that ketosis is the cause.

– Dr. Zeeshan Arain

Hypothyroidism can occur when one thyroid hormone, T4, isn't easily converted into another thyroid hormone, T3. In recent years, some prominent members of the online Paleo community have promulgated the idea that the lack of glucose on a ketogenic diet leads to a diminished capacity for T4 to be converted into T3, leading to hair loss, cold hands and feet, general malaise, and other symptoms associated with low thyroid function. It all sounds so dastardly that you might wonder why anyone would ever go on a very low-carb, ketogenic diet.

MOMENT OF CLARITY The concern about thyroid function reveals a misunderstanding both among the lay public and among doctors themselves. A lower number does not necessarily mean lower function. Often it means better function. As the body is functioning better, thyroid levels go down. This is a very desirable state. This is what distinguishes health and longevity in many instances. Centenarians have lower thyroid than their elderly peers. When people criticize a very low-carbohydrate diet by saying that it causes hypothyroidism, it's not only misleading but overtly wrong.

– Dr. Ron Rosedale

The problem with this criticism is that it is incomplete. While some on a ketogenic diet may experience hypothyroidism if they aren't consuming enough calories, when calories are adequate, hypothyroidism doesn't occur. It's the number of calories, not the ketogenic diet itself, that matters here. In research studies following people on a well-formulated low-carb, moderate-protein, high-fat diet with adequate calories, there has been no occurrence of low thyroid. And as long as the calories are not restricted on a very low-carb diet, thyroid and metabolic function remain normal, without any need for consuming additional glucose. In fact, a diminished thyroid level is not a "pathological condition," says nutritional consultant and educator Nora Gedgaudas. As long as calories are sufficient, a lowered thyroid level is actually a sign of "improved efficiency of metabolic functioning and is literally a desirable longevity marker."

MOMENT OF CLARITY If you happen to have thyroid issues upon embarking on a ketogenic diet, you may experience symptoms of thyroid dysfunction. But people are often very quick to confuse this association with their new diet being the cause. I have never seen the sudden development of non-preexisting thyroid disease in anyone eating a low-carb, high-fat diet. It is true that over time, there may be a slowed conversion of T4 thyroid hormone into active T3 on a well-formulated ketogenic diet. But this doesn't mean there's a problem.

– Nora Gedgaudas

A naturopathic physician named Dr. Chris Decker wrote on this very topic in her online article "Does Paleo Make Us Hypothyroid?", in which she addresses exactly what happens to the thyroid when you are generating ketones while following a low-carb, moderate-protein, high-fat diet:

When we are burning ketones from fat as our primary fuel source, our thyroid just doesn't have to work as hard as it does when it's got to manage bodily metabolism on a less-preferred fuel (glucose). When our organs, against their better judgment, are required to metabolize sugar over fat, more T3 is needed to deal with this less-than-ideal scenario. Our thyroid has to work overtime, and somebody—poor T3!—has got to do the job. But burn fat for fuel instead, and T3 gets to stay home and put its feet up.

So a reduction in T3 levels is in fact a very *good* thing!

MOMENT OF CLARITY What we consider to be a normal level of thyroid function may actually be an elevated level due to a consistently high-carb diet, in which case the lower thyroid function observed on a low-carb, high-fat, ketogenic diet would actually be closer to a normal value.

– Dr. Jay Wortman

Cardiologist Dr. William Davis also says the claims about very low-carb diets and reduced thyroid function are "simply untrue." He says that when someone on a ketogenic diet loses weight, levels of thyroid-stimulating hormone (TSH, one of the three key thyroid hormones checked on a thyroid panel) increase and free T3 (another thyroid hormone that's checked on a more advanced thyroid panel) levels decrease, which some falsely believe indicates hypothyroidism. But Dr. Davis says this is not entirely accurate. "This specific situation does not represent disturbed thyroid function, but rather a physiologic adaptation to limit weight loss by reducing metabolic rate, a survival mechanism that is meant to protect the body from starvation," he explains. "These hormonal adjustments are transient and correct themselves over several weeks after weight has plateaued. But it does not represent thyroid dysfunction."

MOMENT OF CLARITY We see a drop in thyroid hormone levels over the short term on a ketogenic diet, but that's balanced by a more responsive sympathetic nervous system response.

– John Kiefer

As for adrenal fatigue on a ketogenic diet, the thinking has been that a low-carb diet stresses the body, leading to overworked adrenal glands and leaving you feeling tired, fatigued, shaky, unable to recover from workouts, and worse. But what if none of this has anything to do with eating a ketogenic diet? It's more likely that these are symptoms of an underlying issue that was there long before the shift to a ketogenic diet—if not done properly, the transition could trigger a latent problem.

MOMENT OF CLARITY There are anecdotal reports of people experiencing symptoms of adrenal fatigue or hypothyroidism after being in ketosis for extended periods of time; however, to the best of my knowledge, there are no studies corroborating these reports.

– Franziska Spritzler

Being in a state of ketosis *lowers* the amount of stress on the body through the elimination of such culprit foods as sugar, white flour, grains, legumes, and more. Switching over from the unnatural and stressful state of being a sugar-burner to the more relaxed state of being a fat-burner is arguably far less taxing on your adrenal glands. Getting enough sleep, doing some light exercise, and engaging in stress-lowering activities will do more to help with adrenal fatigue than trying to blame it on a ketogenic diet!

DOCTOR'S NOTE FROM DR. ERIC WESTMAN: Any approach to eating that is substantially different metabolically from what most people are doing—like a low-carb, ketogenic diet—may lead to blood values that are outside the "normal range." This doesn't always mean that the value is unhealthy, because the "normal range" is defined by what is most commonly seen. The levels of thyroid hormone, for example, may be outside the normal range and yet perfectly healthy if the body needs less thyroid hormone in the blood because it is more sensitive to it. Similarly, most keto-adapted people have so-called abnormally low blood glucose because they are burning ketones so much that they don't need high glucose levels anymore!

4. LDL and total cholesterol increase to unhealthy levels on a ketogenic diet.

MOMENT OF CLARITY An excess of oxidation-prone LDL particles is, by a long stretch, the most common abnormality in people who develop coronary heart disease and heart attack. People who consume plenty of "healthy whole grains" have astounding excesses of these damaging LDL particles. People who eliminate grains and sugars and enjoy a healthy state of ketosis experience the dramatic reduction, even complete elimination, of these small, dense LDL particles.

– Dr. William Davis

When you consume a low-carb, high-fat diet, HDL cholesterol (the good kind) goes up, triglycerides come way down, and LDL cholesterol particles shift from the dangerous small, dense kind to the much more benign large, fluffy kind. (We talk about all this in much more detail in our book *Cholesterol Clarity*.)

It is true, though, that two numbers on your cholesterol panel—LDL-C and total cholesterol levels—may go up in some people on a ketogenic diet. The question is whether or not that indicates something bad is happening with your health. LDL-C, a calculated measurement, and total cholesterol are actually two of the most uninteresting numbers on your cholesterol panel, and they don't really matter as much to your overall health as other numbers. What does matter is the LDL particle breakdown, which is presented separately in a more advanced cholesterol panel known as the NMR LipoProfile test.

So what should you be paying attention to in your cholesterol tests? Make sure your HDL cholesterol is above 50, ideally higher than 70 (consuming saturated fat helps get you there). Get your triglycerides under 100, ideally under 70 (cutting your carbohydrate intake does this best). Shift your LDL particle size (determined with the NMR LipoProfile test, which any doctor can have run) to mostly the large, fluffy kind (by eating a low-carb, high-fat, ketogenic diet). Additionally, get an hsCRP (high-sensitivity C-reactive protein) blood test to check for signs of inflammation, the *true* culprit in heart disease, and a CT scan of your heart to look for any signs of disease.

And if you are concerned about your cholesterol while on a low-carb, high-fat diet, read *Cholesterol Clarity,* which delves into this topic in great detail.

5. Very low-carb diets induce mucus deficiency, leading to dry eyes and mouth.

MOMENT OF CLARITY The so-called problem of ketogenic diets leading to mucus deficiency is being grossly misinterpreted. First, I have not seen this in decades of using this diet with patients. Second, the claim is that mucus is a glycoprotein that requires glucose, so not eating glucose will diminish its production, resulting in dry eyes and mouth. However, this makes little sense in light of the fact that during starvation, serum glucose is maintained at normal levels almost until death. In other words, there is plenty of glucose available if it is absolutely necessary.

– Dr. Ron Rosedale

This criticism of very low-carb diets simply leaves me crying. Seriously?! The idea is that because our bodies need glucose to make mucus—including saliva, sweat, and tears—if you don't consume enough carbohydrates, you'll be reaching for the Visine early and often. Can I just say how utterly ridiculous this is? As someone who has eaten a low-carb, high-fat diet for over a decade, I've never had an issue with dry eyes and mouth. And I've interacted with tens of thousands of people who eat this way and never once have I ever heard anyone dealing with this issue.

Nutritional consultant and educator Nora Gedgaudas says that "no healthy person adopting a ketogenic diet is going to need to worry about" a mucus deficiency. "I can honestly say I have personally never once encountered a 'mucus deficiency' issue when it comes to this way of eating," she said. Gedgaudas said there is "a lot of fearmongering" that is "absurdly alarmist and completely unrelated to a normal, healthy ketogenic state."

Mucus production happens normally on a very low-carb diet because our bodies can make enough glucose through gluconeogenesis. Unless there is some underlying metabolic issue regarding amino acids, this criticism is really a red herring. Gedgaudas notes that a study published in the June 2006 issue of the *Journal of Nutrition* found that impaired production of mucin (the molecules that make up mucus) has more to do with amino acid imbalances than a "carbohydrate deficiency." Consuming bone broth and pasture-raised gelatin will help restore any amino acid imbalances, she explained.

If someone on a very low-carb, high-fat, ketogenic diet is dealing with dry eyes and mouth, it's more likely that they are simply more prone to this than others. Sensitivities to specific foods or food components could also contribute to these problems. This underscores the importance of tinkering with your own diet to look for things like dairy intolerance, problems with nightshades (tomatoes and peppers, for instance), and more. An autoimmune elimination diet can help you determine if you have a sensitivity to particular foods. To learn more about that diet, check out *The Paleo Approach* by Dr. Sarah Ballantyne.

6. The lack of fiber in a very low-carb diet results in constipation.

Dietary fiber has been given a virtual health halo by nutrition experts as the ideal way to fill you up and keep you regular. So it should come as no surprise that a very low-carb diet would come under fire from these same health gurus. Yes, you do greatly reduce the amount of fiber you consume when you eat a ketogenic diet. However, you can get plenty of fiber from non-starchy and green, leafy vegetables without resort to eating "healthy whole grains." Furthermore, constipation is easily avoided by simply drinking more water and adding more sea salt and magnesium to your diet.

DOCTOR'S NOTE FROM DR. ERIC WESTMAN: Just about everyone notices that they tend to have fewer bowel movements after going on a ketogenic diet. This is not a medical problem that needs to be treated. However, if you have hard stools or hard-to-pass stools during the keto-adaptation period, then drinking water, consuming bouillon broth, and using milk of magnesia are all useful remedies.

7. Very low-carb, ketogenic diets contain major nutrient deficiencies.

MOMENT OF CLARITY People often experience health benefits from going into ketosis. However, if they do not eat sufficient amounts of micronutrients, especially vitamins C, K, and E and plant-based antioxidants, they are likely to develop insufficiency of these nutrients after two or three years of ketosis, as the stores of these nutrients are used up. It is possible to maintain intake of antioxidants and vitamins C, K, and E while in ketosis by eating more organ meats, greens, and sulfur-rich vegetables such as onions, mushrooms, and cabbages.

– Dr. Terry Wahls

Some registered dietitians promote the idea that eating a very low-carb, ketogenic diet will leave you deficient in some key nutrients. What's ironic about this notion is that a healthy low-carb diet includes some of the most nutrient-dense foods on the planet, filled with so many essential vitamins and minerals to help your body thrive. While fruits and vegetables are often assumed to be the sole source of this nutrition, the fact is, plenty of low-carb, high-fat foods are also rich in nutrients.

Ketogenic diet staples such as red meat, eggs, cheese, fish, and nuts offer up something that is completely lacking in a low-fat diet: fat-soluble vitamins! These can only be absorbed when you eat fat, and they're essential for your health. So instead of creating nutrient deficiencies, a low-carb, high-fat diet is actually providing even *more* nutrition than you've probably ever experienced before.

8. On a ketogenic diet, you can develop scurvy due to lack of vitamin C.

MOMENT OF CLARITY Two explorers, Vilhjalmur Stefansson and K. Andersen, lived and traveled with the Inuit for nine years while eating the Inuit's animal-based, low-carb, high-fat diet. These two explorers were later studied for one year at Bellevue Hospital in New York on the all-meat (including organ meat and bone broth) ketogenic diet, and the results were published in 1930. They remained healthy during the one-year study and didn't develop scurvy or any other nutritional deficiencies, as had been predicted by the leading nutritionists of the day.

– Dr. Keith Runyan

The scaremongering continues with the claim that being in a state of ketosis doesn't allow your body to absorb enough vitamin C, which leads to scurvy, a condition that manifests with symptoms of extreme fatigue, spots on the skin, sore and bleeding gums, and depression.

Those who are not extremely sensitive to carbohydrates have the option of eating plenty of excellent, low-carb, non-starchy vegetables that are packed with vitamin C, such as broccoli, kale, and green peppers, for example. But even if these vegetables aren't a major part of your ketogenic diet, there's another key point to remember: because carbs deplete the amount of vitamin C in your body, you won't *need* as much vitamin C when you cut carbs. So eating a high-carb diet full of sugar, grains, and starchy foods actually means you need more vitamin C than when you are in a state of ketosis.

Finally, vitamin C is found in animal-based foods as well, as Arctic explorer and researcher Vilhjalmur Stefansson proved. He studied the nutritional habits of the Inuit population in Alaska for nine years in the early 1900s, and he noticed their diet was mostly fat and protein, with very little carbohydrate consumption for most of the year. In other words, these people are most certainly in ketosis most of the time. After Stefansson returned home and shared his findings, the medical establishment refused to believe he could have been healthy surviving on mostly fat, moderate amounts of protein, and very few carbohydrates.

So he agreed to do a one-year metabolic ward study in which he was locked in a hospital ward so that all of his food intake could be tracked and his health analyzed. At the end of that experiment, during which he consumed a virtually all-meat diet, he exhibited no signs of any health problems and had no vitamin deficiencies. The results of that study were published in the *Journal of Biological Chemistry* in 1930.

So much for trying to scare people away from keto with scurvy fears!

DOCTOR'S NOTE FROM DR. ERIC WESTMAN: I heard a talk given by an expert on the health of the Inuit. She explained that the Inuit never developed scurvy because there was plenty of vitamin C in the foods that they ate. Of course, it was so cold where the traditional Inuit lived that they never *ate fruits or vegetables—just animal products. Just to show you how ingrained the importance of fruit and vegetables is in our culture, at the end of her talk she reminded us that, despite this information, we should* still *eat five servings of fruits and vegetables every day. Go figure.*

9. Consuming a very low-carb diet will increase the occurrence of kidney stones.

MOMENT OF CLARITY The common misinformation that ketosis and low-carb diets cause kidney damage and kidney stones has not been seen in clinical practice, nor has it been demonstrated in the numerous studies done over the last fifteen years or so. Instead, the results we've seen have all been positive.

— Jackie Eberstein

This is another common criticism of very low-carb diets that has no basis in reality. The claim is that people who consume a ketogenic diet are 500 times more likely to develop kidney stones composed of uric acid and 50 times more likely to develop the more common calcium oxalate kidney stones. What is their proposed solution? Eat more carbohydrates like white rice and potatoes.

MOMENT OF CLARITY If a person is uncomfortably symptomatic in some way, then they need to dig deep with a qualified, knowledgeable, and capable professional to determine the underlying problem. Here's one hint: it has nothing to do with a "starch deficiency." Dig deeper! One cannot consume so-called safe starches like white rice and potatoes and expect to maintain a healthy ketogenic state.

— Nora Gedgaudas

Just like the fears about dry eyes and mouth discussed earlier, this could be an example of blaming a ketogenic diet when someone is predisposed to having kidney stones anyway. To help prevent kidney stones, make sure you are properly hydrated, supplement your diet with magnesium and potassium citrate, eliminate soda from your diet (it's full of phosphates that contribute to stone formation), and keep an eye on the pH balance of your urine (you can test it with strips available in any health store and tinker with your diet to get it more alkaline than acidic). One thing to keep in mind is that kidney stone formation is more common on a high-carb diet, not a low-carb one, as shared in a *British Journal of Urology* study published in December 1978.

It's also important to note that many who embark on a low-carb, high-fat, ketogenic diet tend to be those who are dealing with obesity, type 2 diabetes, and metabolic syndrome, all of which are contributing factors in the development of kidney stones. And if your low-carb diet contains higher levels of protein than you need, that, too, can raise your uric acid excretion, which leads to kidney stones (yet another reason to moderate your protein intake and increase the amount of fat you consume). While blood levels of uric acid do indeed increase when you first go ketogenic, those levels normalize within four to eight weeks.

10. Very low-carb diets induce insulin resistance and a "glucose deficiency."

MOMENT OF CLARITY There is no such thing as a "glucose deficiency." This cannot be found in any medical textbook on the planet.

– Nora Gedgaudas

Quite frankly, this is the most laughable criticism of all. The argument is that eating a very low-carb diet leads to a "glucose deficiency," which brings on insulin resistance (in which the body cannot utilize insulin efficiently, leading to blood sugar dysregulation and other weight and health problems). People who say this believe that insulin resistance occurs on a ketogenic diet as a means of protecting glucose for the brain to function properly. Where do you start with such nonsense?

Let's just say right away that there is no such thing as a "glucose deficiency." Your body and brain function perfectly well using ketones as a fuel source. Because fatty acids and ketones are replacing glucose, blood sugar levels fall below what we might consider the "normal" range. But this isn't a bad thing at all.

In fact, the lower need for glucose actually preserves muscle mass, and the hormonal mechanism for blood sugar regulation is inhibited by the presence of fatty acids and ketones, making them an adequate substitute for glucose. Keep in mind that being in a state of ketosis actually *protects* against insulin resistance, which could come on with a vengeance if you began consuming carbohydrates again. This is why if you eat a low-carb, high-fat, ketogenic diet, you should never take an oral glucose tolerance test—the glucose syrup concoction they give you will overload the body and not give an accurate picture of what is actually happening in the body.

The bottom line is this: consuming a diet that is very low in carbohydrates and high in fat *prevents* insulin resistance. The presence of beta-hydroxybutyrate (the ketone body in the blood) increases your resistance to oxidative stress and acts as an anti-inflammatory agent (a very good thing for your overall health!).

Try as they may, the people who are opposed to a healthy ketogenic diet cannot prevent the truth about its incredible therapeutic effects from getting out.

Coming up in the next three chapters, we'll examine the scientific evidence in support of low-carb, moderate-protein, high-fat diets in three waves: what we have solid evidence for, what we have reasonably good evidence for, and what are emerging areas of interest. If a study has shown that ketosis helps with a particular condition, then you'll read about it in the following chapters. Get ready to be amazed!

Key Keto Clarity Concepts

→ The spontaneous reduction in calories consumed is a major benefit of ketosis.

→ Weight loss on any diet begins with the loss of water weight before fat loss commences.

→ The hysteria over very low-carb diets inducing hypothyroidism is unwarranted.

→ Shifting from focusing on LDL-C and total cholesterol to focusing on LDL particles is better for determining actual heart health risk.

→ There is no evidence that a ketogenic diet causes a lack of mucus.

→ Constipation on a low-carb diet can be fixed with vegetables, salt, magnesium, and water.

→ The notion that a ketogenic diet causes nutrient deficiencies is unfounded as long as you consume a variety of nutrient-rich foods.

→ Despite the scaremongering, scurvy from a lack of vitamin C isn't an issue on ketogenic diets.

→ Kidney stones are the result of a high-carb diet, not a low-carb one.

→ Very low-carb diets improve insulin sensitivity rather than inducing insulin resistance.

→ There is no such thing as a "glucose deficiency."

Chapter 16

Solid Science for Using Ketogenic Diets Therapeutically

DOCTOR'S NOTE FROM DR. ERIC WESTMAN: Canadian prime minister Lester B. Pearson once said that "misunderstanding arising from ignorance breeds fear." Perhaps that is what happens when some people, even scientific experts, are asked about low-carb diets. But that is not the appropriate scientific reaction to a lack of knowledge. When there is not a lot of research about a given topic (like low-carb diets), we don't know if it is good or bad. Low-carb, high-fat diets were simply assumed to be bad, and that led to a taboo about studying them that lasted from 1980 to 2002. But over the last twelve years, low-carb diet research has returned, and the results have been overwhelmingly positive. Using the standards of a court of law, the low-carb, high-fat, ketogenic diet should have been innocent until proven guilty. But instead it was deemed guilty until proven innocent.

Everything you have read about up to this point in the book has been based on our collective experience with ketogenic diets. It is quite possible that you want hard proof that there's scientific evidence that what we've been talking about is true, and that's perfectly fair—in fact, we encourage you to question anything and everything you've heard or continue to hear about nutrition from any so-called health expert. Simply trusting what we have always believed to be true about diet and health doesn't cut it anymore. We need real evidence, and in the next few chapters we'll be sharing what the science has proved about low-carb, high-fat diets.

Be a Careful Consumer of Research

Before we begin describing the multitude of studies that support the use of ketogenic diets for a variety of health concerns, we'd like to talk about the different kinds of research that exist and how to sift through and evaluate the overwhelming amount of information that we hear in the news about research. Most journalists do not have the expertise to evaluate the relevance or importance of research studies, so they end up reporting on any press releases they receive from medical journals or research institutes. That research is then regurgitated on the nightly news, in newspapers and magazines, and all across the Internet. The general public, in turn, doesn't have the deep knowledge and experience needed to decipher what the research really means, and many simply embrace whatever they hear as the gospel truth. After all, they conclude, this is what science is showing us.

The first question to ask regarding any research study is this: "Does this study apply to me?" With that question in mind, it's easy to only pay attention to research done with human subjects. Unfortunately, much of the dietary research that we hear about in the news has been conducted on rats or mice, and the findings are then extrapolated to apply to humans. A prime example of this was a study published in the November 1, 2013, issue of *American Journal of Physiology—Endocrinology and Metabolism* that concluded that a low-carb, high-fat, ketogenic diet impairs glucose tolerance, which in turn leads to an increase in insulin resistance. Who were the study subjects? Rats! Of course, none of the gleeful negative reporting on this research mentioned this salient fact.

The reality is that these kind of studies aren't yet ready for prime time—rats and mice just aren't similar enough to people for the results to be immediately applicable to humans. Instead, these studies help scientists develop theories that warrant further testing on larger animals and perhaps eventually humans (at which point the results will be more applicable to us). The reason so much research is done in rats and mice is that it is relatively inexpensive to conduct and the animals can be sacrificed to make measurements using the entire animal body.

But finding the right studies to listen to is a little more complicated than just focusing on human research. There is also something called the "hierarchy of clinical research," which means that some human research is more relevant to an individual than others.

MOMENT OF CLARITY Anecdotal evidence deals with issues where it is hard to make explicit something that is understood intuitively. The best method of research is the one that answers the question, and some questions are well answered by anecdotal evidence.

– Dr. Richard Feinman

An n=1 case study tells the experience of one individual (for our purposes, usually someone making a change in his or her diet). While most people downplay the importance of a study like this, a lot of information can be obtained from one person's experience—especially if that experience is new or unusual. For example, if an alien being came to Earth and we studied it very carefully, would we dismiss the information gleaned simply because the research was done on just one alien? Of course not! And if an explorer reached the North Pole alone and documented that experience, does the fact that he or she did it singlehandedly negate the discoveries made along the way? Not a chance.

DOCTOR'S NOTE FROM DR. ERIC WESTMAN: I look at Jimmy's n=1 experiment, described in chapter 9, like the observations of one of the first Arctic explorers. While his results might not be the same as yours, in my experience, most people who try something similar have similar results.

Then there are several types of research—observational, case-control, cohort, epidemiological—that are intended to be hypothesis-generating; they establish the groundwork that others use by coming up with theories to test in controlled clinical trials. Epidemiological studies, in particular, look at a large amount of data, apply different parameters, and look for patterns, from which they generate a hypothesis that can be tested in future studies. Due the limitations of such research, they are most definitely not relevant to an individual. Their purpose isn't to answer certain questions but rather to set the stage for research that can be applicable to an individual.

Observational studies tend to find correlations between things. But let's be clear (and you may have heard this before): correlation does not equal causation. Just because two things happen at the same time doesn't mean that one thing causes the other. Health blogger and author Denise Minger shared an excellent example of this in a guest blog post on *Mark's Daily Apple*. She noted that cholesterol levels began to fall the year Justin Bieber was born. But as soon as Facebook was invented, the levels went back up again. Therefore, this is "evidence" that Facebook cancelled out the cholesterol-lowering effects of Justin Bieber. Yes, this sounds preposterous, as it should. And yet these kind of "correlation equals causation" relationships are made often in nutrition studies.

MOMENT OF CLARITY Research on the ketogenic diet has been relatively limited because research-funding committees are either ignorant of its potential benefits or biased against it. Therefore, very few people are encouraged to follow this approach.

— Dr. Keith Runyan

Nutritional epidemiological research is a kind of cohort, hypothesis-generating research that has been used inappropriately to draw conclusions about what foods are healthy or unhealthy. For instance, an April 2014 study published in the *Journal of Epidemiology & Community Health* concluded that eating seven or more portions of fruit and vegetables a day reduces your risk of death at any point in time by 42 percent compared to eating less than one portion. How did the researchers come to this revelation? They examined the self-reported food logs of 65,226 British people who participated in an annual survey from 2001 to 2008. These people weren't in a controlled environment, and the study relied heavily on the participants recalling what they ate over the previous year. What the researchers should have done was take the information gathered from their epidemiological research and use the results to form new hypotheses to test in a controlled, clinical setting. That didn't happen. Instead, the headlines all touted the finding of "new evidence linking fruit and vegetable consumption with lower mortality." This is incredibly misleading to the general public, but unfortunately most people don't know this.

Another study, published by Harvard School of Public Health researchers in *Archives of Internal Medicine* on March 12, 2012, concluded that red meat consumption is associated with an increased risk of total, cardiovascular, and cancer mortality. That study pooled the data from 37,698 men from the Health Professionals Follow-up Study for up to 22 years and 83,644 women in the Nurses' Health Study for up to 28 years who were free of cardiovascular disease and cancer at baseline. Here's the kicker: their diets were assessed through questionnaires distributed every four years. Once again, recall of food consumed over the past few years was heavily relied on to generate the information used to make these correlations. But do you remember what you had to eat for lunch two weeks ago, much less three or four *years* ago? No, me either. And yet headlines boldly state "Red meat consumption linked to increased risk of total, cardiovascular, and cancer mortality," making everyone scared to death of eating a steak or hamburger!

The only type of research that can lead to a solid conclusion about what we should do to be healthy is experimental research. You probably remember this from high school biology or chemistry class. You had well-defined substances, maybe chemicals in a test tube, with various controls. It's possible you were asked to repeat the experiment several times to make sure your results were similar. That's because to really know something or to conclude that one thing is caused by another, it is imperative to experiment and then do it again and again to make sure the same result is obtained each time. This is the most relevant research there is when it comes to practical applications. When this kind of study is conducted, it's referred to as a *controlled clinical trial.*

DOCTOR'S NOTE FROM DR. ERIC WESTMAN: Unfortunately, it is very expensive and time-consuming to conduct controlled clinical trials about diet and health with human subjects, and the researchers in charge of designing these studies have been heavily predisposed to study low-fat diets instead of high-fat diets. As a result, compared to low-fat diets or drugs, there is relatively little information about low-carb, high-fat diets.

Controlled studies, which compare one approach to another, fit into one of four categories: a *parallel group,* in which participants are randomly assigned to a specific group; a *crossover,* in which participants are given an intervention in a random sequence over time; a *cluster,* in which preexisting groups are selected at random for some kind of intervention; or a *factorial,* in which participants are assigned at random to a group for a combination of interventions. So this kind of research really is the best way to determine whether an approach really leads to the desired endpoint or outcome. Ideally, a technique known as *randomization* is used to arbitrarily assign people to one treatment or another. In many circles, the gold standard of human clinical research studies is the randomized, controlled clinical trial.

An n=1 case study *can* be a controlled study if an individual tries different diets and keeps everything else the same. In research language this is known as a "multiple-period, within-subject, crossover study." A case series is a research publication that tells the experience of several case studies, with or without the "crossover" on several different diets.

There is no standard definition of what constitutes a small or large study, but in general, a study with fewer than fifty participants is considered a small study while a large study has hundreds of participants. A large study tends to offer up more relevant and applicable results, and the more diverse the participants, the more likely the results will be relevant to you. For example, if the study looked at 8,000 men and you are a woman—well, you get the picture, right?

This leads us to the final rub—there is no one exactly, 100 percent just like you. So even though there's a lot of great research that has been done to this point, none of it may ever be relevant to you! The only way to know for sure if something will work for you is to try it and see. That's why we are huge advocates of self-experimentation and doing what works for you to become optimally healthy. You are your own best health advocate, and you know the most about your own body. Take control of your own health and never fall victim to false interpretations of any research study.

DOCTOR'S NOTE FROM DR. ERIC WESTMAN: Generally speaking, if a study comes from a clinical practice, it is not as highly regarded as a study that had special staff taking measurements, double-checking procedures, and thoroughly documenting events and outcomes.

Now that you know how to discern the difference between strong, solid experimental studies and weak observational studies that often get a lot more attention than they deserve, let's take a look at the science supporting ketogenic diets. Don't worry if you're not a scientist or don't understand all the complex jargon of research papers—we'll explain it all in plain English for you. However, if you do want to dig a little deeper into the research, the citations for all these studies are listed in the back of the book.

Epilepsy

MOMENT OF CLARITY In the case of epilepsy, a state of nutritional ketosis is effective in the treatment of seizures while avoiding the side effects of antiepileptic medications designed to accomplish the same results. Interestingly, valproic acid is a medication used in the treatment of epilepsy and several mood disorders that is an inhibitor of histone deacetylase, as is the ketone beta-hydroxybutyrate. Histone deacetylase inhibitors are currently being investigated for their anticancer and antiaging properties. This may suggest an actual mechanism for the antiseizure properties of beta-hydroxybutyrate.

– Dr. Keith Runyan

We begin with the oldest use of the ketogenic diet. The Bible describes fasting, which as we've noted causes the body to produce ketones, as a treatment for "fits." Other ancient Western medical practitioners advised their patients with recurring seizures not to eat carbohydrates (sugars and starches), which they found worked as well as not eating any food at all. Today, we understand that both "not eating" and "not eating carbohydrates" are the same thing behind the scenes—both make the body use fat for fuel. Of course, eating moderate protein and a lot of fat is the healthy way to sustain fat-burning over a long period of time.

The low-carb, high-fat, ketogenic diet was rediscovered in the early 1900s as a treatment for epilepsy. In many instances, seizures resolve completely when the patient begins eating this way. Endocrinologist H. Rawle Geyelin used this approach with several epileptic patients and presented his promising findings at the 1921 meeting of the American Medical Association. He ultimately developed the low-carb, high-fat, ketogenic nutritional approach to treating epilepsy that would become the go-to means for controlling epileptic seizures until the early 1940s. When prescription medications for epilepsy were developed, reliance on this natural dietary approach began to wane.

MOMENT OF CLARITY More than ninety years of experience and a number of clinical trials show the benefit of the ketogenic diet for children with drug-resistant epilepsy. About one fourth of these children completely stop having seizures and another third have a substantial reduction in the number of seizures. More recently, some adults with epilepsy have benefitted as well.

– Dr. Mary Newport

The Ketogenic Diet (capitalized here to distinguish it as an official medical treatment for epilepsy) became less and less popular as new medications were developed to treat seizures, but there were a few medical centers that continued using this approach because it worked so well. Then in 1997, the Ketogenic Diet received a tremendous boost in popularity with . . . *First Do No Harm,* a made-for-TV movie starring Meryl Streep that was written and directed by Jim Abrahams, cofounder of the advocacy group The Charlie Foundation for Ketogenic Therapies. It details the story of a mom whose son has epilepsy and her frustration with the medical profession refusing to tell her about the Ketogenic Diet as an alternative therapy. The film spawned even more research about the uses of a ketogenic diet to treat epilepsy.

The studies that have been conducted on this nutritional therapy now include several clinical series and randomized, controlled trials that clearly demonstrate that it works for some—but not all—people with epilepsy. There are treatment centers around the world that offer the Ketogenic Diet as a therapy for patients with epilepsy.

 **MOMENT OF CLARITY** The efficacy of ketosis in reducing the frequency of seizures in patients with epilepsy has been in the medical literature since 1928.

— Dr. David Perlmutter

Interestingly, there has been very little conversation between researchers investigating the effects of low-carb, ketogenic diet on weight and general health and researchers investigating the Ketogenic Diet as a treatment for epilepsy. But effective strategies for increasing ketone production may come from the traditional teachings of the Ketogenic Diet, which calls for a fat to protein and carbohydrate ratio of four to one. First, the protein requirement is determined: 1 gram of protein per kilogram of body weight. Then, add in 10 to 15 grams of carbohydrate. The rest of the diet is comprised of fat. So if a child weighs 44 pounds (20 kilograms), the daily protein intake would be 20 grams and carbohydrate intake would be 10 grams, for a total of 30 grams that are not fat. Then, since the ratio of fat to protein and carbohydrate is 4, multiply 4 by 30 to get 120 grams of fat per day.

So, from the historical use of the ketogenic diet, it was discovered that ketone levels could be optimized by keeping carbs and protein low. The effectiveness of this nutritional treatment for epilepsy has resulted in researchers and clinicians trying a ketogenic diet to treat other medical conditions in people who are not responding well to traditional drug therapies.

Diabetes Mellitus (Type 2 Diabetes)

MOMENT OF CLARITY Type 2 diabetes is a state of profound carbohydrate intolerance, and carbohydrate restriction reduces the demand on the pancreas to secrete excessive insulin in the face of insulin resistance while improving glycemic control and facilitating weight loss.

– Dr. Keith Runyan

Fears about using a low-carb, high-fat diet to treat diabetes don't make any sense at all when you consider that for thousands and thousands of years, the human diet didn't include much sugar or starch. In fact, in the late 1800s and early 1900s, a low-carb, high-fat diet was actually the primary treatment for diabetes! Insulin was discovered in 1921, but before that, a diet of 70 percent fat, 22 percent protein, and 8 percent carbohydrate was advocated by people like Frederick M. Allen and Eliot P. Joslin—top luminaries in the world of medicine—to treat diabetes.

MOMENT OF CLARITY I tell my patients that we can learn some important things from evolutionary biology and empirical science. What did our evolutionary ancestors eat? We can't be sure, but we do know it wasn't Twinkies, soda, and pizza! If people eat in a certain way—say the Standard American Diet—and they keep getting sick and fat, that should tell us something about the dangers of consuming processed food. We can argue to the ends of the earth about exactly *why* this type of diet is harmful, but the argument about whether or not it is dangerous is clearly over.

– Dr. Bill Wilson

The modern research on low-carb, high-fat diets for the treatment of type 2 diabetes (also known as *adult-onset diabetes*) includes several randomized, controlled trials that allowed for carbohydrate intake from 20 to 100 grams per day. Overall, the studies found that reducing carbohydrate in the diet results in a greater reduction of blood glucose and less need for diabetes medications. In many instances, the need for diabetes medication was eliminated and blood sugar control was even better than before! A randomized, controlled trial comparing the low-carb, high-fat, ketogenic diet to the low-glycemic, low-calorie diet over a six-month period found that those on the ketogenic diet needed less diabetes medication.

 **MOMENT OF CLARITY** Many patients with type 2 diabetes have noticed a total reversal of their disease off of all medications.

— Dr. Ron Rosedale

The low-carb, high-fat diet as a treatment for diabetes really combines two different approaches: 1) eliminating foods that raise blood sugar levels, and 2) losing weight. Sometimes the food and beverage effect is so great that when carbohydrates are eliminated, there is no longer any need for medication. In these cases, the diabetes was caused by diet. (Of course, in the case of type 1 diabetes, in which the body doesn't produce insulin at all, some medication will still be needed, but even then, a ketogenic diet can reduce how much is required.) If the diabetes is exacerbated by or a result of excessive weight, then it makes sense to treat the obesity as well. Thankfully, research strongly supports the use of a ketogenic diet for diabetes as well as weight loss, which leads us to the next area for which there is strong evidence supporting the ketogenic approach.

Weight Loss

MOMENT OF CLARITY A ketogenic diet may provide weight loss benefits over and above those achieved with carbohydrate restriction alone. It provides all the benefits of a low-carb diet but to a somewhat greater degree, since ketosis increases satiety and provides mental clarity, focus, prolonged concentration, and increased energy.

— Dr. William Davis

The low-carb, high-fat diet is perhaps best known for helping overweight people lose weight. In fact, since the late 1800s, doctors having been using this approach to help people shed pounds, and up until the 1970s it was common knowledge that if you wanted to make the numbers on the scale go down, you just cut back on bread, pasta, and rice. The great benefit of following a ketogenic diet for weight loss is that it greatly reduces and many times eliminates the hunger that accompanies most other diets, which is a big reason why so many people fail on most diets.

The low-carb approach to weight loss was used in the 1990s by a small group of doctors, as outlined in bestselling diet books such as *Dr. Atkins' Diet Revolution* by Dr. Robert Atkins and *Protein Power* by Dr. Michael

Eades and Dr. Mary Dan Eades. Many of these books sold millions of copies, but researchers didn't really examine this approach seriously until about 2004. That's when several randomized, controlled clinical trials were published showing the diet's beneficial effects on weight and metabolism in general, and over the past decade, multiple randomized, controlled trials have shown similar results.

Jacqueline Eberstein, a registered nurse who worked with the late, great Dr. Robert C. Atkins for three decades, said Dr. Atkins never measured blood ketones because it was too expensive. Eberstein noted that the best tool Dr. Atkins and his medical team had for determining if a patient was in ketosis was urine ketone testing strips, which she said were "used for every patient on every visit." The initial baseline reading almost always came back negative, so they were able to track when ketone production began. The Atkins Center later added a large, cumbersome machine that could analyze the breath for ketones. Routine calibration was needed to keep it operating. These days, the technology is a lot more sophisticated and user-friendly than it was in the 1970s and 1980s, and better ketone monitoring can help you determine if you are burning sugar or fat.

Getting into ketosis may not immediately kick-start weight loss. But the presence of ketones is a clear indication that your body is primed to burn fat for fuel, and that means you'll lose weight.

Cardiovascular Disease, Metabolic Syndrome, and Contributing Factors

MOMENT OF CLARITY For over two decades I have been using a low-carb, high-fat diet to treat very sick diabetic and cardiovascular patients. I have noticed a vast improvement in diabetes, cardiovascular disease, and obesity in nearly all of my patients on the diet.

– Dr. Ron Rosedale

Most of us have been taught that a low-fat diet is the healthiest, most nutritious diet, especially for cardiovascular health. At the same time, we've been told that a high-fat diet is completely unhealthy because it raises cholesterol, which in turn "clogs your arteries" and leads to heart disease (an erroneous idea that we debunked in *Cholesterol Clarity*). In the 1950s and 60s, virtually every major health organization came out against high-fat diets even though there was no direct evidence that they were harmful to anyone's health. They simply believed the hypothesis, promoted by Ancel Keys, that saturated fat raises cholesterol, which in turn increases your risk for heart disease. That concept was never actually tested by researchers.

This teaching was based entirely on a prediction of what *might* happen, not on any direct research on the effects of a high-fat diet. Today, all of the studies directly examining the low-carb, high-fat diet have shown these fatalistic predictions to be wrong—dead wrong! The ketogenic diet does not worsen the state of metabolism; instead, it improves it!

MOMENT OF CLARITY The most beneficial aspect of a strongly ketogenic environment and metabolism is that they protect us from nearly all the modern diseases plaguing us today, including heart disease and obesity.

– John Kiefer

The understanding of the causes of heart disease has changed, too, over the last ten years—so it can be confusing to doctors and the public alike. The umbrella term *metabolic syndrome* now encompasses all of the various contributors to heart disease: increased abdominal circumference, high blood pressure, elevated blood sugar, high blood triglycerides, and low HDL cholesterol (the "good" cholesterol). It turns out that the low-carb, high-fat, ketogenic diet improves all of these telltale signs of metabolic syndrome.

In fact, the scientific evidence shows that the ketogenic diet reduces belly fat, lowers blood pressure and blood sugar levels, reduces triglycerides, increases good cholesterol (HDL), and so much more. Researchers Dr. Richard Feinman and Dr. Jeff Volek published a study in the November 16, 2005, issue of the journal *Nutrition & Metabolism* that concluded all of the markers of metabolic syndrome are the same ones that are improved by carbohydrate restriction. This is not a coincidence.

DOCTOR'S NOTE FROM DR. ERIC WESTMAN: Good cholesterol (HDL) rises in most people who are following a low-carb, high-fat diet, which is one of the reasons why the diet doesn't increase the risk of heart disease. The best way to raise the HDL cholesterol is by eating eggs and saturated fat (seriously!).

Polycystic Ovary Syndrome (PCOS)

PCOS is a common hormonal disorder that affects women of reproductive age and is a major cause of infertility. It is usually associated with an irregular or absent menstrual cycle, excessive body hair, obesity, and type 2 diabetes. PCOS often occurs alongside insulin resistance, and because the two are so closely related, it stands to reason that PCOS is helped immensely by a ketogenic diet.

A clinical study on PCOS and the ketogenic diet was conducted by Dr. Eric Westman and others and published in the medical journal *Nutrition & Metabolism* in 2005. Five women with PCOS were put on a low-carb, high-fat, ketogenic diet for a period of six months, and these women had an average weight loss of 12 percent as well as improvements in their hormonal measurements. In fact, two of the five women became pregnant during the study despite previously experiencing infertility problems.

Irritable Bowel Syndrome (IBS)

IBS is a common disorder in the United States, affecting 10 to 15 percent of the adult population. People with IBS tend to experience stomach discomfort, pain, and bloating. This condition is divided into "diarrhea-predominant" and "constipation-predominant" types depending upon which symptom is experienced more often. It's a miserable condition, and some people suffering from it feel hopeless about making any progress through diet changes.

In fact, the idea of a low-carb, high-fat diet for someone with IBS may not be very appealing at first glance. After all, eating more fat can lead to even more diarrhea at first. But soon after, the symptoms all start to clear up and you feel normal again. This improvement is not an uncommon experience based on the many anecdotal experiences shared across the Internet. But additionally, several clinical trials have shown that a diet low in sugar can improve IBS.

A study published in the June 2009 issue of *Clinical Gastroenterology and Hepatology* looked at thirteen patients who used a low-carb, high-fat, ketogenic diet for diarrhea-predominant IBS over a four-week period and saw an improvement in stool frequency, stool consistency, abdominal pain, and quality of life. The ketogenic diet is giving people suffering with this uncomfortable condition hope.

GERD and Heartburn

Gastroesophageal reflux disease (GERD), generally experienced as heartburn, is a common disorder that affects 20 to 30 percent of Americans at least once a week. The medical costs associated with treating GERD are estimated to be in excess of $9 billion annually. We hear all the time that when people stop eating carbohydrates, the burning sensation from GERD improves or completely goes away.

Whole grains and sugars, in particular, are the main culprits in GERD, which is why you will find relief so quickly when eating keto. Some people with autoimmune conditions also need to cut out nightshades like tomatoes and peppers. Far too many people are reaching for over-the-counter heartburn relief from products, like Rolaids or Tums, and even prescription medications like Nexium and other such drugs that rake in billions of dollars in revenue annually. Can a simple diet change really help?

You bet it can! A study published in the July 27, 2006, issue of the journal *Digestive Diseases and Sciences*, featuring contributions from Dr. Eric Westman, measured stomach acidity after eight study participants with GERD were placed on a low-carb, high-fat, ketogenic diet. Each of them had a small tube threaded into the nose and down to their stomach for a period of twenty-four hours to measure stomach and esophageal acidity before and after changing the diet. Over just three to six days on the ketogenic diet, all eight individuals showed improvement in the severity of their heartburn and a reduction in the acidity at the lower esophagus—which is usually the cause of heartburn. They found relief simply by making changes to their diet.

Nonalcoholic Fatty Liver Disease (NAFLD)

Nonalcoholic fatty liver disease (NAFLD) is commonly found in individuals with obesity. It can become so severe that it leads to liver failure, and without a liver transplant, liver failure is a fatal condition. When fat in the liver accounts for more than 10 percent of the liver's weight, insulin can no longer properly control your blood sugar—a condition known as *insulin resistance*—which can lead to some serious damage to your health.

Interestingly, the fat in the liver doesn't come from dietary fat but rather from carbohydrates. The liver turns dietary carbohydrates into a blood fat called *triglycerides*, and it's this fat that is stored in the liver. This is why corn, a high-carbohydrate grain that many think is a vegetable, is used to fatten up pigs, and why it's also used to fatten the livers of ducks and geese for foie gras (which literally means "fatty liver"!).

In a study published in the September 2006 issue of *Digestive Diseases and Sciences,* ten healthy volunteers experienced fat loss in the liver after following a low-carb diet for ten days. But another clinical study (again by Dr. Eric Westman and other researchers) published in the February 2007 issue of the same journal looked at five patients with NAFLD who were all put on a low-carb, high-fat, ketogenic diet for a period of six months. The four people who followed the instructions given by the researchers showed significant weight loss and improvement or even resolved the fatty liver according to their follow-up biopsy. Even the severe scarring (known as *fibrosis*) that can accompany NAFLD improved on a ketogenic diet.

It seems that increasing saturated fat intake and reducing carbohydrate consumption can bring about phenomenal reductions in liver fat. A May 2011 study published in the *American Journal of Clinical Nutrition* placed eighteen study participants with NAFLD on either a very low-carb diet or very low-calorie diet, and the low-carb diet reduced triglycerides in the liver (called *hepatic fat*) because of the fat-burning effect brought on by ketosis. This is very strong support for the positive health effects that happen as a result of being in a ketogenic state.

We've shared some pretty compelling information in this chapter about how to distinguish good science from bad, and we have detailed the strong scientific evidence in support of low-carb, high-fat, ketogenic diets. Coming up in the next chapter, we'll take a look at the health conditions that there's good evidence may be helped by ketosis; we anticipate that this evidence will become even stronger as research continues in the coming years.

Key Keto Clarity Concepts

→ **Learning to distinguish between strong and weak research is critical.**

→ **All studies are not made the same—most research is observational, not controlled.**

→ **Determining if a study applies to you is the first question you must always ask.**

→ **Animal studies should only be used to form hypotheses for human studies.**

→ **N=1 case studies can be helpful in revealing unusual responses to a given stimuli.**

→ **Correlation should never be assumed to equal causation without further research.**

→ **Experimental research in a controlled clinical trial provides the most reliable study data.**

→ **Adding randomization to a controlled clinical trial makes it the gold standard in human research.**

→ **In the end, every person is different, and no study can tell you exactly what will work for you.**

→ **Controlling epileptic seizures with the Ketogenic Diet has been around since the early 1900s.**

→ **Type 2 diabetes responds well to ketogenic diets because of its insulin-lowering effect.**

→ **Most people associate low-carb, high-fat diets with weight loss, and they are quite effective for making that happen.**

→ **Studies have shown that heart disease and metabolic syndrome greatly improve on a ketogenic diet.**

→ **Women with PCOS see improvement when they start eating a low-carb, high-fat diet.**

→ **IBS can be virtually eliminated through the strategic use of a ketogenic diet.**

→ **GERD and heartburn are no longer an issue when you remove the carbohydrate-based foods that increase stomach acid.**

→ **Nonalcoholic fatty liver disease is caused by the consumption of carbs, not fat.**

Chapter 17
Good Evidence of Benefits from Ketosis

MOMENT OF CLARITY I haven't encountered a lot of stigma about ketogenic diets. I think scientists are much more open-minded than physicians. It was actually very easy for me to find mentors who were interested in low-carb, high-fat diets.

— Bryan Barksdale

We've already seen the wealth of scientific evidence that strongly supports low-carb, high-fat, ketogenic diets. But the evidence doesn't stop there; there is also very good, though less definitive, scientific research underway on many other common diseases. The effects of ketosis on the conditions covered in this chapter haven't been examined in long-term studies—all the studies outlined lasted one year or less—but they seem to respond quite well to a ketogenic nutritional therapy and show great promise for future controlled clinical trials, if and when the funding for such research can be obtained.

Alzheimer's Disease (AD), Parkinson's Disease, and Dementia

MOMENT OF CLARITY Increased ketone availability has been demonstrated to improve cognitive function in patients with mild Alzheimer's disease. The science is so compelling that the FDA has actually approved a medical food that increases ketone availability as an Alzheimer's treatment. In one study, a ketogenic diet provided more improvement in functionality for Parkinson's patients than pharmaceutical intervention.

— Dr. David Perlmutter

The human brain needs fat and cholesterol for proper functioning, and it can be fueled by either glucose or ketones. After keto-adaptation from consuming a low-carb, high-fat diet, the brain gets most of its energy from ketone bodies. This becomes an important factor when we begin looking at the diseases of the brain such as Alzheimer's, Parkinson's, and dementia. We know that being in a state of ketosis lowers chronic inflammation levels, provides a fantastic fuel source for the brain, and significantly reduces the production of insulin—which have all been implicated in the development of these neurological diseases.

Alzheimer's disease (AD), commonly referred to in research circles now as "type 3 diabetes," is a progressive dementia leading to memory loss and loss of function due to a lack of insulin sensitivity in the brain, and unfortunately there is no good treatment for it. Just as insulin resistance in the liver leads to the development of type 2 diabetes, so too does insulin resistance in the brain lead to the development of Alzheimer's disease. When the brain cannot receive the primary fuel source (glucose), signs of mental decline begin.

MOMENT OF CLARITY The human brain is operating at its most efficient in an effective state of ketosis, which is increasingly being examined by researchers as a viable means of addressing—and possibly preventing or reversing—premature cognitive decline, dementia, and even Alzheimer's. It is well understood by neurologists that dietary fat in the absence of sugar and starch is enormously stabilizing to the human brain and nervous system, potentially even enhancing cerebral blood flow by a whopping 39 percent!

— Nora Gedgaudas

There is a strong theoretical basis for putting a patient with Alzheimer's on a low-carb, high-fat diet as a means for preventing the further progression of AD because the inflammation caused by gluten, carbohydrates, and high blood glucose levels has been associated with the development of this disease. Additionally, ketone bodies are readily taken in by the brain as an alternative fuel source when glucose is not present. In fact, the idea of delivering ketones instead of glucose to the brain to treat dementia-related diseases has led to the development of a new medical food called Axona. A randomized, controlled clinical trial showed that over a period of ninety days, increased blood ketone levels led to a slight improvement in brain function in patients with dementia, which, without treatment, almost invariably leads to Alzheimer's or Parkinson's.

Dr. Mary Newport knows a thing or two about Alzheimer's disease. Her husband, Steve, was diagnosed with early-onset Alzheimer's at the age of fifty-one, and she quickly became frustrated by the lack of meaningful therapies to help slow its progression, much less reverse the damage that had already been done. But when Dr. Newport started feeding Steve large amounts of coconut and MCT oil while cutting out carbohydrate-based foods like bread, rice, and pasta, he started to "climb out of the Alzheimer's abyss." She shares the details of Steve's miraculous turnaround in her book *Alzheimer's Disease: What If There Was a Cure?*

Dr. Newport's experience isn't isolated. She has heard from hundreds of caregivers whose Alzheimer's, Parkinson's, and dementia patients have found varying levels of improvements following the same protocol that she did. Some of these patients have been stable for upwards of four years because they found success in ketosis. Thanks to a grant from a private foundation, a clinical study is already underway at the University of South Florida to examine the impact of coconut oil–induced ketosis on Alzheimer's. Results from this study could help further the efficacy of the ketogenic diet in the treatment of Alzheimer's disease.

MOMENT OF CLARITY I find the evidence that the brain prefers ketone bodies for fuel quite compelling. In addition, the fact that ketones are involved in lowering oxidative stress throughout the body begins to explain some of the remarkable improvements we see in health when folks switch to a ketogenic diet.

— Dr. Jay Wortman

The mechanisms of Parkinson's disease are extremely similar to those of Alzheimer's, which is why diet is also theorized to be an effective treatment for Parkinson's. In an uncontrolled clinical study published in the February 22, 2005, issue of the journal *Neurology,* five patients who followed a very low-carb (2 percent of calories), very high-fat (90 percent of calories) diet for twenty-eight days showed improvement as measured by the Unified Parkinson's Disease Rating Scale. Their balance improved, their tremors and shaking ceased, and their overall mood was much happier. The brain loves ketones, especially when it has become impaired by Alzheimer's or Parkinson's.

Schizophrenia, Bipolar Disorder, and Other Mental Illnesses

MOMENT OF CLARITY As a neuroscientist, I find the most interesting beneficial aspects of being in ketosis to be the cognitive benefits. The research supports a general enhancement in things like short-term memory, verbal memory, and mood. Ketones have neuroprotective properties, which mean they protect your brain cells. They provide a clean-burning energy source, increase antioxidants, and decrease inflammation.

— Bryan Barksdale

Interestingly, it is being theorized that the root cause of many mental illnesses isn't in the brain: it's in the gut. Poor gut health can be brought on by a high-carb, grain-based diet; an overuse of antibiotics; common over-the-counter drugs; and even the state of your mother's gut health when you were born. A low-carb, high-fat, ketogenic diet gives you a fighting chance to improve your mental health by stabilizing your brain chemistry through the changes made in the gut.

The possible link between gluten, a substance found in grains, and schizophrenia was first suspected when researchers noticed that there were fewer hospitalizations for this condition during World War II, when grains were rationed. In 1965, an uncontrolled clinical study showed that a ketogenic diet could decrease schizophrenia symptoms. And a more recent case study (whose researchers included my coauthor, Dr. Eric Westman) published in the February 26, 2009, issue of the journal *Nutrition & Metabolism* found that schizophrenic symptoms resolved after a ketogenic diet was begun for weight loss. There are also two other case studies showing that bipolar disorder similarly improves on a ketogenic diet.

MOMENT OF CLARITY Because of my interest in neuroscience, I am most impressed with the ability of a ketogenic diet to improve brain function. This is not just true for people with obvious brain disorders—it also applies to those who are quite healthy. In this complex world full of daily stresses, getting a leg up when it comes to brain function can improve your life in a multitude of ways. On the other hand, if you want to guarantee declining brain function, I suggest sticking with the Standard American Diet!

— Dr. Bill Wilson

When Hollywood actress Catherine Zeta-Jones checked herself into a clinic for help in dealing with her bipolar II disorder in 2011 and again in 2013, it shone a spotlight on this very serious mental condition. Depression and manic episodes are the hallmarks of bipolar disorder (bipolar I disorder tends to involve more obvious fits of full-blown mania, while bipolar II disorder can be milder in nature but still life-altering). Its primary treatment tends to be the exact same anticonvulsant medications that are also used to treat epilepsy. And as you learned in the previous chapter, a ketogenic diet was traditionally used to treat epileptic seizures. Could a low-carb, moderate-protein, high-fat nutritional approach help bipolar disorder as well?

The answer to that question is not as definitive as we might hope. Fueling the brain with ketone bodies instead of glucose should, theoretically, reduce the activity of neurotransmitters, helping to stabilize mood. But in an Israeli case study published in the February 2002 issue of the medical journal *Bipolar Disorders*, a bipolar patient who was nonresponsive to medication was put on a ketogenic diet for one month. Doctors even added MCT oil to the diet to help boost ketone production. But the patient saw no improvement.

MOMENT OF CLARITY The latest science is showing how ketone bodies provide better focus, less anxiety, and improved overall mental health.

– Maria Emmerich

That doesn't really prove that the ketogenic diet does not help bipolar disorder, and there are plenty of anecdotal success stories being reported all across the Internet. More significantly, in a case study published in the October 2013 issue of the journal *Neurocase,* two women with bipolar II disorder who maintained a state of ketosis for more than two years both saw better mood stabilization than they had achieved with medication, and they tolerated the diet as a bona fide lifestyle change remarkably well, with no significant adverse effects.

Given the conflicting results of past case studies, a randomized, controlled trial examining the effects of a ketogenic diet on schizophrenia, bipolar disorder, and other mental illnesses is sorely needed.

Narcolepsy and Other Sleep Disorders

MOMENT OF CLARITY Concerns about the human brain's need for carbohydrates are entirely unfounded. If you cease consumption of all carbohydrates in your diet, then you will undoubtedly survive, even thrive, though you may have to endure several weeks of metabolic conversion to fatty acid oxidation, which can cause temporary fatigue.

– Dr. William Davis

Narcolepsy is a serious neurological disorder that leads to excessive daytime sleepiness and "sleep attacks." Medications may help with some of the sleep issues related to narcolepsy, but they can become less and less effective over time.

In a clinical study published in the June 2004 issue of the medical journal *Neurology,* nine patients with narcolepsy were placed on a low-carb, high-fat, ketogenic diet for a period of eight weeks. One patient was unable to complete the study, but the rest experienced less sleepiness during the day, had fewer sleep attacks, and saw other improvements in the severity of their narcolepsy. The researchers concluded that all these improvements were likely due to lower glucose levels while the study participants were in ketosis.

Most people in ketosis report that they sleep better and do not feel tired after meals. For those with narcolepsy, this is a much-needed respite from the living hell of their condition. Melissa, one of my blog readers, suffered from narcolepsy before she found the benefits of ketosis. She dealt with narcolepsy from an early age and as a child slept virtually all the time. Melissa employed various distraction techniques to keep herself awake, but most of them didn't help.

It wasn't until she reached the age of forty that the doctors even diagnosed Melissa with narcolepsy. After trying all the best drugs for treating it, she heard about the ketogenic diet and decided to give up all whole grains, sugar, and starchy carbohydrates while eating a lot more saturated fat in her diet, with the goal of producing more ketone bodies. The results were astonishing. Melissa described it this way: "I was alive again." Today she continues to eat this way, which helps her stay awake when she needs to during the day. Of course, Melissa's story is only anecdotal, but it underscores the need for more research into how a low-carb, high-fat, ketogenic diet can help those dealing with sleep disorders.

Exercise Performance

The US Defense Advanced Research Projects Agency (DARPA) has been investigating ketosis as a secret weapon for boosting soldiers' mental and physical performance under battlefield conditions. Why? Because as a soldier's blood glucose drops, he or she becomes confused, sometimes resulting in friendly fire. So they tested a highly ketogenic fuel source on rats and found that it boosted physical and mental performance—the rats became much healthier, lost body fat, had lower levels of triglycerides (fatty acids) in their blood, and had lower blood sugar levels, with zero harmful side effects. That same fuel is now under development for soldiers.

– Ben Greenfield

Obviously exercise isn't a disease, but it's included here because some exciting things are happening for athletes who eat a low-carb, moderate-protein, high-fat, ketogenic diet. Dr. Stephen Phinney, the ketogenic diet researcher we have referenced often throughout this book, was one of the first to study the impact of ketosis on exercise performance way back in 1983. His landmark study, published in the August 1983 issue of the journal *Metabolism,* looked at how a ketogenic diet affected the endurance training of five elite cyclists.

After four weeks of eating ketogenic, with less than 20 daily grams of carbohydrate in their diet, the athletes did not see their performance compromised by being in ketosis because they had shifted from sugar-burners to fat-burners. Although their glycogen stores at the end of the four weeks were considerably lower than at baseline, not only did they not crash from hypoglycemia, they actually improved their overall output. This is when Dr. Phinney coined the phrase *nutritional ketosis* to describe the state in which someone is keto-adapted. For these elite athletes, their fuel source had shifted fully from carbohydrates (glucose) to fat and ketones.

A strategic use of ketosis has been the only way I've been able to stay lean without a lot of effort, and this holds true for my clients as well. For athletes, it's the only method available for losing extreme amounts of body fat while maintaining, or even increasing, performance.

– John Kiefer

The 1983 study was almost ended prematurely. The cyclists' response to the diet in the first couple of weeks resulted in a decline in performance, and the researchers thought the nutritional changes were proving to be more detrimental than helpful. But Dr. Phinney fortuitously decided to press on for at least one more week. That's when keto-adaptation happened, and the improvements in key data points such as oxygen utilization (VO2 max), respiratory quotient, amount of glycogen in the muscle, and more all began to manifest. Can you imagine how that study would have turned out if they stopped after only two weeks?

Dr. Phinney notes the importance of this period of adaptation in an August 27, 2004, paper entitled "Ketogenic Diet and Physical Performance" published in the journal *Nutrition & Metabolism*. You can Google the title of this paper to read it for yourself; it complements everything we've been sharing with you in this book. Additionally, Dr. Phinney, along with his research partner Dr. Jeff Volek, cowrote a book in 2012 that chronicles a lot more about this information and what they've learned using a low-carb, high-fat approach with athletes called *The Art and Science of Low Carbohydrate Performance*.

Although the research on athletics and ketogenic diets is still emerging (another study featuring elite gymnasts was published in the *Journal of the International Society of Sports Nutrition* in 2012), many elite athletes are willingly and openly trying it for themselves with great success. One such endurance athlete is Timothy Allen Olson, an Oregon-based long-distance runner who ran in the 2012 Western States 100-Mile Endurance Run to show the world what a ketogenic runner could do. Did he win the race? You bet he did, and his time was twenty-one minutes faster than the previous course record!

Ben Greenfield is a triathlete who followed a strict ketogenic diet for sixteen weeks during his training for the Ironman Canada and Ironman Hawaii races in 2013. He consumed far fewer carbohydrates (less than 200 grams) than the typical Ironman triathlete would—they often consume 600 to 800 grams of carbohydrate on a training day—and supplemented with coconut oil and MCT oil to help his body shift to using fat for fuel. Here are the major benefits Greenfield found from being in ketosis:

▸ **Increased metabolic efficiency and enhanced fat burning, which lets him "get stronger as the day gets longer."** This is especially useful for endurance athletes, such as those participating in Ironman competitions and long-distance marathons.

- ▶ **Sparing of glycogen stores, which also leads to increased endurance.** He uses less stored muscle and liver carbohydrates because he's able to burn fat more efficiently.

- ▶ **Lowered inflammation, which enables his body to recover faster after a workout** due to the decreased formation of free radicals and reactive oxygen species (molecules that can damage cells) from a high amount of sugar intake.

- ▶ **More stable energy levels** because his blood sugar levels don't fluctuate as they would on a carbohydrate-based diet.

MOMENT OF CLARITY Ketone bodies have become known as a superfuel because they provide more energy per unit of oxygen than other metabolic fuels. This improved metabolic efficiency was first shown in sperm cells, in which exposure to ketone bodies decreased oxygen consumption while increasing mobility. This was later confirmed in a study that showed ketone bodies increased the heart's hydraulic work capacity while simultaneously decreasing oxygen consumption. This may explain why there is a flourishing community of keto-adapted athletes that is rapidly increasing.

— Dr. Bill Lagakos

And, finally, there's Olaf Sorenson, a forty-year old long-distance runner who is putting the idea of getting into ketosis for athletic performance to the test himself. At the time of writing, he is documenting his low-carb, high-fat experience in a movie tentatively called *Two Forty, Forty One*, a reference to his stated goal to run the marathon in less than two hours, forty minutes, and forty-one seconds.

Why is this time so significant? In 1952, Sorenson's grandfather qualified for the Olympics with that time. Now he's attempting to match it while in ketosis from consuming a lots of healthy saturated fats and ditching carbohydrates. Sorenson's progress and state of health during his marathon training are being tracked by the College of Health and Human Performance at the University of Florida.

We've got some really good evidence in support of ketogenic diets that certainly could use more clinical, human research on a wider scale in the coming years. There are many more conditions that may improve on a low-carb, high-fat diet, but the evidence is less clear—we only have animal models or anecdotal stories in support of the theory. The therapeutic use of ketones for these conditions is an emerging area of research that should be much more closely examined in the coming years, and we'll take a look at these health conditions in the next chapter.

Key Keto Clarity Concepts

→ **We have good evidence, from studies less than a year in duration, that many conditions are improved by a ketogenic diet.**

→ **Alzheimer's, Parkinson's, and dementia are all shown to get better on a low-carb, moderate-protein, high-fat diet.**

→ **Schizophrenia, bipolar disorder, and other mental illnesses get better with ketones.**

→ **Narcolepsy and other sleep disorders show modest improvement in people in ketosis.**

→ **Better exercise performance is emerging as a huge benefit of eating a low-carb, high-fat diet.**

Chapter 18

Emerging Areas of Research on the Use of Ketones

MOMENT OF CLARITY Ketones are excellent fuel for our mitochondria, and for most of human history we were in ketosis for much of the year. Certainly every winter we were in ketosis. Our diet was also much lower in carbs. Therefore we were consuming either more protein or more fat in the diet, or both. We did not have high-glycemic food in our diet. We were eating low-glycemic green, leafy vegetables, tubers (most often raw), only occasional fruit, and more meat, and fat in the meat.

– Dr. Terry Wahls

In the last two chapters, we've looked at conditions for which there is strong evidence and good evidence that a ketogenic lifestyle may be beneficial. But just because there isn't any research to speak of on other conditions in relation to ketosis doesn't mean ketones won't benefit these health problems as well. There is hope for people dealing with many other health issues that a natural, nutritional solution may exist for their conditions.

We want to explore with you some emerging areas of research and how a low-carb, high-fat diet could be used to improve health. No solid claims have been made for treating any of the health conditions in this chapter with a ketogenic diet, but we wouldn't be surprised to see a major paradigm shift in the way these diseases are treated in the near future. Are you ready to see what's coming down the pipeline?

Cancer

MOMENT OF CLARITY A ketogenic approach is the single most effective dietary treatment for any and all forms of cancer and other immune-related illnesses. By robbing cancer of its needed fuel source (sugar) and relying on ketones and free fatty acids instead (which cancer cannot make use of), you can create an internal and epigenetic environment conducive to keeping cancers under control or even preventing them from being able to get a foothold in the first place. With a growing level of environmental toxicity and skyrocketing cancer rates, this particular way of eating could just be the best preventative foundational approach of all.

– Nora Gedgaudas

Cancer cells like to use glucose as a fuel; in fact, doctors inject tagged glucose into cancer patients to find the exact location of tumors. Shouldn't it tell you something that doctors look for cancerous tumors by using sugar to make PET scans light up like a Christmas tree? The theory behind using the ketogenic diet to treat and prevent cancer is that cutting out glucose starves the cancer cells, and it has been shown to produce benefits in animal studies. Unfortunately there have not been any human clinical studies yet.

However, a story published in *Time* magazine on September 17, 2007, entitled "Can a High-Fat Diet Beat Cancer?" examined the idea. Featuring researchers Dr. Melanie Schmidt and Dr. Ulrike Kammerer, both from the University of Wurzburg in Germany, the article discusses the work of a German Nobel Prize–winning scientist named Otto Warburg, who in 1924 posited that "the prime cause of cancer is the replacement of the respiration of oxygen in normal body cells by a fermentation of sugar."

MOMENT OF CLARITY I've worked with a woman who had stage IV cancer. She was told to go see her family and friends right away, because she had less than three months to live. That was six months ago, and now she has a clean bill of health and is planning a two-month vacation in Europe. The power of ketogenic diets is simply astonishing. More accurately, it's astonishing to see how poisonous carbohydrates can be.

– John Kiefer

Warburg's hypothesis goes like this: remove the sugar (and the carbohydrates that turn to sugar in the body), replace it with more fat, and the cancer cells will die. It was a brilliant idea that was lauded by the scientists and health advocates of his day, but somehow today it has been largely forgotten and is often ridiculed as too extreme.

Not by Dr. Schmidt and Dr. Kammerer, though.

They've taken Warburg's lifetime of work and run with it. By removing sugar from the diet of cancer patients, can they stop the cancer from spreading? The results of their preliminary research treating five patients over a three-month period with a ketogenic diet were promising: all of them survived, their cancer either stabilized or improved, and the tumors either grew slower, stopped, or even shrank. With these results, Dr. Schmidt and Dr. Kammerer expanded their research, which we will be hearing more about in the coming years.

In a second study, published in the July 27, 2011, issue of *Nutrition & Metabolism,* they treated sixteen patients with advanced cancer with a ketogenic diet. Eight had to drop out of the study for a variety of reasons, but of the remaining eight, six saw improvements in their quality of life and a slowdown in the progression of their tumors. We need more curious researchers who are willing to use a high-fat, low-carb ketogenic diet with cancer patients who have run out of other treatment options. Thankfully there are a few.

Neurologist Dr. Thomas Seyfried from Boston College has been doing some extraordinary work looking into a calorie-restricted ketogenic diet as a treatment for brain tumors. Although his research has only been in mice, he sees this as a "non-toxic approach to the management of cancer" for humans. His 2012 book, *Cancer as a Metabolic Disease,* should be required reading for anyone interested in the impact of nutrition on cancer. Dr. Seyfried's work is paving the way for human research on a much wider scale.

MOMENT OF CLARITY Dr. Eugene Fine's paper on treating advanced cancer patients received such a good reception because everybody intuitively understood its value and the study should have been done twenty years ago. Dr. Fine's hypothesis was that if we think of cancer in terms of genetics, we can think of cancer cells as having evolved through the life of the individual, an individual whose system, in a modern setting, would be unlikely to have any significant level of ketosis. It would be highly unlikely to provide any selective pressure for adaptation to the use of ketone bodies as a fuel source. Incidentally, the patients who became stable or showed partial remission in his experiment had the highest level of ketone bodies.

– Dr. Richard Feinman

Another researcher looking at using a low-carb, high-fat, ketogenic diet with cancer patients is Dr. Eugene Fine from the Albert Einstein College of Medicine in New York. His RECHARGE (Reduced Carbohydrates Against Resistant Growth Tumors) trial examined the safety and feasibility of a twenty-eight-day ketogenic diet in ten cancer patients who had exhausted every other treatment option. Changes were monitored with PET scans at the beginning and end of the trial. The results of this small study were published in the October 2012 issue of the journal *Nutrition*. Four of the patients continued to have progressive disease on the diet, five stabilized and had no further progression, and one had a partial remission. Those who had the best metabolic results—their insulin went down the most and ketones went up the most—saw the best improvements in their disease progression.

Other researchers looking at this issue include Dr. Colin Champ, from the University of Pittsburgh Cancer Institute in Pittsburgh, and Dr. Dominic D'Agostino from the University of South Florida. I wouldn't be surprised to see even more researchers in the future look further into the ketogenic diet for treating what is arguably one of the most horrific diseases of our time. Wouldn't it be amazing if the cure for cancer was right under our noses the entire time—a low-carb, high-fat nutritional approach?

Autism

MOMENT OF CLARITY   Some children with autism seem to respond to a low-carb, high-fat and/or high–MCT oil diet.

– Dr. Mary Newport

A pilot study published in the February 2003 issue of the *Journal of Child Neurology* examined thirty children between the ages of four and ten who exhibited autistic behavior. They were put on the ketogenic diet intermittently for six months, with four weeks on and two weeks off. While not all of the children did well tolerating the low-carb, high-fat diet (seven of the patients dropped out immediately and another five discontinued after one to two months), most of those who stuck with it saw improvements in the parameters set out by the Childhood Autism Rating Scale. This study wasn't spectacular by any means, but it did show some promise in using a ketogenic diet to treat autism.

Fibromyalgia, Chronic Pain, and Migraines

MOMENT OF CLARITY We have a grant pending to study a nutrient-dense, low-glycemic diet and a ketogenic diet for treating fibromyalgia.

– Dr. Terry Wahls

There are currently no published studies on treating fibromyalgia, chronic pain, or migraines with a low-carb, high-fat, ketogenic diet. While many practitioners and patients who use this nutritional approach have reported improvement with all of these conditions, these anecdotal stories need to be supported by quality clinical research.

There was one study published in the December 2013 issue of the *Journal of Musculoskeletal Pain* that examined the effects of a non-ketogenic low-carb diet on fibromyalgia symptoms, including pain, mood, and energy levels, in thirty-three middle-aged women. The results? Their symptom scores were lower on the Fibromyalgia Impact Questionnaire and they had increased energy and less pain. Whether a ketogenic diet would have similar or even better results remains to be seen.

Traumatic Brain Injury and Stroke

MOMENT OF CLARITY Our lab is studying the ketogenic diet for the treatment of multiple sclerosis. In my traumatic brain injury clinic and my therapeutic lifestyle clinic, I push for a low-glycemic, nutrient-dense diet for everyone, and we offer a ketogenic version of it for patients who want to try it.

– Dr. Terry Wahls

A review of the ketogenic diet for treating traumatic brain injury and stroke published in the September 2006 issue of the journal *Behavioural Pharmacology* noted the role beta-hydroxybutyrate (the ketone body in the blood) plays in protecting the brain by reducing inflammation and protecting neurons. There was also a May 2009 study published in the journal *Brain Injury* that put the neuroprotective properties of a ketogenic diet to the test on sixty rats with traumatic brain injury. Although it was just an animal study, the results were very positive for the effects of the ketones in the treatment of brain injury.

Researchers at the University of Copenhagen, Denmark, began recruiting study participants in November 2013 for a clinical trial into the effects of a ketogenic diet on acute stroke. The purpose of this controlled, randomized intervention is to investigate whether eating a low-carb, high-fat diet for one week has a positive effect on blood sugar, mortality, and function in patients hospitalized with acute stroke, compared to the effect of a typical diet. The hypothesis is that brain function will improve because of reduced glucose availability to brain cells.

Gum Disease and Tooth Decay

Because there are no grains or sugars in a ketogenic diet, gum disease and tooth decay virtually disappear. A story that aired on NPR on February 24, 2013, looked at the teeth of our early ancestors and found them to be very healthy despite the lack of toothbrushes, toothpaste, or dental floss. The story blames our consumption of sugar and carbohydrates for the cavities and gum disease we are plagued with today.

Personally, I noticed that years of tooth decay from crunching hard candy came to a complete halt once I embraced a low-carb, high-fat diet. Furthermore, the build-up of plaque and tartar is much less now than it was when I was consuming lots of processed grains and sugars. We definitely need more published research into this, since the health of our teeth and gums can play a negative role in other aspects of our health, including cardiovascular health—gum disease raises inflammation in the body, which in turn can increase the risk of a heart attack. (If you're interested in this, check out Episode 364 of *The Livin' La Vida Low-Carb Show* podcast, in which holistic dentist Kevin Boehm explains more about the connection between dental health and cardiovascular health.)

Acne

A review of the research looking at the "therapeutic potential of ketogenic diets" in treating acne by Italian researcher Antonio Paoli was published in the April 2012 issue of the journal *Skin Pharmacology and Physiology*. He outlined the physiological and biochemical reasons why a low-carb, high-fat diet might be beneficial for treating acne—the theory is that acne is one manifestation of insulin resistance—but no long-term studies have been done. (*The Dietary Cure for Acne,* by well-known Paleo author Loren Cordain, explores this idea in detail.) Paoli joined Dr. Jeff Volek and other researchers in a review of the uses of a ketogenic diet beyond weight loss published in the May 29, 2013, issue of the *European Journal of Clinical Nutrition* that calls for randomized clinical trials to examine this issue further.

Eyesight

While there is currently no published data about the effects of a ketogenic diet on eyesight, there is plenty of anecdotal evidence from people who began a low-carb, high-fat diet and noticed improvements in their vision. Because elevated blood sugar levels can lead to blurred vision, it may be that the normalization of blood sugar levels in ketosis brings about the improvements. My wife, Christine, who is blind in one eye and has had poor vision ever since she was given too much oxygen at birth, actually improved her eyesight for the first time in her life when she had it checked in October 2011 after getting serious about eating a low-carb, high-fat diet. Far too many people who get into ketosis report similar stories for the research community to continue to ignore this.

Amyotrophic Lateral Sclerosis (ALS; also known as Lou Gehrig's Disease)

In the search for a more natural treatment for amyotrophic lateral sclerosis (ALS), also known as Lou Gehrig's disease, researcher Dr. Carl E. Stafstrom published an argument for considering a ketogenic diet in the April 9, 2012, issue of the journal *Frontiers in Pharmacology*. A study published in the April 3, 2006, issue of the journal *BMC Neuroscience* examining the ketogenic diet for treating ALS looked at how increased ketone levels affected mice with the disease. This was the first study of its kind to show improvements in ALS brought about through diet changes. Hopefully it spawns more research in the coming years.

Multiple Sclerosis (MS) and Huntington's Disease (HD)

There have been several animal studies in recent years looking at the effect of ketogenic diets on multiple sclerosis and Huntington's disease, but no human studies have been done. A May 2, 2012, study published in the journal *PLOS ONE* found that in mice with MS, the ketogenic diet lowered brain inflammation and acted as a protective measure. And a study published in the July 6, 2011, issue of *Physiology & Behavior* showed that in mice, a ketogenic diet delayed the typical weight loss that occurs with HD. Whether these results would also be seen in humans is a question for future research to answer.

Pay close attention to the work of Dr. Terry Wahls, author of the 2014 book *The Wahl's Protocol: How I Beat Progressive MS Using Paleo Principles and Functional Medicine.* Dr. Wahls overcame secondary progressive multiple sclerosis by going into a mild state of nutritional ketosis, allowing her brain and body to function well on fat and ketones. She is seeking funding for more thorough research into the precise mechanism through which ketosis may help MS.

Aging

People are always looking for ways to slow down the aging process, and in yeast, worms, fruit flies, and mice, restricting the amount of calories in the diet can result in a longer lifespan. It appears that the lower the insulin level, the longer the lifespan, because of the decrease in oxidative stress, which reduces our ability to detoxify and repair cells. So, in theory, a diet that keeps the insulin level low—like the low-carb, high-fat, ketogenic diet—would lead to a longer lifespan.

(M)OMENT OF CLARITY I believe that what we are really doing with the ketogenic diet is slowing the rate of aging and, especially, increasing the rate of repair. Therefore all of the symptoms of aging, which we are calling the diseases of aging, can be very effectively treated if not totally reversed by this diet, and I believe it is currently the only way to do so.

— Dr. Ron Rosedale

In 2014, the Anti-Ageing & Aesthetic Medicine Conference in Melbourne, Australia, hosted by the AustralAsian Academy of Anti-Ageing Medicine, focused on the role that a ketogenic diet plays in obesity, metabolic syndrome, and aging. There is great worldwide interest in the impact of diet on the aging process, and human research could soon begin to look at this nutritional approach as an anti-aging therapy.

Kidney Disease

Neurologist and endocrinologist Dr. Charles Mobbs conducts research on lab mice using ketogenic diets at the Mount Sinai School of Medicine in New York. In an April 20, 2011, study published in the journal *PLOS ONE*, Dr. Mobbs noted that the low-carb, high-fat diet could possibly replace dialysis if the results he found in animals also appear in humans. Looking at mice with both type 1 and type 2 diabetes and early-stage kidney disease, researchers saw significant improvement in the kidney disease as well as blood sugar and insulin levels (an expected outcome) among those that were on the ketogenic diet. It's still very early in the research to extrapolate these findings to humans, but it certainly sets the stage for some potentially exciting developments.

Restless Legs Syndrome (RLS)

No research exists looking at a connection between restless legs syndrome and a ketogenic diet. But one of my forum members reported that shifting to a ketogenic lifestyle and weight lifting regimen cured her RLS completely, and other anecdotal reports confirm that this is something that needs to be investigated further.

Arthritis

It stands to reason that because being in a state of ketosis is anti-inflammatory, it would be beneficial for people suffering from arthritis. But to date we've seen no scientific proof that a ketogenic diet can help with this. Nevertheless, many people are convinced their arthritis improved once they started eating a low-carb, high-fat diet.

Alopecia and Hair Loss

Some people think that a ketogenic diet is the cause of hair loss—mostly because some people get too few calories on this diet, which can cause hair loss. But if you're getting enough calories, it's not an issue with a ketogenic diet. Even better, wellness expert Maria Emmerich says she has seen hundreds of clients who suffered from alopecia for years suddenly grow a full head of hair on a ketogenic diet. It's a condition with potentially positive results that is certainly worth further research.

GLUT1 Deficiency Syndrome

GLUT1 deficiency syndrome is an extremely rare genetic disease, affecting around 300 people worldwide, whose neurological symptoms can include an inability to speak. A July 18, 2013, article on the *Daily Mail* website MailOnline tells the story of a three-year-old with this condition who showed improvement and began to speak for the first time after consuming a low-carb, high-fat diet that produced ketone bodies for her brain to use as an alternative fuel source. Yes, this is only anecdotal evidence, but doesn't this demonstrate the need for even more research into the therapeutic uses of the ketogenic diet? You bet it does!

I truly believe we are only beginning to scratch the surface of the potential positive health impact that a ketogenic diet can have. If the effects of a low-carb, moderate-protein, high-fat diet were seen in a prescription medication, the scientific community would be heralding it as the greatest medical discovery in the history of the world. But since there's no money to be made from a simple yet effective diet change, all we get is a collective yawn from the purveyors of conventional health wisdom. This needs to change, and the ketogenic diet deserves a fair shake in the health conversation.

Now that we've looked at all the areas of health that ketosis helps to improve, let's go shopping for the foods that will help rev up those ketones and put your body in the best possible position to heal and thrive as it was intended. Coming up in the next chapter, we'll share a convenient food shopping list to help you choose the right kinds of foods to get into a state of nutritional ketosis.

Key Keto Clarity Concepts

→ While there may not be research on it yet, many health conditions are being reported anecdotally to improve with a ketogenic diet.

→ Cancer is perhaps the most exciting area of development where a low-carb, high-fat diet may help.

→ Ketogenic therapy shows promise for autism, fibromyalgia, chronic pain, and migraines.

→ Studies are beginning to look at the ketogenic diet for treating traumatic brain injury and stroke.

→ People in ketosis are reporting that gum disease, tooth decay, acne, and eyesight are all improved.

→ Lou Gehrig's disease, multiple sclerosis, and Huntington's disease are all ripe for more research looking at the effects of a ketogenic diet.

→ Ketogenic diets may slow aging and increase the rate of cell repair.

→ In rats, kidney disease has been shown to reverse with a ketogenic diet.

→ Restless legs syndrome, arthritis, hair loss, and GLUT1 deficiency syndrome are more health issues that need more research to confirm the beneficial effects of keto.

→ If the health effects of ketosis were found in a drug, it would be heralded as the greatest medical discovery in the history of the world.

Chapter 19
Food Shopping List for Creating Ketosis

MOMENT When your body is breaking down fat for energy, most of that fat OF CLARITY gets converted into ATP energy (the form of energy cells use). In that process, ketones are produced. When you eat fewer carbohydrates, your body turns to fat as its primary energy source and generates lots of ketones in the process. Some of those ketones are used directly for energy. As a matter of fact, some of your body's organs, such as your heart, diaphragm, and kidneys, actually prefer ketones to glucose. And most cells in your body, including brain cells, are also able to use ketones for much of their energy.

– Ben Greenfield

Perhaps the question I'm asked most frequently about eating a ketogenic diet is, "What can I eat?" This has always been a bit strange to me, because the answer is right there in the description of a ketogenic diet: eat low-carb, moderate-protein, and high-fat. Follow those guidelines, bearing in mind your personal carbohydrate and protein thresholds, and you're good to go.

But eating a ketogenic diet does introduce a new way to think about the food you are consuming and the choices you make about what to put in your mouth. This chapter will be your personal shopping guide for what to eat on your ketogenic lifestyle. Keep in mind that there may be some foods on these lists that are not appropriate for you personally. A ketogenic diet will vary from person to person; some are able to tolerate more vegetables and other carbohydrate-based foods better than others. Use the tools in chapters 5, 6, 7, and 8 to determine what works best for you.

I tell people to increase their fat intake by, for instance, eating the fat on pork and beef, seeking out fatty cuts, eating the dark meat and skin on poultry, consuming bone marrow, and boiling bones for soup without skimming off the fat or gelatin when it cools. I ask them to add more coconut oil, extra virgin olive oil, and organic ghee or butter to their foods. If ketosis is still not achieved, it is then time to count carbohydrates.

– Dr. William Davis

Although it's a real challenge to create a universal food shopping list for creating ketosis, I believe seeing a list of foods to buy in the store can help you begin thinking about what it takes to produce more ketones. At the very least, you will be moving in the right direction in your grocery shopping habits to make ketosis become a reality.

Let's take a look at each of the three major macronutrients (carbohydrates, proteins, and fats) to help you find the best foods in each category. Keep in mind that although many of these foods contain a mix of macronutrients, they are categorized according to which macronutrient is predominant. Are you ready to see what you can eat on a ketogenic diet? Check out all these delicious foods!

Carbohydrates

Ketosis is primarily induced by carbohydrate restriction. The level of dietary carbohydrates that is conducive to ketosis is generally dependent on energy balance.

– Dr. Bill Lagakos

This list of carbohydrate-based foods is rather lengthy, but that doesn't mean you will be able to consume all of these as part of your ketogenic diet. While it is possible that some people will be able to reach ketosis eating plenty of the foods you see on this list, many others must limit their consumption to the green, leafy vegetables on this list or even omit carbs entirely. Again, figure out what your carbohydrate tolerance is first and then choose wisely.

- ► Arugula
- ► Artichokes
- ► Asparagus
- ► Blackberries
- ► Blueberries
- ► Bok choy
- ► Broccoli
- ► Brussels sprouts
- ► Cabbage
- ► Cauliflower
- ► Celery
- ► Chicory greens
- ► Cranberries
- ► Cucumbers
- ► Eggplant

- ► Garlic
- ► Green beans
- ► Jicama
- ► Kale
- ► Leeks
- ► Lemon
- ► Lettuce
- ► Lime
- ► Mushrooms
- ► Okra
- ► Onions
- ► Parsley
- ► Peppers
- ► Pumpkin
- ► Radicchio

- ► Radishes
- ► Raspberries
- ► Rhubarb
- ► Scallions
- ► Shallots
- ► Snow peas
- ► Spaghetti squash
- ► Spinach
- ► Strawberries
- ► Summer squash
- ► Tomatoes
- ► Watercress
- ► Wax beans
- ► Zucchini

Proteins

MOMENT OF CLARITY If ketosis is needed for its therapeutic effects, some protein limitation may be needed if carbohydrate restriction alone does not achieve the target ketone levels.

– Dr. Keith Runyan

As we discussed in chapter 6, moderating your protein intake to your personal threshold is critically important for producing ketones. And since dietary fat is crucial for ketosis, look for the fattiest cuts of proteins to make the most of your food. Needless to say, chicken breasts that are 99 percent fat-free are probably not a very good option (particularly if you are sensitive to carbohydrates, which means you'll also need to be careful about the absolute amount of protein you eat). Ideally, the fat-to-protein ratio of a food should be one-to-one or higher. If you look at the nutritional facts label and see that a product has 7 grams of fat and 7 grams of protein, you're good to go. The higher the percentage of fat in a food, though, the better.

- Bacon (not turkey bacon)
- Beef jerky (watch out for added sugars)
- Beef ribs
- Beef roast
- Bratwurst
- Chicken (choose the darkest cuts, skin on)
- Duck
- Eggs (whole)
- Fish (salmon, bass, carp, flounder, halibut, mackerel, sardines, trout)
- Ground beef (not lean)
- Goose
- Ham
- Hot dog (Nathan's brand is the best)
- Kielbasa
- Pepperoni
- Pheasant
- Pork chops
- Pork ribs
- Pork rinds
- Pork roast
- Quail
- Salami
- Sausage
- Shellfish (scallops, shrimp, crab meat, mussels, oysters)
- Steak (the fattier the better)
- Tuna
- Turkey (darker pieces are best)
- Veal

Fats

MOMENT OF CLARITY The benefit of ketosis is that it utilizes our fat stores and dietary fat as they were meant to be used—for energy. We all have plenty of stored energy that can meet our needs rather than processed, nutrient-empty, high-carb foods.

– Jackie Eberstein

And finally we come to what is arguably the best part of being on a ketogenic diet—the abundance of delicious, satisfying, and nutritious fats you can eat! I don't care what anyone else says about fat, it's where the flavor comes from, and that makes this way of eating so enjoyable and, more important, sustainable for the rest of your life. (How many people can honestly say that about a low-fat diet?) I encourage you to fill up on fat in your meals to zap your hunger completely. Fat is where it's at, and these are the best ones for your ketogenic kitchen.

▶ Almonds

▶ Almond butter

▶ Almond milk, unsweetened

▶ Almond oil

▶ Avocado

▶ Avocado oil

▶ Beef tallow

▶ Blue cheese

▶ Brazil nuts

▶ Butter (Kerrygold is a high-quality brand)

▶ Cheese (cheddar, Colby, feta, mozzarella, provolone, ricotta, Swiss, and others)

▶ Chia seeds

▶ Chicken fat

▶ Coconut

▶ Coconut cream

▶ Coconut milk, unsweetened

▶ Coconut oil

▶ Cream cheese

▶ Dark chocolate (80 percent or higher)

▶ Fish oil (Carlson brand is a fabulous cod liver oil)

▶ Flax seeds and oil (men should probably not consume this because of possible prostate cancer risks)

▶ Ghee

▶ Greek yogurt

▶ Heavy whipping cream

▶ Lard

▶ Macadamia nut oil

▶ Macadamia nuts

▶ Mayonnaise (see recipe in chapter 20)

▶ Olive oil

▶ Pecans

▶ Pili nuts

▶ Pistachios

▶ Sour cream

▶ Sunflower seeds

▶ Walnuts

Remember, if you eat the foods on this list and are still having difficulty producing ketones or controlling your blood sugar levels, look first at your carbohydrates and then at your proteins. Make sure you are using the KETO formula (**K**eep carbs low, **E**at more fat, **T**est ketones often, **O**verdo-ing protein is bad) and sticking to your personal carbohydrate and protein thresholds with unlimited fats from the list above. If you do that, you can't help but find great success on your ketogenic diet.

Keep carbs low

Eat more fat

Test ketones often

Overdoing protein is bad

Coming up in the next chapter, we'll provide you with some delicious and nutritious keto-friendly recipes from many of my favorite Paleo and low-carb cookbook authors and bloggers. My mouth is already watering!

MOMENT OF CLARITY I think it is beneficial to include nutrient-dense foods such as organ meats, bone broths, fermented foods and sea vegetables in our diet while in ketosis.

– Bryan Barksdale

Chapter 20

Low-Carb, High-Fat Recipes for Nutritional Ketosis

 **MOMENT OF CLARITY** The lower the carbohydrate and higher the fat in the diet, the higher one can expect the beta-hydroxybutyrate level to be.

– Dr. Mary Newport

While I do enjoy cooking low-carb, moderate-protein, high-fat meals in my own kitchen (and my wife says I do a pretty good job at it), and I will share a few of my favorite ketogenic dishes with you in the pages that follow, there are many other amazing recipe creators in the Paleo and low-carb health communities whom I am privileged to call my friends, and I'm thrilled to present their keto culinary delights in this chapter.

These recipes are all very low in carbohydrates, moderate in protein, and very high in dietary fat. If you are able to tolerate more carbs and protein in your diet and still get into ketosis, then feel free to add them to your meals. At the same time, if a recipe contains more carbohydrates or protein than your body can handle, then adjust the ingredients to fit your personal situation. Only you can determine what is best for you. And when in doubt, add more fat!

Jimmy Moore's Keto Eggs

Serves: 1 to 2   ◆   Prep time: 5 minutes   ◆   Cook time: 15 minutes

This is one of my absolute favorite dishes, and it helps me rock the ketones. It's extremely easy to make and quite tasty, even if I do say so myself. Keep in mind that it's very important to get the high-fat versions of these meats (no turkey bacon or sausage!) for maximum ketogenic effect. The brand of sausage I use, Swaggerty's Farm from Sam's Club, contains 13 grams of fat and 5 grams of protein per patty—a spectacularly high amount of fat (117 of the 140 total calories) compared to the protein (just 20 calories). This is something to look for when making your food choices.

Ingredients

3 thick slices bacon or 2 sausage patties

¼ to ⅓ cup grass-fed butter or coconut oil

4 to 5 pastured eggs

Sea salt

Parsley (or your favorite seasoning)

¼ cup grated full-fat cheese (optional)

3 tablespoons sour cream, to serve

½ avocado, to serve

1. In a medium skillet or sauté pan, fry the bacon or sausage patties over medium heat until cooked through. Use a slotted spoon to remove the bacon or sausage and set aside, leaving the grease in the pan.

2. Add the butter, then once it's melted, crack the eggs directly into the pan. Add the salt, parsley, and cheese. Scramble all the ingredients together with a spatula until fully mixed and cooked to your liking.

3. Serve the eggs and meat together with the sour cream and avocado.

Keto Pizza Frittata

by Diane Sanfilippo (BalancedBites.com)

Author of the *New York Times* bestselling books *Practical Paleo: A Customized Approach to Health and a Whole-Foods Lifestyle*, *The 21-Day Sugar Detox*, and *The 21-Day Sugar Detox Cookbook*

Serves: 6   ♦   Prep time: 15 minutes   ♦   Cook time: 35 minutes

Who doesn't like pizza, right? You might think that on a ketogenic diet, it would be off-limits. But this mouthwatering recipe from one of my favorite cookbook authors fits the bill perfectly, without the wheat-bomb crust that is typical of most pizzas. When you choose food that's made from quality ingredients, that won't have a negative metabolic impact on your body, and that will nourish your body well, then you have discovered the mindset that it takes to successfully manage your weight and health. Congratulations!

Ingredients

ITALIAN SAUSAGE SPICE BLEND

1 teaspoon sea salt

1 tablespoon fennel seeds, ground

1 tablespoon ground sage

1 tablespoon onion powder

¼ teaspoon white pepper or 1 teaspoon black pepper

2 teaspoons dried parsley

½ pound ground pork

8 eggs

1¼ teaspoon sea salt, divided

½ teaspoon freshly ground black pepper

½ cup tomato sauce

½ teaspoon dried basil

½ teaspoon dried oregano

½ teaspoon granulated garlic

1 tablespoon coconut oil or butter

1 bell pepper, seeded and sliced

5 white mushrooms, sliced

3 green onions (scallions), sliced

½ cup sliced olives

1. Preheat the oven to 400°F.

2. In a small bowl, combine all the spice blend ingredients and set aside. Only 1 tablespoon will be used in this recipe; the rest can be stored in an airtight container for up to 6 months.

3. Heat a large, oven-safe skillet over medium heat. While the skillet is heating up, combine the ground pork and 1 tablespoon of the spice blend in a medium mixing bowl and mix them together until the spices are evenly distributed. Add the meat to the skillet and cook until just a little pink is visible, about 10 minutes, breaking up the meat with a heat-safe spatula or wooden spoon. Remove the pork from the pan and set aside. (Do not wash the pan; you will use it again.)

4. In a small bowl, whisk together the eggs, 1 teaspoon of the salt, and the pepper. In another small bowl, stir together the tomato sauce, basil, oregano, granulated garlic, and the remaining ¼ teaspoon of salt. Set both bowls aside.

5. Melt the coconut oil over medium heat in the same pan you used to cook the pork, then add the bell pepper and cook until it starts to soften, about 5 minutes. Add the mushrooms and cook for 2 minutes, or until they soften slightly. Put the meat back into the pan along with the majority of the green onions (reserving some for garnish) and the olives and stir to combine all the ingredients.

6. Pour in the egg mixture and tilt the pan back and forth until the eggs cover the entire bottom of the pan. If necessary, give the ingredients a gentle stir to distribute them evenly. Let cook for about 5 minutes, or until the edges begin to set.

7. Drizzle the tomato sauce mixture over the eggs, then place the pan in the oven and cook for 8 to 10 minutes, or until the eggs are set. To check, use a knife to make a cut in the center of the frittata—if raw egg runs along the cut, cook for another 2 to 3 minutes and check again. Let sit for 5 minutes before slicing and serving.

Perfect Roast Keto Chicken

by Elana Amsterdam (ElanasPantry.com)

Author of *Paleo Cooking from Elana's Pantry: Gluten-Free, Grain-Free, Dairy-Free Recipes*

Serves: 4 ◆ Prep time: 10 minutes ◆ Cook time: 1½ hours

Note from Elana: This recipe is based on one from Ina Garten's *The Barefoot Contessa Cookbook*. My best friend from childhood, Helen, introduced me to Ina, and I have been hooked on her books ever since. While Ina's recipe calls for wheat flour, chicken stock, and butter, mine is a tad simpler and gluten-free as well. I make this go-to dish at least once a week and use the carcass for chicken stock. My boys love this!

Ingredients

1 (2- to 3-pound) whole chicken

Sea salt

Freshly ground black pepper

1 bunch fresh thyme

1 lemon, halved

1 head garlic, peeled and cut in half crosswise

2 tablespoons extra virgin olive oil

1 medium onion, quartered

1. Preheat the oven to 425°F.

2. Remove the chicken giblets, rinse the chicken inside and out, and pat dry. Place the chicken in a 9-by-13-inch baking dish and liberally sprinkle the inside of the chicken with salt and pepper.

3. Stuff the cavity with the thyme, lemon, and garlic. Brush the outside of the chicken with the olive oil and sprinkle with salt and pepper.

4. Tie the legs together with kitchen string and tuck the wings under the body. Place each onion quarter into a corner of the baking dish. Roast the chicken for 1 ½ hours, or until the juices run clear. Allow to cool slightly and serve.

Almond Butter Keto Bombs
by Dietitian Cassie (DietitianCassie.com)

Yield: 16 pieces ◆ Prep time: 5 minutes ◆ Cook time: 2 hours to freeze

Note from Cassie: My favorite bedtime snack is one that promotes stable blood sugars through a combination of healthy fat and a little bit of carbohydrate, and one that also provides a touch of sweetness without unnecessary sugar. These Almond Butter Keto Bombs are the result of my experimenting with my three favorite healthy fats!

Ingredients

1 cup almond butter

¾ cup organic, unrefined coconut oil

2 tablespoons unsalted butter

2 to 3 teaspoons stevia powder extract

1. Place all the ingredients in a large bowl and microwave for 45 seconds.

2. Whisk the ingredients together and pour the mixture into ice cube trays. Freeze for 2 hours.

3. Once they're frozen, you can pop the fat bombs out of the ice cube trays and store them in an airtight container in the freezer, or keep them stored in the ice cube trays!

Camille's Keto Energy Bars
by Camille Macres (CamilleMacres.com)

Author of *Paleogasm: 150 Grain, Dairy and Sugar-free Recipes That Will Leave You Totally Satisfied and Begging for More*

Yield: 18 to 24 bars ◆ Prep time: 10 minutes ◆ Cook time: 3 hours to chill

Note from Camille: This is my favorite snack recipe by *far*. It is loaded with healthy fats and protein, so it's wonderful to have on-hand to keep blood sugar stable throughout the day. These bars are also awesome to eat pre-workout.

Although you can use any brand of protein powder, I prefer Sun Warrior Vanilla Protein Powder, as it has just a couple ingredients and no soy or dairy, and it's sweetened with stevia, which gives the bars some sweetness without any sugar.

Ingredients

1 cup coconut oil, melted

1 cup almond butter, macadamia nut butter, or cashew butter

½ cup protein powder

1 cup shredded unsweetened coconut

½ cup dried cranberries, raisins, or dried cherries

1 cup slivered almonds, pecans, walnuts, or hazelnuts

½ cup cacao nibs

1 teaspoon cinnamon (optional)

¼ teaspoon sea salt

1. In a medium bowl, whisk together the coconut oil, nut butter, and protein powder until smooth. Add the remaining ingredients and stir.

2. Line a baking sheet or cake pan with parchment paper, making sure it goes all the way up the sides. Pour in the batter (don't let the batter touch the actual pan or it will be very messy and difficult to remove). Cover and refrigerate for about 3 hours, or until solid.

3. Lift the bars off the baking sheet with the parchment paper underneath and cut into squares for serving.

4. Store the bars in the refrigerator! If they get too warm, the coconut oil will melt and they will turn into a puddle.

Jimmy Moore's Homemade Keto Béarnaise Sauce

Yield: 1 cup ◆ Prep time: 5 to 10 minutes ◆ Cook time: 20 to 25 minutes

When you've eaten keto for an extended period of time, you're always on the lookout for ways to squeeze even more healthy fats, especially saturated fat, into your meals. Browsing around online, I found inspiration in a post on Diet Doctor (DietDoctor.com), the blog of a Swedish physician friend of mine named Dr. Andreas Eenfeldt. He showed a picture of a typical low-carb meal in his home: a steak, some veggies cooked in butter, and a béarnaise sauce. Honestly, I'd never made a béarnaise sauce before, but it looked easy enough. It turned out to be an amazing discovery that I think you're gonna love too.

Ingredients

5 tablespoons salted grass-fed butter (I like Kerrygold brand)

12 pastured eggs

¼ cup white wine vinegar

Pinch of dried basil or another spice of your choice (such as Italian seasoning or tarragon)

Pinch of sea salt

Pinch of freshly ground black pepper

1. In a small skillet over medium-high heat, add the butter. While it melts, in a large mixing bowl separate the egg yolks from the egg whites, discarding the whites. Beat the yolks thoroughly until smooth and creamy.

2. To the skillet, add the white wine vinegar, dried basil, sea salt, and pepper and reduce the heat to medium-low. Allow to simmer for 10 to 15 minutes, stirring occasionally.

3. Remove from heat and let cool for 10 minutes, then pour the butter mixture slowly into the beaten egg yolks, stirring constantly. Once all the butter is in the bowl, whisk briskly until a beautiful creamy sauce emerges.

4. Use immediately and pour on top of spaghetti squash, grass-fed steak, or anything you want to add more fat to.

Mushroom Burger Scramble
by Linda Genaw (Genaw.com/LowCarb)

Serves: 6 to 8 ◆ Prep time: 10 minutes ◆ Cook time: 45 to 50 minutes

Note from Linda: This has become one of my favorite dishes, and I make it a couple times a month. It makes a lot, so it's great for leftovers. I use ground beef with the highest percentage of fat, and I don't drain the fat after browning the meat. The fat will settle on the bottom of the casserole as it cools, and while that doesn't bother me, you can skip the Parmesan cheese topping and stir the dish occasionally as it cools to redistribute the fat, if you like.

Ingredients

2 pounds grass-fed ground beef

1 small onion, chopped

2 cloves garlic, minced

16 ounces fresh mushrooms, sliced

8 ounces cream cheese, softened

½ cup grated Parmesan cheese (2 ounces), plus additional for topping (optional)

½ cup heavy cream

½ teaspoon garlic powder

1½ teaspoons sea salt

½ teaspoon freshly ground black pepper

Butter, lard, or tallow, to grease the pan

1. Preheat the oven to 350°F.

2. In a large pot or Dutch oven over medium-high heat, brown the hamburger, onion, and garlic; drain the fat if desired (I keep the fat in). Stir in the mushrooms. Cook, stirring occasionally, until the mushrooms are tender, about 5 minutes.

3. Add the softened cream cheese, mashing it into the meat to blend well. Stir in the Parmesan cheese and cream; mix well. Add the garlic powder, salt, and pepper, and adjust to taste.

4. Grease a 2-quart casserole dish and pour in the mixture. Sprinkle some extra Parmesan cheese over the top, if desired. Bake, uncovered, for 30 to 35 minutes, until bubbly and browned.

Coconut Almond Porridge
by Louise Hendon (AncestralChef.com)

Author of *30-Minute Paleo Dessert Recipes: Simple Gluten-Free and Paleo Desserts for Improved Weight Loss*

Serves: 1 ◆ Cook time: 10 minutes

Note from Louise: I love trying out cuisines from other countries, and it's one of the main reasons why my husband and I are embarking on a four-year around-the-world trip! Many of my recipes are inspired by dishes from various countries across the globe. The original inspiration for this one was amlou, a Moroccan sweet almond paste that's often served at breakfast.

It can be difficult to find coconut cream without added sugar. A good alternative is to skim the cream from the top of a can of refrigerated coconut milk. And for a less creamy version, you can use straight coconut milk.

Ingredients

¾ cup coconut cream

½ cup almonds, ground

Stevia

1 teaspoon ground cinnamon

Pinch of nutmeg

Pinch of cloves

Pinch of cardamom (optional)

1. Heat the coconut cream in a small saucepan on medium heat until it forms a liquid.

2. Add the ground almonds and stevia to taste and mix well. Keep stirring for approximately 5 minutes, until the mixture begins to thicken.

3. Add the cinnamon, nutmeg, cloves, and cardamom; taste and add more if desired. Serve hot.

Bacon Brussels Sprouts
by Abel James and Alyson Rose (FatBurningMan.com)

Serves: 2 to 3 ◆ Prep time: 10 minutes ◆ Cook time: 30 minutes

Simplicity in a recipe is always a good thing. Take four amazing, keto-friendly ingredients and you've got the makings for an incredible side dish to complement your lunch or dinner. My friends Abel and Alyson realize the importance of dietary fat in fat-burning, and this tasty recipe infuses plenty of it.

Ingredients

3 slices bacon

3 cups halved Brussels sprouts

1 tablespoon garlic powder

Sea salt

1. In a skillet or sauté pan, cook the bacon, remove from pan, and set aside.

2. Add the Brussels sprouts to the pan and cook in the bacon grease over medium-low heat until brown and soft, about 18 minutes, stirring every 3 minutes. While the sprouts cook, crumble or slice the cooked bacon into bits.

3. Add the bacon bits and garlic powder to the Brussels sprouts, and salt to taste.

Baked Creamed Spinach
by Carrie Brown (CarrieBrown.com)

Serves: 4 to 6 ◆ Prep time: 10 minutes ◆ Cook time: 50 minutes

Note from Carrie: Struggling to get your greens in? I hated spinach with a passion for years, until one day I decided that I had to find a way to make it delicious. It's amazing what the addition of some healthy fats can do for a pile of leafy greens! Now I eat spinach all the time, and this recipe is one of my favorite vegetable dishes. Yum!

Konjac flour and glucomannan powder can be found in health food or supplement stores, but you might find it easiest to order them online from Amazon.com.

Ingredients

2 pounds fresh spinach

1 tablespoon coconut oil

1 pound onions, chopped

2 teaspoons konjac flour or glucomannan powder

2 cups coconut milk, divided

¼ cup heavy cream

Pinch of sea salt

Pinch of freshly ground black pepper

1 teaspoon ground nutmeg

2 eggs, separated

1. Preheat the oven to 350°F.

2. Place the spinach in a dry large pan, cover, and cook over medium heat for 10 minutes, or until completely wilted. Remove the spinach from the pan, drain well, chop finely, and set aside.

3. In the same pan, melt the coconut oil over medium heat. Add the chopped onions and cook until transparent, about 5 minutes.

4. Add the konjac flour to a small bowl and quickly whisk in 1 cup of the coconut milk. Add the konjac milk mixture to the onions and stir until the mixture has thickened, about 2 minutes. Stir in the remaining 1 cup of coconut milk, the cream, salt, pepper, ground nutmeg, egg yolks, and chopped spinach, and stir until completely mixed. Reduce heat to low and let simmer until the egg whites are ready to add.

5. In a small bowl, use a hand mixer on high to beat the egg whites until very stiff. Remove the pan with the spinach from heat and quickly and carefully fold in the stiff egg whites. Tip the spinach mixture into an ovenproof dish and place in the oven 30 minutes, or until the top just starts to brown.

Keto Skordalia (Greek Garlic Dip)
by Maria Emmerich (mariamindbodyhealth.com)

Author of *Keto-Adapted: Your Guide to Accelerated Weight Loss and Healthy Healing* and *The Art of Healthy Eating—Savory: Grain Free Low Carb Reinvented*

Serves: 12 ◆ Prep time: 10 minutes

◆ Cook time: 40 minutes to 1 hour to roast the garlic

Note from Maria: Years ago, my husband, Craig, and I were at a Greek restaurant called Shish on Grand Avenue in St. Paul, Minnesota. Craig had the kebabs with a fantastic garlic dip. It was full of flavor, and I decided to make it myself at home. When I looked it up, I discovered it was made with potatoes, so I decided to create a keto-friendly version with lots of healthy fats and very few carbohydrates.

Roasted garlic gives the dish a sweeter and milder garlic profile, but you can use raw garlic, too.

Ingredients

1 head garlic

¾ cup MCT oil

½ teaspoon sea salt

2 large ripe avocados, peeled, halved, and pitted

¼ cup fresh lemon juice

1 tablespoon coconut vinegar or apple cider vinegar

½ teaspoon freshly ground black pepper

1. Preheat the oven to 400°F.

2. Place the head of garlic on a baking sheet and sprinkle with a dash of MCT oil. Bake for 40 minutes to 1 hour; when the garlic is soft and squeezable, it is ready. Remove the garlic from the oven and let cool, then remove the cloves. Eight cloves will be used in this recipe; reserve the rest for later use.

3. Place 8 garlic cloves and the salt in a blender or food processor and puree until smooth. Add the avocados and puree.

4. Gradually add the MCT oil, lemon juice, and vinegar, rotating between the three and pureeing in between. Add the pepper and use a fork to mix briskly until very smooth.

5. Serve with kebabs or sliced bell peppers. The dip will keep in the refrigerator for about 1 week. Bring to room temperature several hours before serving.

Healthified Keto "Refried Beans"
by Maria Emmerich (mariamindbodyhealth.com)

Author of *Keto-Adapted: Your Guide to Accelerated Weight Loss and Healthy Healing* and *The Art of Healthy Eating—Savory: Grain Free Low Carb Reinvented*

Serves: 4   ◆   Prep time: 10 minutes   ◆   Cook time: 25 to 30 minutes

Note from Maria: Refried beans are traditionally made with pinto beans, but beans are high in carbohydrates and can be counterproductive for people who want to get into ketosis. Plus, the refried beans you purchase at the grocery store can have some iffy ingredients, so it's good to have an alternative. This "refried beans" recipe is low in starch and grain- and bean-free. I know it sounds crazy, but this dish is so good! So many people have told me that their spouses had no clue it wasn't real refried beans.

If you're a vegetarian, you can omit the bacon and smoke the eggplant instead for a natural bacon flavor: Peel and slice the eggplant, wrap it in tinfoil, and place it in a wood smoker for 2 hours. Then cube the eggplant and skip the stir-fry instructions, going straight to pureeing the eggplant instead.

Ingredients

1 eggplant or zucchini, peeled and cubed (about 4 cups)

4 slices bacon

1 cup chopped yellow onions

1 tablespoon minced garlic

1 tablespoon minced, seeded jalapeño pepper

1 tablespoons chili powder

1 teaspoon ground cumin

½ teaspoon sea salt

Pinch of cayenne pepper

½ teaspoon chopped oregano

½ cup grated queso blanco or cheddar cheese, for garnish (optional)

¼ cup minced fresh cilantro, for garnish (optional)

1. In a skillet or sauté pan over medium-high heat, stir-fry the eggplant and bacon until the bacon is fried and the eggplant is very soft, about 10 minutes. Reserve the bacon fat. Transfer the eggplant and bacon to a food processor and puree until smooth.

2. In a large, heavy skillet, heat the reserved bacon fat over medium-high heat. Add the onions and cook, stirring continuously, until soft, about 3 minutes. Add the garlic, jalapeño, chili powder, cumin, salt, and cayenne pepper. Cook, stirring continuously, until fragrant, about 45 seconds to 1 minute. Add the eggplant puree and the oregano, and stir to combine.

3. Cook, stirring continuously with a heavy wooden spoon, until the mixture forms a thick paste, about 5 to 10 minutes, adding water 1 tablespoon at a time to keep it from getting dry. Garnish with the cheese and cilantro, and serve.

Jimmy Moore's Bacon-Wrapped Salmon

Serves: 2 ◆ Prep time: 5 to 10 minutes ◆ Cook time: 20 to 25 minutes

My wife, Christine, absolutely loves salmon. I usually cook it for her at least once a week. One night I decided to do something a little bit different and wrapped some bacon around the salmon before placing it in the skillet. I think she died and went to heaven when she saw this meal that she already loved become even better with bacon. It's a fatty, yummy way to make you a ketone-burning machine!

Ingredients

2 tablespoons grass-fed butter

6 thick slices bacon (don't get the thinner kind; it won't work)

2 fillets wild Alaskan salmon

4 tablespoons sour cream

Garlic salt

1. In a skillet over medium heat, add the butter. While it is melting, wrap 3 slices of thick bacon around each salmon fillet, completely covering it. The bacon should hold to the salmon pretty well.

2. Carefully place the bacon-wrapped salmon fillets into the skillet and cook for 7 to 8 minutes, until brown and crispy. Flip the salmon and splash the hot butter up along the sides to help evenly cook the bacon and salmon.

3. Mix the sour cream with garlic salt to taste, divide into two equal portions, and serve with the salmon.

Gary the Primal Guy's Keto Chocolate
by Gary Collins (PrimalPowerMethod.com)

Yield: 6 to 8 ounces ◆ Serves: 2 to 4
◆ Cook time: 15 minutes, plus 15 to 30 minutes to chill

Note from Gary: This healthy chocolate recipe has very little sugar compared to store-bought chocolate, and it's far more nutritious. It's loaded with healthy fats and contains no dairy or grains at all, and it's completely gluten-free. Of course it is primal, ketogenic, low-carb, and Paleo-approved.

Cacao butter and cacao powder, the key ingredients, are the less-refined versions of cocoa products. They can be found in most health-food stores. It may take a couple of batches of experimenting with the amounts of cacao butter and cacao powder to get your preferred flavor.

Use as small a pan as possible—the smaller the pan, the easier it is to keep the ingredients well mixed.

Ingredients

2 tablespoons coconut oil

2 heaping tablespoons cacao butter

3 tablespoons cacao powder

3 to 4 tablespoons coconut milk or almond milk (optional)

1 teaspoon vanilla extract

1 teaspoon cinnamon

Pinch of sea salt

Stevia

1. In a skillet over very low heat, melt the coconut oil and cacao butter. Do not allow to boil; the slower they melt, the better. Once the mixture is completely melted, turn off the heat and mix in the cacao powder. Melted homemade chocolate is runnier than store-bought chocolate, but it should look dark and somewhat creamy.

2. Mix in the coconut milk if you want more of a milk chocolate flavor. Add the vanilla extract, cinnamon, and salt, and add stevia to taste. Stir well to combine.

3. Allow the chocolate mixture to cool in the pan until it reaches room temperature. Once at room temperature, taste and adjust the seasoning as preferred. Stir well once more, cover, and put in the refrigerator for 30 minutes or the freezer for 15 minutes, until it becomes solid. If you refrigerate it, check it every 5 or 10 minutes and mix it with a spoon two to three times until it starts to solidify, as the oils tend to separate. (This step isn't necessary if you freeze it.)

4. Once the chocolate is solid, break it apart and put in a glass container. Real chocolate has a lower melting temperature than store-bought chocolate, so store it in the refrigerator.

Skinny Keto Pizza

by Bob Montgomery (NotSoFastFood.com)

Owner and operator of the Not So Fast! food truck in San Diego, California

Serves: 4 ◆ Prep time: 15 minutes ◆ Cook time: 45 minutes

Note from Bob: When I lived in Dallas, Texas, from 2006 to 2008, I really got into bodybuilding and what I thought was healthy eating. In reality, I was on a terrible diet that led to weight gain and lethargy. My search for an alternative eventually led me to a low-carb, high-fat, ketogenic way of eating. When I started getting lean and gaining strength by eating this way, I felt fantastic, but I have to admit, I missed pizza. I found a keto-friendly recipe online that used pork rinds for the crust and cream cheese, mozzarella cheese, and Parmesan cheese for toppings. Since my body doesn't respond well to dairy except for a little bit of grass-fed, raw milk cheese, I decided to rework the recipe to make it good for someone like me. This is by far one of my favorite recipes ever. Feel free to add more cheese if your body can handle it, and add any keto-friendly toppings—I like Applegate Farms uncured pepperoni, chicken thighs, or roasted bone marrow. Enjoy!

Ingredients

½ cup ground pork skins or rinds

¾ cup ground chicken skins

2 teaspoons Italian seasoning

1 teaspoon garlic powder

4 large brown eggs

Butter or ghee, to grease the baking sheet

½ cup marinara sauce, BBQ sauce, or other sauce

½ cup raw milk Parmesan cheese

1. Preheat the oven to 335°F.

2. In a medium bowl, combine the ground pork skins, ground chicken skins, Italian seasoning, and garlic powder. In a separate large bowl, beat the eggs. Stir the dry ingredients into the eggs to form pizza dough. Flatten the dough by hand or roll it out to the desired size.

3. Grease a baking sheet with butter or ghee, spread the pizza dough on the sheet, and bake in the oven for 20 to 25 minutes, until the crust turns golden-brown and crispy. Remove from the oven and let rest for 5 minutes.

4. Spread the sauce over the crust and add your toppings of choice. Return to the oven and bake until the cheese is melted, about 12 to 15 minutes. Devour.

Keto Beef Stroganoff
by Freda Mooncotch (Keto-Coach.com)

Author of Defying Age with Food: Reclaim Your Health, Energy & Vitality!

Serves: 4 ◆ Prep time: 10 minutes ◆ Cook time: 20 to 30 minutes

Freda, whose inspiring story appeared in chapter 13, has created a nostalgic, keto-friendly recipe for those of us who grew up on Hamburger Helper. I used to cook for our family when I was a kid, and Hamburger Helper Stroganoff was a staple in our house. But since I don't want to feed my body pasta or artificial ingredients anymore, this recipe from a bona fide ketogenic success story is perfect—it has all the taste that I love and remember without any ketone-busting ingredients.

For a more nutrient-dense version, add 3 ounces of grated, frozen grass-fed liver to the ground beef. No one will ever know!

Ingredients

1 tablespoon grass-fed butter

1 medium onion, chopped

2 to 3 cloves garlic, chopped

1 pound grass-fed ground beef

2 to 3 ounces cheddar or another hard cheese, shredded

2 tablespoons cream

Sea salt and freshly ground black pepper

2 bunches fresh spinach or other greens, to serve

1. Add the butter to a heated cast iron pan over medium-high heat. When it has melted, add the onion and garlic and cook until translucent, about 5 to 7 minutes.

2. Add the ground beef and cook to desired doneness, breaking up the beef as it cooks. Reduce heat to low, add the cheese, and gently melt.

3. Turn off the heat. Add cream until the desired texture is achieved. Salt and pepper to taste and stir well.

4. Serve on a bed of spinach and enjoy!

Jimmy Moore's Homemade Really Real Keto Mayo

Yield: 1⅓ cup   ◆   Prep time: 5 to 10 minutes

When I first began my low-carb, high-fat, ketogenic diet in 2004, I started looking at nutritional labels to find the foods that were low in carbohydrates and had plenty of fat. What I didn't realize at the time was that there is a huge difference between the saturated and monounsaturated fats found in real foods (like the saturated fat in coconut oil and butter and the monounsaturated fat in avocadoes and olive oil) and the polyunsaturated fats found in vegetable oils, including soybean, corn, cottonseed, and canola oil. It's these polyunsaturated fats that are highly inflammatory and should be limited.

Unfortunately, virtually all of the commercially sold mayonnaise products contain soybean oil—even if they try to spin it by calling it "real" mayonnaise or attempt to fool people by putting "with olive oil" on the label, it is still predominantly soybean oil. And when you take into account all the sugar and other dubious ingredients added to this science experiment in a jar, it only makes sense to make your own mayonnaise at home. It's a whole lot easier than you think. This recipe gives you a flavorful source of dietary fat without all the added sugar.

Instead of olive oil in this recipe, try using the same amount of bacon fat. You haven't lived until you've experienced bacon mayo!

Ingredients

2 large eggs

2 egg yolks

½ teaspoon sea salt

1 tablespoon mustard

2 tablespoons lemon juice

1 tablespoon white wine vinegar

½ cup extra virgin olive oil

½ cup coconut oil

1. Add all of the ingredients to a large bowl, if you're using an immersion blender, or food processor. Blend until it thickens to the desired consistency.

2. Store in a glass jar or sealable container in the refrigerator for up to 10 days (but it won't last that long!).

West African Chicken Stew
by Melissa Joulwan (TheClothesMakeTheGirl.com)

Author of *Well Fed: Paleo Recipes for People Who Love to Eat* and *Well Fed 2: More Paleo Recipes for People Who Love to Eat*

Serves: 4 ◆ Prep time: 10 minutes ◆ Cook time: 1 hour

Note from Melissa: I have a thing for peanut butter, by which I mean that I love it to distraction. I especially adore peanut butter in unexpected places, like soups and savory dishes. It was a heartbreaking day for me when I learned that peanuts are a legume and, therefore, do not love me back. But almond butter is an excellent rebound partner, and this stew will win you over with its savory combination of creamy almond butter, just the right bite of heat from the ginger and cayenne, and the underlying sweetness of vanilla and coriander.

Ingredients

1 pound boneless, skinless chicken thighs

Sea salt and freshly ground black pepper

1 tablespoon coconut oil

½ medium onion, diced (about ½ cup)

1 (1-inch) piece fresh ginger, grated (about 1 tablespoon)

3 cloves garlic, minced (about 1 tablespoon)

½ tablespoon ground coriander

½ teaspoon cayenne pepper

1 bay leaf

1 cup canned crushed tomatoes

¼ cup water

¼ cup almond butter (no sugar added)

¼ teaspoon vanilla extract

Minced parsley, for garnish

Butter (optional, for added fat)

1. Sprinkle the chicken enthusiastically with salt and pepper. Heat a large soup pot over medium-high heat, about 3 minutes. Add the coconut oil and allow it to melt. Add the chicken in a single layer and brown well on both sides, about 10 minutes. (Don't crowd the pan; cook in batches if you need to.) Transfer the chicken to a bowl.

2. In the same pot, cook the onion and ginger until soft, about 5 to 7 minutes. Add the garlic, coriander, cayenne, and bay leaf, and cook until fragrant, about 30 seconds. Add the tomatoes and water, stirring to combine. Nestle the chicken into the sauce, along with any juices it released into the bowl. Increase the heat to bring the pot to a boil, then reduce to a simmer and cook, covered, for 25 minutes.

3. Remove the chicken from the pot; it will be very tender. Break the chicken into large pieces with the side of a wooden spoon. Add the almond butter and vanilla to the pot and mix to combine. Return the chicken to the pot and cover. Heat through, about 5 minutes, then serve, sprinkled with parsley. Add butter on top if you desire more fat.

Macadamia Avocado Freezer Fudge

by Shelby Malaterre (CavemanTruck.com)

Owner and operator of the Caveman Truck food truck in Indianapolis, Indiana

Yield: 2 cups ◆ Prep time: 15 minutes
◆ Cook time: 10 minutes, plus 3 hours to freeze

Note from Shelby: This recipe was inspired by my love of dark chocolate and desire to create something with a fudge-like texture. I was encouraged when I started to see similar recipes online. The problem with a lot of these recipes, though, was that they relied heavily on honey and bananas for consistency and sweetness, and I wanted something that could be used as a treat on a low-carb, high-fat, ketogenic diet. After several variations I came up with this recipe, and it was everything I was hoping for.

Ingredients

½ cup macadamia nuts

¼ cup grated or shaved dark chocolate (100% cacao) (2 ounces)

¼ cup ghee

¼ cup coconut butter

Liquid stevia, to taste

¼ teaspoon vanilla extract

⅛ teaspoon sea salt

4 large egg yolks

1 medium avocado, peeled, halved, and pitted

2 tablespoons MCT oil

1. In the top of a double boiler, combine the macadamia nuts, chocolate, ghee, coconut butter, stevia, vanilla, and salt. Place about 1½ cups of water in the bottom of the double boiler, set the chocolate mixture on top, and place over medium-high heat. Let the chocolate fully melt, stirring occasionally.

2. Once the mixture is melted and combined, pour it into a blender and blend until the nuts are smooth. Because they were heated in the double boiler, this process is fairly quick. Once the mixture is smooth, add the egg yolks, avocado, and MCT oil. Blend to smooth it out again.

3. You should now have a fairly dense, warm pudding. It can be eaten right away or frozen to solidify. To freeze, transfer the mixture to bowls, cookie cutter shapes, or, for easy removal, a silicone muffin pan and place in the freezer for 3 hours.

4. Keep in the refrigerator or freezer (depending on the density and temperature you like best) and pop them out as an easy way to get some nutrient-dense, high-fat calories in a hurry.

Luscious Lemon Bars
by Caitlin Weeks (GrassFedGirl.com)

Author of *Mediterranean Paleo Cookbook: Over 135 Grain-Free Recipes to Tempt Your Palate*

Yield: 9 squares ◆ Prep time: 15 minutes
◆ Cook time: 5 minutes, plus 2 hours to chill

Note from Caitlin: You may not have heard of chia seeds, but they are a very healthy source of omega-3 fatty acids and a great substitute for eggs. Chia seeds do tend to have a gritty texture that some people find undesirable, so I encourage you to grind them up to make them smooth and easy to work with. (You can also buy ground chia seed.) There's a lot of healthy fats to bring about ketosis in this recipe.

Ingredients

2 cups full-fat coconut milk

½ cup water

1 heaping tablespoon grass-fed gelatin

1 teaspoon stevia powder extract

2 tablespoons lemon juice

2 teaspoon lemon zest

2 tablespoons chia seeds

1 cup almond flour

¼ teaspoon sea salt

¼ cup coconut oil, melted

Butter or coconut oil, to grease the pan

1. Heat the coconut milk and water in a saucepan over medium heat. Add the gelatin and whisk until dissolved. Stir in the stevia, lemon juice, and lemon zest, remove from heat, and set aside.

2. In a coffee grinder, grind the chia seeds to a fine powder. In a medium bowl, mix the ground chia seeds, almond flour, sea salt, and melted coconut oil until well combined.

3. Grease an 8-by-8-inch glass baking dish and pour in the chia seed mixture, using your fingers to evenly spread it over the bottom of the dish. Pour the lemon gelatin over the crust and refrigerate for 2 hours. Slice and serve.

Pan-Fried Breaded Pork Chops with Sautéed Kale
by Kelsey Albers (IgniteNourishThrive.com)

Serves: 2 ◆ Prep time: 10 minutes ◆ Cook time: 20 minutes

Note from Kelsey: My Grandpa Suma loved breaded pork chops. He loved them so much that he would gnaw at them until all the meat and gristle was gone. As a kid, I was filled with pride and excitement when I helped my mom make them for him.

Grandpa Suma was a man who could have benefited greatly from books like this one. He was diabetic, and his doctors pulled fried and breaded foods like pork chops out of his diet and replaced them with diet sodas, sugar-free treats, and low-carb, "healthy" whole grains.

When I recently I bought a couple of pork chops on sale from my farmer, I was struck by the memory of my grandpa enjoying breaded chops, and the scrumptious, comforting recipe below was born. I wish my grandpa were still with us so I could share my recipe, but I'll just be happy with dedicating it to his memory. I hope it can help you or a loved one transition to a real-foods lifestyle!

Ingredients

2 tablespoons coconut flour

¾ teaspoon onion powder, divided

½ teaspoon garlic powder

½ teaspoon sea salt, divided

½ teaspoon freshly ground black pepper, divided

2 pork chops (5½ ounces total)

2 tablespoons coconut oil

½ clove garlic, minced

½ bunch kale, stemmed and chopped

1. In a medium bowl, mix together the coconut flour, ½ teaspoon of the onion powder, the garlic powder, ¼ teaspoon of the salt, and ¼ teaspoon of the pepper. Dredge each pork chop in the mixture until it's well coated.

2. In a cast iron skillet over medium-high heat, melt the coconut oil. Add the pork chops and cook for 4 to 6 minutes per side, or until golden-brown. Remove from heat and let sit for 5 minutes before serving.

3. While the pork chops are resting, in the same skillet, lightly sauté the garlic for 2 minutes. Add the kale, the remaining ¼ teaspoon of onion powder, remaining ¼ teaspoon of salt, and remaining ¼ teaspoon of pepper. Sauté until the kale is slightly wilted, usually 5 minutes. Serve and enjoy!

Keto Pot Roast
by Lori Pratt (a reader from Orland Park, Illinois)

Serves: 4 ◆ Prep time: 10 minutes ◆ Cook time: 3½ hours

Note from Lori: When I started eating ketogenic, I already loved to cook and was excited to see what I could come up with. This recipe helps keep me from cheating at all because it tastes so good. In fact, it smells so good while I'm making it that my dogs start crying! I always feel energetic after eating a meal like this; it's perfect for anyone following a low-carb, high-fat diet.

Ingredients

3 pounds chuck roast, room temperature

Sea salt and freshly ground black pepper

2 tablespoons coconut oil

¼ cup beef broth

2 small onions, halved

1 teaspoon minced garlic

2 pounds large mushrooms, halved

¼ cup grass-fed butter

1. Rub the roast on both sides with salt and pepper. In a Dutch oven over high heat, add the coconut oil and wait 1 minute, until it becomes hot. Add the chuck roast and sear on each side until brown, about 4 minutes. Reduce the heat to low and add the beef broth. Cover and simmer for 2½ hours.

2. Put the onion halves underneath the bottom of the roast to lift it out of the accumulating liquid. Add the garlic, mushrooms, and butter and continue to cook for 1 hour.

3. Discard the onions, slice the roast (which should practically fall apart), and serve.

Spaghetti Squash Alfredo
by Jimmy Moore

Serves: 2 ◆ Prep time: 5 minutes ◆ Cook time: 40 to 55 minutes

When I was addicted to carbohydrates, I used to think it was the alfredo sauce in fettuccine alfredo that was going to clog my arteries and give me a heart attack. But now I know it's the wheat-based pasta that was the problem, which is why I've replaced that truly unhealthy ingredient with a delicious and nutritious low-carb one: spaghetti squash! Once you get a taste of this, you'll never miss the high-carb version again.

Ingredients

1 spaghetti squash

3 tablespoons grass-fed butter

1 cup heavy cream or coconut milk

2 pinches of garlic salt

2 tablespoons grated Parmesan cheese

Pinch of dried basil

1. Preheat the oven to 375°F.

2. Slice the spaghetti squash in half lengthwise and remove the seeds and pulp. Wrap both halves in aluminum foil, place face-up on a baking sheet, and bake for 30 to 40 minutes. Let cool, then scoop out the flesh with a fork and set aside.

3. In a skillet, melt the butter over medium heat and add the heavy cream, garlic salt, Parmesan cheese, and basil. Cook for 10 to 15 minutes at a light simmer, stirring occasionally.

4. Add the cooked spaghetti squash, mix thoroughly, and enjoy.

Pan-Fried Avocado
by Wendy McCullough

(a reader from Bicknell, Indiana, who blogs at TheLowCarbMom.blogspot.com)

Serves: 2 ◆ Prep time: 5 minutes ◆ Cook time: 5 minutes

Note from Wendy: I started making this recipe when I had several avocados that weren't quite ripe yet when I needed to use them (if you've ever bought avocados, you know exactly what I mean). I was inspired by a recipe for baked avocado and eggs, but I was out of eggs when I wanted to make it. Then it occurred to me that maybe the heat would soften the unripe avocados and make them edible. It did and they were. I like to serve this with scrambled eggs or bacon. How's that for a keto recipe?

Ingredients

1 avocado, firm and unripe

4 tablespoons butter

Sea salt, to taste

1. Cut avocado in half and remove the pit. Peel and cut into 1-inch cubes.

2. In a skillet over medium heat, melt the butter. Add the avocado and cook, covered, until browned, about 5 minutes. Stir occasionally. Season to taste with salt.

Keto Vanilla Ice Cream
by Kent Altena (YouTube.com/Bowulf)

Contributor to *Low-Carbing Among Friends, Volume 1* and *Low-Carbing Among Friends, Volume 3*

Yield: ½ cup ◆ Prep time: 2 minutes ◆ Cook time: 5 minutes to set

Note from Kent: After running the Minneapolis Marathon in June 2010 with temperatures in eighties, I was seriously craving ice cream. I was hot, exhausted, and aching, so when I got home, my kids came up with this recipe for low-carb, high-fat ice cream for me. This simple, three-ingredient recipe has all the flavor of rich vanilla ice cream without the sugar and chemicals that are in most ice cream from the grocery store. It's a perfectly ketogenic way to quench that craving for ice cream.

Ingredients

½ cup heavy cream

6 to 9 drops liquid stevia (equivalent to 1 tablespoon sugar)

½ teaspoon vanilla extract

3 cups ice

6 tablespoons sea salt

1. Pour the heavy cream, liquid stevia, and vanilla extract into a plastic bag and shake briefly to combine.

2. Place the ice and salt in an airtight container. Set the plastic bag on top of the ice and close the container. Vigorously shake for 2 to 5 minutes to set the ice cream.

3. Remove the plastic bag from the container and rinse any excess salt from the bag. Serve immediately.

Jimmy Moore's Keto Chocolate Shell Topping

Yield: ¼ cup ◆ Prep time: 5 to 10 minutes

Lightning struck in the Moore household when I came up with this heckuva ice cream topping. When I started eating a low-carb, high-fat diet, I missed having Magic Shell topping—that chocolate syrup that magically solidifies when you pour it on ice cream. By pure dumb luck, I came up with this fascinating and delightful keto-friendly version, which now goes on top of any cold dessert that I make. I had no idea at first that it solidified on ice cream; I was just making a chocolate syrup. Then I poured it on my wife's vanilla ice cream and handed it to her, and as I was walking back to the kitchen to fix mine, I heard her screech with excitement, "Where did you get the Magic Shell, and is this really low-carb?" I had no idea what she was talking about until I noticed that the chocolate coating had turned hard. What a cool discovery, and it's very ketogenic!

Use dark chocolate with the highest percentage of cacao you can tolerate. I love Taza brand at 87% cacao.

Ingredients

1 teaspoon water

1 tablespoon coconut oil

3 ounces dark chocolate (at least 80% cacao)

1. In a microwavable bowl, combine the water, coconut oil, and dark chocolate. Microwave in several 15- to 20-second cycles until the almost all the chocolate is completely melted, stirring well between cycles.

2. Continue stirring the runny chocolate until it is completely liquid and smooth. Immediately serve on top of anything cold.

Easy Cheesy Cauliflower Gratin
by Nicole Wiese

(a reader from Las Vegas, Nevada, who blogs at menusforlife.wordpress.com)

Serves: 6 ◆ Prep time: 10 minutes ◆ Cook time: 45 minutes

Note from Nicole: The cheese is the star of this dish. Although you can use any cheeses you like, according to your tastes and budget, I think the best texture and creaminess comes from a combination of primarily medium-soft cheese (Havarti, fontina) or firm to semi-firm (cheddar, Swiss, Gouda, Edam, Colby, Monterey Jack), a bit of sharply flavored hard cheese (Asiago, Parmesan, Romano), and a small amount of tangy soft cheese (goat cheese, cream cheese, mascarpone). I personally like to make this with about 1½ cups sharp cheddar, ⅓ cup goat or cream cheese chopped into little chunks, and a bit of freshly grated Romano, but any real, full-fat cheeses you have in the house will do.

This is a fantastic dish to make as a side to a richly flavored meat dish, especially a slow cooker meal.

Ingredients

1 large head cauliflower

2 cups shredded cheese, any combination

2 cups heavy cream

¼ teaspoon freshly ground black pepper

⅛ teaspoon sea salt

¼ teaspoon grated nutmeg

1. Preheat the oven to 400°F.

2. Chop the cauliflower into bite-sized pieces and place in a steamer basket. Add an inch or two of water to a pot, cover, and bring to a boil over high heat. Once the water is boiling, lower the heat to keep the water at a simmer, add the cauliflower in the steamer basket, and cover again. Steam the cauliflower for 10 to 15 minutes, or until it is fork-tender, and remove from heat.

3. While the cauliflower is cooking, mix the cheese and heavy cream in a 9-by-9-inch baking dish. Stir in the black pepper, salt, and nutmeg.

4. Add the cauliflower to the cheese mixture and mix until the cauliflower is well coated. Bake for 30 minutes, or until the top of gratin is nicely browned. Check at the halfway point, and if the

top is already browned, cover the dish with a lid or aluminum foil until it is done.

5. Remove from the oven and let rest for 5 to 10 minutes to allow the sauce to thicken a bit.

6. To make this in the microwave, heat on high for 5 minutes, let sit for 2 minutes, and stir. Continue to microwave in 5-minute increments, wait 2 minutes after each cooking cycle, check if the cauliflower is tender, and repeat if necessary. If you want to brown the top, heat under the broiler until bubbly, but check it frequently because cheese can burn quickly.

How's that to get your low-carb, moderate-protein, high-fat diet started with a bang? Now that you are armed with some incredible ketogenic recipes, read on for a plan for keto success that will help you create keto habits that will last a lifetime. Coming up in the next chapter, we'll outline our 21-Day Kick-start Keto Meal Plan, which will have you rolling in ketones in no time.

MOMENT OF CLARITY Probably the most common mistakes I see people make when they're attempting to get into ketosis are consuming "hidden" dietary carbohydrates ("Whaddaya mean fruit counts?!" or "You mean corn is a grain? I thought it was a vegetable!") or excessive protein consumption, followed by insufficient dietary fat. "If in doubt, cut the carbs even more, eat less protein, and eat more fat!" This often makes the difference for many people.

– Nora Gedgaudas

Chapter 21

21-Day Kick-start Keto Meal Plan

MOMENT OF CLARITY The quality of macronutrients is just as important as the proportion of macronutrients. Carbs should come from above-ground vegetables. Where possible, protein should be animal-based, and dietary fat should come from saturated and monounsaturated fat and less polyunsaturated fat, ideally with a 1:1 ratio of omega-3 to omega-6.

– Dr. Zeeshan Arain

Now that you've learned all about ketogenic diets; why you might want to be eating low-carb, moderate-protein, and high-fat; the scientific evidence for eating this way for therapeutic purposes; and what eating keto can look like in terms of recipes, let's get you going on our 21-Day Kick-start Keto Meal Plan to put you on the clear pathway to success.

Keep in mind that this meal plan is simply a suggestion. If you really like a particular meal and it satisfies your hunger, there is no harm in eating it again and again (this is sometimes referred to as *mono eating*). And remember, we all have different levels of tolerance for carbohydrate and protein. So attempting to exactly replicate these twenty-one days' worth of meals is not necessarily the point. Rather, use this as a general guideline and then adapt it to what works best for you.

You'll notice that this meal plan doesn't refer to specific serving sizes or mealtimes such as breakfast, lunch, and dinner. This is by design. While some people like the traditional three-meals-and-snacks routine, others are able to eat one to two somewhat larger meals daily once they are in ketosis. You may even find yourself gradually reducing the frequency of your meals over time. Keep in mind that if you are hungry enough to eat again just a few hours after your last meal, you probably didn't eat enough fat and/or food in that meal.

MOMENT OF CLARITY Reaching and sustaining a constant state of ketosis is not an easy process. It takes a lot of major lifestyle changes to even get your brain to understand the metabolic shift from using glucose for fuel to using ketone bodies.

– Stephanie Person

Learning to distinguish true hunger from other reasons we eat, as we discussed in chapter 11, and adjusting your eating routine accordingly will help you succeed in your keto journey, especially if you are struggling to produce ketones. Stick to your personal carbohydrate tolerance level and individual protein threshold, consume unlimited fats to satiety, and watch your ketones soar. Some may see success within three weeks, while others may need six weeks or longer before experiencing the positive effects of ketosis. Be patient. Once you get into ketosis, the health benefits will begin to happen in earnest. It's worth the effort, and you'll be glad you persevered.

So let's take a look at a progressive 21-Day Kick-start Keto Meal Plan. It starts with three meals a day in the first week, but consider the second meal optional—if you're not hungry, just skip it. The plan cuts back to two meals a day in the second week and to one meal a day in the third week. If you get hungry at any time, eat a high-fat snack (and consider adding more fat to your next meal so you can stay satisfied longer). Please don't feel that you need to follow this meal plan exactly; just use it as a general way to get started on your ketogenic diet. After twenty-one days, you can fall back into the pattern of eating that works best to keep you in ketosis.

MOMENT OF CLARITY Most commonly, people do not achieve ketosis because they are getting carbs from unexpected sources. For instance, a single 12-ounce glass of orange juice provides an astounding 36 grams of carbs. The other part of the story is that for ketosis to work, you've got to be careful not to overindulge in terms of protein consumption.

– Dr. David Perlmutter

21-Day Kick-start Keto Meal Plan

Day 1

- ▸ **Meal 1:** Jimmy Moore's Keto Eggs (page 245)
- ▸ **Meal 2:** Pork roast cooked in butter and broccoli topped with melted cheddar cheese (optional)
- ▸ **Meal 3:** Perfect Roast Keto Chicken (page 248)
- ▸ **Snack:** Macadamia nuts (optional)

Day 2

- ▸ **Meal 1:** Mushroom Burger Scramble (page 252)
- ▸ **Meal 2:** Halibut cooked in coconut oil with green beans cooked in butter (optional)
- ▸ **Meal 3:** Bratwurst with Bacon Brussels Sprouts (page 254)
- ▸ **Snack:** Pork rinds with cream cheese (optional)

Day 3

- ▸ **Meal 1:** Camille's Keto Energy Bars (page 250)
- ▸ **Meal 2:** Pepperoni slices and mozzarella cheese cooked with butter and garlic salt (optional)
- ▸ **Meal 3:** Jimmy Moore's Bacon-Wrapped Salmon (page 258) topped with Jimmy Moore's Homemade Keto Béarnaise Sauce (page 251)
- ▸ **Snack:** Gary the Primal Guy's Keto Chocolate (page 259) (optional)

Day 4

- ▸ **Meal 1:** Almond Butter Keto Bombs (page 249)
- ▸ **Meal 2:** Tuna with Jimmy Moore's Homemade Really Real Keto Mayo (page 262) and blueberries (optional)
- ▸ **Meal 3:** Keto Beef Stroganoff (page 261)
- ▸ **Snack:** Macadamia Avocado Freezer Fudge (page 264) (optional)

Day 5

- ▸ **Meal 1:** 4 pork sausage patties

- ▸ **Meal 2:** Ham and Colby Jack cheese roll-up dipped in Jimmy Moore's Homemade Really Real Keto Mayo (page 262) (optional)

- ▸ **Meal 3:** Pan-Fried Breaded Pork Chops with Sautéed Kale (page 266)

- ▸ **Snack:** Luscious Lemon Bars (page 265) (optional)

Day 6

- ▸ **Meal 1:** Cucumber slices with Keto Skordalia (page 256)

- ▸ **Meal 2:** Almond butter and dark chocolate (87% cacao) (optional)

- ▸ **Meal 3:** Keto Pot Roast (page 267)

- ▸ **Snack:** Keto Vanilla Ice Cream (page 270) with Jimmy Moore's Keto Chocolate Shell Topping (page 271) (optional)

Day 7

- ▸ **Meal 1:** Celery and Healthified Keto "Refried Beans" (page 257)

- ▸ **Meal 2:** Beef ribs with snow peas cooked in butter (optional)

- ▸ **Meal 3:** 6-ounce sirloin steak cooked in butter and Baked Creamed Spinach (page 255)

- ▸ **Snack:** Beef jerky (optional)

After the first week, you should notice a discernable improvement in your hunger and cravings. In fact, it's possible you've already "forgotten" to eat a meal. If so, don't panic. That's totally normal as your body adjusts from running on sugar to running on fat.

Like the first week, the second week of the meal plan includes snacks in case you get hungry between meals. (But remember, if you're getting hungry between meals, that's your cue to add more fat to your meals.) You are under no obligation to eat all of the meals and snacks listed, but they're there in case you need them. Keep in mind that your first meal of the day could be at noon or beyond.

MOMENT OF CLARITY To maintain some degree of ketones, we must restrict the intake of carbohydrates to no more than about 50 grams daily. It is essential to control not only the quantity of carbs but the quality as well. Allowing only those carbs with a low glycemic load will eliminate foods with added sugars and highly refined, processed items. This is closer to the whole-foods diet that was consumed decades ago when we were a far slimmer and much healthier nation.

– Jackie Eberstein

Day 8

- ▶ **Meal 1:** Keto Pizza Frittata (page 246)
- ▶ **Meal 2:** Hamburger patty cooked in butter, bacon, and Swiss cheese topped with a mixture of sour cream and garlic salt (optional)
- ▶ **Snack:** Raw almonds (optional)

Day 9

- ▶ **Meal 1:** Roasted duck with Coconut Almond Porridge (page 253)
- ▶ **Meal 2:** Salami and cheese (optional)
- ▶ **Snack:** Deviled eggs made with Jimmy Moore's Homemade Really Real Keto Mayo (page 262) (optional)

Day 10

- ▶ **Meal 1:** Eggs fried in coconut oil, bacon, and avocado
- ▶ **Meal 2:** Pan-seared scallops cooked in lard and raw spinach salad topped with olive oil and lemon juice (optional)
- ▶ **Snack:** Cashew butter mixed with cream cheese, a touch of cinnamon, and a few drops of your favorite liquid sweetener (optional)

Day 11

- ▶ **Meal 1:** West African Chicken Stew (page 263)
- ▶ **Meal 2:** Veal cooked in ghee with Parmesan cheese and bell peppers (optional)
- ▶ **Snack:** Pork rinds with sour cream (optional)

Day 12

- ▶ **Meal 1:** Chicken drumsticks with Spaghetti Squash Alfredo (page 268)

- ▶ **Meal 2:** Shrimp cooked in macadamia nut oil with Jimmy Moore's Homemade Keto Béarnaise Sauce (page 251) and asparagus cooked in beef tallow (optional)

- ▶ **Snack:** Heavy cream with unsweetened cocoa powder and a few drops of your favorite liquid sweetener (optional)

Day 13

- ▶ **Meal 1:** 2 Nathan's hot dogs cooked in butter and topped with melted Provolone cheese, and Pan-Fried Avocado (page 269)

- ▶ **Meal 2:** Turkey (dark meat) and kale salad with blue cheese crumbles and avocado oil (optional)

- ▶ **Snack:** String cheese with cream cheese (optional)

Day 14

- ▶ **Meal 1:** Rotisserie chicken (dark meat) with Easy Cheesy Cauliflower Gratin (page 272)

- ▶ **Meal 2:** Skinny Keto Pizza (page 260) (optional)

- ▶ **Snack:** Strawberries and homemade whipped cream (optional)

After two weeks, you may already be experiencing benefits for your weight and health, particularly with your blood sugar and ketones.

Let's put ketosis to the test in the third week and see how well it will keep your hunger completely satisfied on just one meal a day. I haven't provided any snacks for this week, but I don't think you're going to need them. As we stated in chapter 11, a good sign of what we're calling your "keto fitness level" is the ability to go eighteen to twenty-four hours between meals rather easily. At this point your body has likely shifted to burning fat and ketones efficiently, and you're ready to see how you do. Of course, if at any time you get hungry during the week, you know what you're supposed to do—*eat*!

To be satisfied on just one meal each day, you'll need to be careful to get enough food in that meal to sustain you. This isn't the time to skimp on portion size. Each meal may seem like a lot of food to eat at one time, but it provides the same number of calories that would typically be broken up into three meals and snacks. That's not to say that you should try to gorge yourself or force food down your throat that you cannot eat. Just consume enough food to satisfy your hunger, adhere to your carbohydrate tolerance and protein threshold, and fill up on dietary fat so you can go up to twenty-four hours between meals. Remember, if you like a certain meal and feel comfortable eating it again and again during the week, then go for it!

MOMENT OF CLARITY Keep in mind that a ketogenic diet isn't necessarily healthy unless high-quality food and dietary fats are a meaningful part of the equation. Hospital-prescribed ketogenic prepackaged "food-like substances" include partially hydrogenated fats and oils, high fructose corn syrup, and highly processed, denatured protein powders. "Ketogenic" can mean all kinds of things. I am very careful to focus on foods that most closely mimic what we ate as ancient hunter-gatherers.

– Nora Gedgaudas

Just one meal a day is actually my usual pattern of eating, and I enjoy the freedom that comes with not having to worry about what I'm putting in my mouth. Remember, you won't be eating this way very long—just one more week on the kick-start meal plan—so give it your best shot. If you get hungry four to twelve hours after eating, then you didn't eat enough food and/or enough fat. Bump it up in the next meal by adding more butter or your favorite fat and see how you do.

Being satisfied on just one meal a day isn't impossible, and I think you might be surprised at how well you can endure the periods of intermittent fasting this week. And don't lose sight of why you are doing this: those periods of fasting will help you produce more therapeutic ketones.

MOMENT OF CLARITY Nutritional ketosis is a natural consequence of following a ketogenic diet of whole foods consisting of meat, poultry, fish, and eggs, along with non-starchy vegetables; low-sugar fruits, including olives, avocados, and berries; nuts and seeds; and added natural fats, including tallow, lard, butter, cream, aged cheese, and coconut and olive oils.

– Dr. Keith Runyan

Day 15

▸ **Meal 1:** Jimmy Moore's Keto Eggs (page 245) and Macadamia Avocado Freezer Fudge (page 264)

Day 16

▸ **Meal 1:** Beef hamburger patty cooked in coconut oil, cheese, bacon, Jimmy Moore's Homemade Really Real Keto Mayo (page 262), and Almond Butter Keto Bombs (page 249)

Day 17

▸ **Meal 1:** Jimmy Moore's Bacon-Wrapped Salmon (page 258) topped with Jimmy Moore's Homemade Keto Béarnaise Sauce (page 251), and Luscious Lemon Bars (page 265)

Day 18

▸ **Meal 1:** 6-ounce sirloin steak cooked in butter and cucumber slices with Keto Skordalia (page 256)

Day 19

▸ **Meal 1:** Pepperoni slices and mozzarella cheese cooked with butter and Gary the Primal Guy's Keto Chocolate (page 259)

Day 20

▸ **Meal 1:** A whole rotisserie chicken and Keto Vanilla Ice Cream (page 270) with Jimmy Moore's Keto Chocolate Shell Topping (page 271)

Day 21

▸ **Meal 1:** Keto Pot Roast (page 267) and Bacon Brussels Sprouts (page 254)

Eating keto may seem daunting at first, but it's really not as hard as you think, and once you commit fully to becoming ketogenic to improve your health (and, for some people, to shed some pounds) it becomes even easier. Find the pattern of eating that works best for you and enjoy your pursuit of nutritional ketosis.

I'm excited to hear about your keto journey, so let me know how you are doing by e-mailing me at livinlowcarbman@charter.net. I'm always thrilled to hear how a low-carb, moderate-protein, high-fat, ketogenic lifestyle is working for others. Once you're there, the sky truly is the limit.

MOMENT OF CLARITY By definition, when fat, protein, and carbohydrate are manipulated to produce ketosis, a reduction in carbohydrates is a fundamental part of the diet. For diabetics, this means a reduction in insulin output and lower insulin levels.

– Dr. Mary Newport

Epilogue

Now That You've Been Enlightened, What Happens Next?

> **MOMENT OF CLARITY** I find I have much better drive and focus when in a state of ketosis. I have a lot more mental clarity and productivity.
>
> — Bryan Barksdale

When I stopped believing that I had to eat a low-fat, high-carb diet in order to lose weight and get healthy, it was perhaps one of the defining moments of my entire life. Never again would I look at nutrition and its impact on health in the same way. I hope that reading this book has been a similarly transformative experience for you, and that the knowledge and wisdom within these pages leads you to all the health benefits ketosis brings.

> **MOMENT OF CLARITY** Many cultures throughout time would have experienced long-term nutritional ketosis.
>
> — Dr. Zeeshan Arain

So many people who would benefit from a low-carb, moderate-protein, high-fat, ketogenic diet haven't even heard of it, because it's not well understood or represented in the mainstream media. That to me is the biggest travesty of all. How many people in your life are suffering from one of the many conditions that have been shown to improve on a ketogenic diet—type 2 diabetes, obesity, epilepsy, cardiovascular disease, metabolic syndrome, irritable bowel syndrome, and so many more? Don't they deserve to know about a completely natural nutritional therapy that could be more effective than drugs and other treatments? You bet they do! And that's what inspired me write this book: to share honest, practical information about ketosis in everyday language. I wanted to empower you with the knowledge, wisdom, and experience to feel confident about pursuing ketosis as a viable means for bringing about major improvements in your health.

 **MOMENT OF CLARITY** People are now living longer but are sicker, destined to experience decades of poor health before they finally kick the bucket. And it's all because they have lost their connection to ketone bodies. Virtually every chronic disease that physicians deal with every single day is caused by eating a diet high in simple sugars and processed food.

– Dr. Bill Wilson

The ball is now in your court. Your friends, family, and even your doctor may wonder what in the world you are doing eating this way. But now you should feel confident enough to be a living, breathing example of the great things that can happen if you dare to give ketogenic eating a go.

MOMENT OF CLARITY Being in ketosis forces a physiological shift from a sugar-based metabolism to a fatty acid– and ketone-based metabolism. Nutritional ketosis suppresses insulin and forces a "fat-adapted state" that produces a wide range of health benefits. Especially when combined with resistance training, nutritional ketosis typically produces dramatic body composition alterations and improvements in overall metabolic profile.

– Dr. Dominic D'Agostino

Your keto journey begins right here, right now.

MOMENT OF CLARITY Nutritional ketosis may not be required for general health, but it may very well be a conduit to optimal health.

– Dr. Bill Lagakos

Resources

Scientific Studies

General

Boling, C. L., E. C. Westman, W. S. Yancy Jr. "Carbohydrate-Restricted Diets for Obesity and Related Diseases: An Update." *Current Atherosclerosis Reports* 11.6 (2008): 462-9.

Cahill, G. F., Jr. "Fuel Metabolism in Starvation." *Annual Review of Nutrition* 26 (2006): 1-22.

Feinman, R. D., M. Makowske. "Metabolic Syndrome and Low-Carbohydrate Ketogenic Diets in the Medical School Biochemistry Curriculum." *Metabolic Syndrome and Related Disorders* 1.3 (2003): 189-197.

Liu, Y. M. "Medium-Chain Triglyceride (MCT) Ketogenic Therapy." *Epilepsia* 49.Suppl 8 (2008): 33-6.

Manninen, A. H. "Is a Calorie Really a Calorie? Metabolic Advantage of Low-Carbohydrate Diets." *Journal of the International Society of Sports Nutrition* 1.2 (2004): 21-6.

McClernon, F. J., et al. "The Effects of a Low-Carbohydrate Ketogenic Diet and a Low-Fat Diet on Mood, Hunger, and Other Self-Reported Symptoms." *Obesity* (Silver Spring) 15.1 (2007): 182-7.

Paoli, A., A. Rubini, J. S. Volek, K. A. Grimaldi. "Beyond Weight Loss: A Review of the Therapeutic Uses of Very-Low-Carbohydrate (Ketogenic) Diets." *European Journal of Clinical Nutrition* 67 (2013): 789–796.

Veech, R. L. "The Therapeutic Implications of Ketone Bodies: The Effects of Ketone Bodies in Pathological Conditions: Ketosis, Ketogenic Diet, Redox States, Insulin Resistance, and Mitochondrial Metabolism." *Prostaglandins, Leukotrienes and Essential Fatty Acids* 70.3 (2004): 309-19.

Veech, R. L., et al. "Ketone Bodies, Potential Therapeutic Uses." *IUBMB Life* 51 (2001): 241-7.

Volek, J. S., C. E. Forsythe. "The Case for Not Restricting Saturated Fat on a Low Carbohydrate Diet." *Nutrition & Metabolism* 2 (2005):21.

Volek, J. S., C. E. Forsythe. "Very-Low-Carbohydrate Diets." In *Essentials of Sports Nutrition and Supplements,* edited by Jose Antonio, Douglas Kalman, Jeffrey R. Stout, Mike Greenwood, Darryn S. Willoughby, and G. Gregory Haff, 581-604. Totowa, NJ: Humana Press, 2008.

Westman, E. C. "A Review of Very Low Carbohydrate Diets for Weight Loss." *Journal of Clinical Outcomes Management* 6.7 (1999): 36-40.

Westman, E. C. "Is Dietary Carbohydrate Essential for Human Nutrition?" *American Journal of Clinical Nutrition* 75.5 (2002): 951-953; author reply 953-954.

Westman, E. C., et al. "Effect of 6-Month Adherence to a Very Low Carbohydrate Diet Program." *American Journal of Medicine* 113.1 (2002): 30-36.

Westman, E. C., et al. "Low-Carbohydrate Nutrition and Metabolism." *American Journal of Clinical Nutrition* 86 (2007): 276-84.

Westman, E. C., J. Mavropoulos, W. S. Yancy Jr., J. S. Volek. "A Review of Low-carbohydrate Ketogenic Diets." *Current Atherosclerosis Reports* 5.6 (2003): 476-483.

Westman, E. C., W. S. Yancy Jr., M. C. Vernon. "Is a Low-Carb, Low-Fat Diet Optimal?" *Archives of Internal Medicine* 165.9 (2005): 1071-1072.

Weight Loss/Metabolic Syndrome/Insulin Resistance

Al-Sarraj, T., H. Saadi, J. S. Volek, M. L. Fernandez. "Carbohydrate Restriction Favorably Alters Lipoprotein Metabolism in Emirati Subjects Classified with the Metabolic Syndrome." *Nutrition, Metabolism & Cardiovascular Disease* 20 (2010): 720-726.

Al-Sarraj, T., H. Saadi, J. S. Volek, M. L. Fernandez. "Metabolic Syndrome Prevalence, Dietary Intake, and Cardiovascular Risk Profile among Overweight and Obese Adults 18-50 Years Old from the United Arab Emirates." *Metabolic Syndrome and Related Disorders* 8.1 (2010): 39-46.

Bailey, W. A., E. C. Westman, M. L. Marquart, J. R. Guyton. "Low Glycemic Diet for Weight Loss in Hypertriglyceridemic Patients Attending a Lipid Clinic." *Journal of Clinical Lipidology* 4.6 (2010): 508-14.

Foster, G. D., et al. "A Randomized Trial of a Low-Carbohydrate Diet for Obesity." *New England Journal of Medicine* 348.21 (2003): 2082-2090.

LeCheminant, J. D., et al. "Comparison of a Low Carbohydrate and Low Fat Diet for Weight Maintenance in Overweight or Obese Adults Enrolled in a Clinical Weight Management Program." *Nutrition Journal* 6 (2007): 36.

Noakes, M., P. Foster, J. Keogh, P. Clifton. "Very Low Carbohydrate Diets For Weight Loss And Cardiovascular Risk." *Asia Pacific Journal of Clinical Nutrition* 13.Suppl (2004): S64.

Phelan, S., et al. "Three-Year Weight Change in Successful Weight Losers Who Lost Weight on a Low-Carbohydrate Diet." *Obesity* (Silver Spring) 15 (2007): 2470–2477.

Ruano, G., et al. "Physiogenomic Analysis of Weight Loss Induced by Dietary Carbohydrate Restriction." *Nutrition & Metabolism* 3 (2006): 20.

Shai, I., et al. "Weight Loss with a Low-Carbohydrate, Mediterranean, or Low-Fat Diet." *New England Journal of Medicine* 359 (2008): 229-241.

Sharman, M. J., J. S. Volek. "Weight Loss Leads to Reductions in Inflammatory Biomarkers after a Very-Low Carbohydrate Diet and a Low-Fat Diet in Overweight Men." *Clinical Science* 107.4 (2004): 365-369.

Sumithran, P., et al. "Ketosis and Appetite-Mediating Nutrients and Hormones after Weight Loss." *European Journal of Clinical Nutrition* 67.7 (2013): 759-64.

Tay, J., et al. "Metabolic Effects of Weight Loss on a Very-Low-Carbohydrate Diet Compared with an Isocaloric High-Carbohydrate Diet in Abdominally Obese Subjects." *Journal of the American College of Cardiology* 51.1 (2008): 59-67.

Vernon, M. C., et al. "Clinical Experience of a Carbohydrate-Restricted Diet for the Metabolic Syndrome." *Metabolic Syndrome and Related Disorders* 2.3 (2004): 180-6.

Volek, J. S., E. C. Westman. "Very-Low-Carbohydrate Weight-Loss Diets Revisited." *Cleveland Clinic Journal of Medicine* 69.11 (2002): 849, 853, 856-848 passim.

Volek, J. S., et al. "Body Composition and Hormonal Responses to a Carbohydrate-Restricted Diet." *Metabolism* 51.7 (2002): 864-870.

Volek, J. S., et al. "Carbohydrate Restriction Has a More Favorable Impact on the Metabolic Syndrome than a Low Fat Diet." *Lipids* 44.4 (2009): 297-309.

Volek, J. S., et al. "Comparison of Energy-Restricted Very Low-Carbohydrate and Low-Fat

Diets on Weight Loss and Body Composition in Overweight Men and Women." *Nutrition & Metabolism* 1.1 (2004): 13.

Volek, J. S., R. D. Feinman. "Carbohydrate Restriction Improves the Features of Metabolic Syndrome. Metabolic Syndrome May Be Defined by the Response to Carbohydrate Restriction." *Nutrition & Metabolism* 2 (2005): 31.

Westman, E. C. "A Review of Very Low Carbohydrate Diets for Weight Loss." *Journal of Clinical Outcomes Management* 6.7 (1999): 36-40.

Westman, E. C., et al. "Effect of 6-month Adherence to a Very Low Carbohydrate Diet Program." *American Journal of Medicine* 113.1 (2002): 30-36.

Westman, E. C., W. S. Yancy Jr., M. D. Haub, J. S. Volek. "Insulin Resistance from a Low Carbohydrate, High Fat Diet Perspective." *Metabolic Syndrome and Related Disorders* 3.1 (2005): 14-18.

Yancy, W. S., Jr., et al. "Effects of Two Weight-Loss Diets on Health-Related Quality of Life." *Quality of Life Research* 18.3 (2009): 281-289.

Yancy, W. S., Jr., et al. "A Randomized Trial of a Low-Carbohydrate Diet vs Orlistat Plus a Low-Fat Diet for Weight Loss." *Archives of Internal Medicine* 170.2 (2010): 136-145.

Gastrointestinal Diseases/IBS/GERD/NAFLD

Austin, G. L., et al. "A Very Low Carbohydrate Diet Improves Gastroesophageal Reflux and Its Symptoms." *Digestive Diseases and Sciences* 51.8 (2006): 1307-1312.

Austin, G. L., et al. "A Very-Low-Carbohydrate Diet Improves Symptoms and Quality of Life in Diarrhea-Predominant Irritable Bowel Syndrome." *Clinical Gastroenterology and Hepatology* 7.6 (2009): 706-708.

Tendler, D., et al. "The Effect of a Low-Carbohydrate, Ketogenic Diet on Nonalcoholic Fatty Liver Disease: A Pilot Study." *Digestive Diseases and Sciences* 52.2 (2007): 589-93.

Yancy, W. S., Jr., D. Provenzale, E. C. Westman. "Improvement of Gastroesophageal Reflux Disease after Initiation of a Low-Carbohydrate Diet: Five Brief Case Reports." *Alternative Therapies in Health and Medicine* 7.6 (2001): 116-120.

Polycystic Ovary Syndrome (PCOS)

Mavropoulos, J., W. S. Yancy Jr., J. Hepburn, E. C. Westman. "The Effects of a Low-Carbohydrate, Ketogenic Diet on the Polycystic Ovary Syndrome: A Pilot Study." *Nutrition & Metabolism* 2 (2005): 35.

Epilepsy

Barañano, K. W., A. L. Hartman. "The Ketogenic Diet: Uses in Epilepsy and Other Neurologic Illnesses." *Current Treatment Options in Neurology* 10.6 (2008): 410-9.

Dressler, A., et al. "Type 1 Diabetes and Epilepsy: Efficacy and Safety of the Ketogenic Diet." *Epilepsia* 51.6 (2010): 1086–1089.

Greene, A. E., M. T. Todorova, T. N. Seyfried. "Perspectives on the Metabolic Management of Epilepsy through Dietary Reduction of Glucose and Elevation of Ketone Bodies." *Journal of Neurochemistry* 86.3 (2003): 529–537.

Peterson, S. J., et al. "Changes in Growth and Seizure Reduction in Children on the Ketogenic Diet as a Treatment for Intractable Epilepsy." *Journal of the American Dietetic Association* 105.5 (2005): 718-25.

Diabetes

Accurso, A., et al. "Dietary Carbohydrate Restriction in Type 2 Diabetes Mellitus and Metabolic Syndrome: Time for a Critical Appraisal." *Nutrition & Metabolism* 5 (2008): 9.

Allen, F. M. "Studies Concerning Diabetes." *Journal of the American Medical Association* 63.11 (1914): 939-943.

Boden, G., et al. "Effect of a Low-Carbohydrate Diet on Appetite, Blood Glucose Levels, and Insulin Resistance in Obese Patients with Type 2 Diabetes." *Annals of Internal Medicine* 142.6 (2005): 403-411.

Brand-Miller, J., S. Hayne, P. Petocz, S. Colagiuri. "Low-Glycemic Index Diets in the Management of Diabetes: A Meta-Analysis of Randomized Controlled Trials." *Diabetes Care* 26.8 (2003): 2261-2267.

Dashti, H. M., et al. "Beneficial Effects of Ketogenic Diet in Obese Diabetic Subjects." *Molecular and Cellular Biochemistry* 302.1 (2007): 249-256.

Feinman, R. D., J. S. Volek. "Carbohydrate Restriction as the Default Treatment for Type 2 Diabetes and Metabolic Syndrome." *Scandinavian Cardiovascular Journal* 42.4 (2008): 256-263.

Feinman, R. D., J. S. Volek, E. Westman. "Dietary Carbohydrate Restriction in the Treatment of Diabetes and Metabolic Syndrome." *Clinical Nutrition Insight* 34.12 (2008): 1-5.

Gannon, M. C., F. Q. Nuttall. "Effect of a High-Protein, Low-Carbohydrate Diet on Blood Glucose Control in People with Type 2 Diabetes." *Diabetes* 53.9 (2004): 2375-2382.

Hussain, T. A., et al. "Effect of Low-Calorie Versus Low-Carbohydrate Ketogenic Diet in Type 2 Diabetes." *Nutrition* 28.10 (2012): 1016-21.

Mobbs, C. V., J. Mastaitis, F. Isoda, M. Poplawski. "Treatment of Diabetes and Diabetic Complications with a Ketogenic Diet." *Journal of Child Neurology* 28.8 (2013): 1009-14.

Nielsen, J. V., E. Joensson. "Low-Carbohydrate Diet in Type 2 Diabetes: Stable Improvement of Bodyweight and Glycemic Control During 44 Months Follow-Up." *Nutrition & Metabolism* 5 (2008): 14.

Nielsen, J. V., E. Jonsson, A. Ivarsson. "A Low Carbohydrate Diet in Type 1 Diabetes: Clinical Experience—A Brief Report." *Upsala Journal of Medical Sciences* 110.3 (2005): 267-273.

Nielsen, J. V., E. Jonsson, A. K. Nilsson. "Lasting Improvement of Hyperglycaemia and Bodyweight: Low-Carbohydrate Diet in Type 2 Diabetes. A Brief Report." *Upsala Journal of Medical Sciences* 110.2 (2005): 179-183.

Nielsen, J. V., P. Westerlund, P. Bygren. "A Low-Carbohydrate Diet May Prevent End-Stage Renal Failure in Type 2 Diabetes. A Case Report." *Nutrition & Metabolism* 3 (2006): 23.

Vernon, M. C., et al. "Clinical Experience of a Carbohydrate-Restricted Diet: Effect on Diabetes Mellitus." *Metabolic Syndrome and Related Disorders* 1.3 (2003): 233-238.

Westman, E. C., et al. "The Effect of a Low-Carbohydrate, Ketogenic Diet Versus a Low-Glycemic Index Diet on Glycemic Control in Type 2 Diabetes Mellitus." *Nutrition & Metabolism* 5 (2008): 36.

Westman, E. C., W. S. Yancy Jr., M. Humphreys. "Dietary Treatment of Diabetes Mellitus in yhe Pre-Insulin Era (1914-1922)." *Perspectives in Biology and Medicine* 49.1 (2006): 77-83.

Yancy, W. S., Jr., M. C. Vernon, E. C. Westman. "A Pilot Trial of a Low-Carbohydrate, Ketogenic Diet in Patients with Type 2 Diabetes." *Metabolic Syndrome and Related Disorders* 1.3 (2003): 239-243.

Yancy, W. S., Jr., M. Foy, M. C. Vernon, E. C. Westman. "A Low-Carbohydrate Ketogenic Diet to Treat Type 2 Diabetes." *Nutrition & Metabolism* 2 (2005): 34.

Mental Health

Kraft, B. D., E. C. Westman. "Schizophrenia, Gluten, and Low-Carbohydrate, Ketogenic Diets: A Case Report and Review of the Literature." *Nutrition & Metabolism* 6 (2009): 10.

McClernon, F. J., et al. "The Effects of a Low-Carbohydrate Ketogenic Diet and a Low-Fat Diet on Mood, Hunger, and Other Self-Reported Symptoms." *Obesity* (Silver Spring) 15.1 (2007): 182-7.

Pacheco, A., W. S. Easterling, M. W. Pryer. "A Pilot Study of the Ketogenic Diet in Schizophrenia." *American Journal of Psychiatry* 121 (1965): 1110-1111.

Phelps, J. R., S. V. Siemers, R. S. El-Mallakh. "The Ketogenic Diet for Type II Bipolar Disorder." *Neurocase* 19.5 (2013): 423-6.

Yancy, W. S., Jr., et al. "Effects of Two Weight-Loss Diets on Health-Related Quality of Life." *Quality of Life Research* 18.3 (2009): 281-289.

Cardiovascular Disease/Cholesterol

Austin, M. A., J. E. Hokanson, K. L. Edwards. "Hypertriglyceridemia as a Cardiovascular Risk Factor." *American Journal of Cardiology* 81.4A (1998): 7B-12B.

Dashti, H. M., et al. "Ketogenic Diet Modifies the Risk Factors of Heart Disease in Obese Patients." *Nutrition* 19.10 (2003): 901-902.

Dashti, H. M., et al. "Long Term Effects of Ketogenic Diet in Obese Subjects with High Cholesterol Level." *Molecular and Cellular Biochemistry* 286.1-2 (2006): 1-9.

deOgburn, R., et al. "Effects of Increased Dietary Cholesterol with Carbohydrate Restriction on Hepatic Lipid Metabolism in Guinea Pigs." *Comparative Medicine* 62.2 (2012): 109-115.

Feinman, R. D., J. S. Volek. "Low Carbohydrate Diets Improve Atherogenic Dyslipidemia Even in the Absence of Weight Loss." *Nutrition & Metabolism* 3 (2006): 24.

Hickey, J. T., et al. "Clinical Use of a Carbohydrate-Restricted Diet to Treat the Dyslipidemia of the Metabolic Syndrome." *Metabolic Syndrome and Related Disorders* 1.3 (2003): 227-232.

Karam, J., F. Nessim, S. McFarlane, R. Feinman. "Carbohydrate Restriction and Cardiovascular Risk." *Current Cardiovascular Risk Reports* 2.2. (2008): 88-94.

LeCheminant, J. D., et al. "Comparison of a Reduced Carbohydrate and Reduced Fat Diet for LDL, HDL, and VLDL Subclasses during 9 Months of Weight Maintenance Subsequent to Weight Loss." *Lipids in Health and Disease* 9 (2010): 54.

Lofgren, I., et al. "Weight Loss Associated with Reduced Intake of Carbohydrate Reduces the Atherogenicity of LDL in Premenopausal Women." *Metabolism* 54.9 (2005): 1133-1141.

Mutungi, G., et al. "Carbohydrate Restriction and Dietary Cholesterol Modulate the Expression of HMG-CoA Reductase and the LDL Receptor in Mononuclear Cells from Adult Men." *Lipids in Health and Disease* 6 (2007): 34.

Noakes, M., et al. "Comparison of Isocaloric Very Low Carbohydrate/High Saturated Fat and High Carbohydrate/Low Saturated Fat Diets on Body Composition and Cardiovascular Risk." *Nutrition & Metabolism* 3 (2006): 7.

Nordmann, A. J., et al. "Effects of Low-Carbohydrate Vs Low-Fat Diets on Weight Loss and Cardiovascular Risk Factors." *Archives of Internal Medicine* 166.3 (2006): 285-293.

Samaha, F. F., G. D. Foster, A. P. Makris. "Low-Carbohydrate Diets, Obesity, and Metabolic Risk Factors for Cardiovascular Disease." *Current Athersclerosis Reports* 9.6 (2007): 441-447.

Sharman, M. J., A. L. Gomez, W. J. Kraemer, J. S. Volek. "Very Low-Carbohydrate and Low-Fat Diets Affect Fasting Lipids and Postprandial Lipemia Differently in Overweight Men." *Journal of Nutrition* 134.4 (2004): 880-885.

Sharman, M. J., et al. "A Ketogenic Diet Favorably Affects Serum Biomarkers for Cardiovascular Disease in Normal-Weight Men." *Journal of Nutrition* 132.7 (2002): 1879-1885.

Sharman, M. J., et al. "Replacing Dietary Carbohydrate with Protein and Fat Decreases the Concentrations of Small LDL and the Inflammatory Response Induced by Atherogenic Diets in the Guinea Pig." *Journal of Nutritional Biochemistry* 19.11 (2008): 732-738.

Siri-Tarino, P. W., Q. Sun, F. B. Hu, R. M. Krauss. "Meta-Analysis of Prospective Cohort Studies Evaluating the Association of Saturated Fat with Cardiovascular Disease." *American Journal of Clinical Nutrition* 91.3 (2010): 535-46.

Torres-Gonzalez, M., et al. "Carbohydrate Restriction and Dietary Cholesterol Distinctly Affect Plasma Lipids and Lipoprotein Subfractions in Adult Guinea Pigs." *Journal of Nutritional Biochemistry* 19.12 (2008): 856-863.

Volek, J. S., et al. "Comparison of a Very Low-Carbohydrate and Low-Fat Diet on Fasting Lipids, LDL Subclasses, Insulin Resistance, and Postprandial Lipemic Responses in Overweight Women." *Journal of the American College of Nutrition* 23.2 (2004): 177-184.

Volek, J. S., et al. "A Hypocaloric Very Low Carbohydrate Ketogenic Diet Results in a Greater Reduction in the Percent and Absolute Amount of Plasma Triglyceride Saturated Fatty Acids Compared to a Low Fat Diet." Paper presented at the Annual Scientific Meeting of the North American Association for the Study of Obesity, Boston, Massachusetts, October 20-24, 2006.

Volek, J. S., et al. "An Isoenergetic Very Low-Carbohydrate Diet Is Associated with Improved Serum High-Density Lipoprotein Cholesterol (HDL-C), Total Cholesterol to HDL-C Ratio, Triacylglycerols, and Postprandial Lipemic Responses Compared to a Low-Fat Diet in Normal Weight, Normolipidemic Women." *Journal of Nutrition* 133.9 (2003): 2756-2761.

Volek, J. S., M. J. Sharman, C. E. Forsythe. "Modification of Lipoproteins by Very Low-Carbohydrate Diets." *Journal of Nutrition* 135.6 (2005): 1339-42.

Volek, J. S., M. L. Fernandez, R. D. Feinman, S. D. Phinney. "Dietary Carbohydrate Restriction Induces a Unique Metabolic State Positively Affecting Atherogenic Dyslipidemia, Fatty Acid Partitioning, and Metabolic Syndrome." *Progress in Lipid Research* 47.5 (2008): 307-318.

Westman, E. C., et al. "Effect of a Low-Carbohydrate, Ketogenic Diet Program Compared to a Low-Fat Diet on Fasting Lipoprotein Subclasses." *International Journal of Cardiology* 110.2 (2006): 212-216.

Westman, E. C., J. S. Volek. "Postprandial Triglycerides in Response to High Fat: Role of Dietary Carbohydrate." *European Journal of Clinical Investigation* 34.1 (2004): 74; author reply 75.

Westman, E. C., J. S. Volek, R. D. Feinman. "Carbohydrate Restriction Is Effective in Improving Atherogenic Dyslipidemia Even in the Absence of Weight Loss." *American Journal of Clinical Nutrition* 84.6 (2006): 1549; author reply 1550.

Wood, R. J., et al. "Carbohydrate Restriction Alters Lipoprotein Metabolism by Modifying VLDL, LDL, and HDL Subfraction Distribution and Size in Overweight Men." *Journal of Nutrition* 136.2 (2006): 384-389.

Wood, R. J., et al. "Effects of a Carbohydrate-Restricted Diet on Emerging Plasma Markers for Cardiovascular Disease." *Nutrition & Metabolism* 3.1 (2006): 19.

Yancy, W. S., Jr., et al. "A Low-Carbohydrate, Ketogenic Diet Versus a Low-Fat Diet to Treat Obesity and Hyperlipidemia: A Randomized, Controlled Trial." *Annals of Internal Medicine* 140.10 (2004): 769-777.

Cancer

Fine, E. J., et al. "Targeting Insulin Inhibition as a Metabolic Therapy in Advanced Cancer: A Pilot Safety and Feasibility Dietary Trial in 10 Patients." *Nutrition* 28.10 (2012): 1028-35.

Mavropoulos, J. C., et al. "The Effects of Varying Dietary Carbohydrate and Fat Content on Survival in a Murine LNCaP Prostate Cancer Xenograft Model." *Cancer Prevention Research* 2 (2009): 557-565.

Schmidt, M., et al. "Effects of a Ketogenic Diet on the Quality of Life in 16 Patients with Advanced Cancer: A Pilot Trial." *Nutrition & Metabolism* 8.1 (2011): 54.

Seyfried, T. N., et al. "Metabolic Management of Brain Cancer." *Biochimica et Biophysica Acta (BBA)—Bioenergetics* 1807.6 (2011): 577–594.

Simone, B. A., et al. "Selectively Starving Cancer Cells through Dietary Manipulation: Methods and Clinical Implications." *Future Oncology* 9.7 (2013): 959-76.

Zhou, W., et al. "The Calorically Restricted Ketogenic Diet, an Effective Alternative Therapy for Malignant Brain Cancer." *Nutrition & Metabolism* 4 (2007): 5.

Kidney Disease

Poplawski, M. M., et al. "Reversal of Diabetic Nephropathy by a Ketogenic Diet." *PLOS ONE* 6.4 (2011): e18604.

Anti-Aging

Rosedale, R., E. C. Westman, J. P. Konhilas. "Clinical Experience of a Diet Designed to Reduce Aging." *Journal of Applied Research* 9 (2009): 159-165.

Brain Disorders/Alzheimer's/Parkinson's/ALS

Gasior, M., M. A. Rogawski, A. L. Hartman. "Neuroprotective and Disease-Modifying Effects of the Ketogenic Diet." *Behavioural Pharmacology* 17.5-6, (2006): 431-9.

Henderson, S. T. "Ketone Bodies as a Therapeutic for Alzheimer's Disease." *Neurotherapeutics* 5.3 (2008): 470-80.

Henderson, S. T., et al. "Study of the Ketogenic Agent AC-1202 in Mild to Moderate Alzheimer's Disease: A Randomized, Double-Blind, Placebo-Controlled, Multicenter Trial." *Nutrition & Metabolism* 6 (2009): 31.

Husain, A. M., et al. "Diet Therapy for Narcolepsy." *Neurology* 62 (2004): 2300-2302.

Maalouf, M., J. M. Rho, M. P. Mattson. "The Neuroprotective Properties of Calorie Restriction, the Ketogenic Diet, and Ketone Bodies." *Brain Research Reviews* 59.2 (2009): 293-315.

Stafstrom, C. E., J. M. Rho. "The Ketogenic Diet as a Treatment Paradigm for Diverse Neurological Disorders." *Frontiers in Pharmacology* 3 (2012): 59.

Vanitallie, T. B., et al. "Treatment of Parkinson's Disease with Diet-Induced Hyperketonemia: A Feasibility Study." *Neurology* 64 (2005): 728-30.

Yang, X., B. Cheng. "Neuroprotective and Anti-inflammatory Activities of Ketogenic Diet on MPTP-induced Neurotoxicity." *Journal of Molecular Neuroscience* 42.2 (2010): 145-153.

Zhao, Z., et al. "A Ketogenic Diet as a Potential Novel Therapeutic Intervention in Amyotrophic Lateral Sclerosis." *BMC Neuroscience* 7 (2006): 29.

Autism

Evangeliou, A., et al. "Application of a Ketogenic Diet in Children with Autistic Behavior: Pilot Study." *Journal of Child Neurology* 18.2 (2003): 113-8.

Acne

Paoli, A., et al. "Nutrition and Acne: Therapeutic Potential of Ketogenic Diets." *Skin Pharmacology and Physiology* 25.3 (2012): 111-7.

Exercise Performance

Paoli, A., et al. "Ketogenic Diet Does Not Affect Strength Performance in Elite Artistic Gymnasts." *Journal of the International Society of Sports Nutrition* 9 (2012): 34

Phinney, S. D. "Ketogenic Diets and Physical Performance." *Nutrition & Metabolism* 1.1 (2004): 2.

Phinney, S. D., et al. "The Human Metabolic Response to Chronic Ketosis without Caloric Restriction: Preservation of Submaximal Exercise Capability with Reduced Carbohydrate Oxidation." *Metabolism* 32.8 (1983): 769-776.

Other Recommended Resources

Books

Atkins, Dr. Robert C. *Dr. Atkins' Diet Revolution.* New York: Bantam, 1972.

Atkins, Dr. Robert C. *Dr. Atkins' New Diet Revolution.* New York: Harper, 2002.

Briffa, Dr. John. *Waist Disposal: The Ultimate Fat-Loss Manual for Men.* New York: Hay House, 2011.

Cantin, Elaine. *The Cantin Ketogenic Diet: For Cancer, Type I Diabetes & Other Ailments.* Williston, VT: Elaine Cantin, 2012.

Carlson, Dr. James. *Genocide: How Your Doctor's Dietary Ignorance Will Kill You.* James Carlson, 2007.

Carpender, Dana. *200 Low-Carb, High-Fat Recipes: Easy Recipes to Jumpstart Your Low-Carb Weight Loss.* Minneapolis, MN: Fair Winds Press, 2014.

Carpender, Dana, Amy Dungan, and Rebecca Latham. *Fat Fast Cookbook: 50 Easy Recipes to Jump Start Your Low Carb Weight.* Las Vegas, NV: CarbSmart Press, 2013.

David, Ellen. *Fight Cancer with a Ketogenic Diet: A New Method for Fighting Cancer,* Second Edition. 2014. Ebook.

Emmerich, Maria. *Keto-Adapted: Your Guide to Accelerated Weight Loss and Healthy Healing.* Maria and Craig Emmerich, 2013. Kindle edition.

Groves, Dr. Barry. *Natural Health & Weight Loss.* London: Hammersmith Press, 2007.

Kiefer, John. *The Carb Nite Solution: The Physicist's Guide to Power Dieting.* Kiefer Productions, 2005.

Kossoff, Dr. Eric H., Dr. John M. Freeman, Zahava Turner, and Dr. James E. Rubenstein. *Ketogenic Diets: Treatments for Epilepsy and Other Disorders,* Fifth Edition. New York: Demos Health, 2011.

McCleary, Dr. Larry. *The Brain Trust Program: A Scientifically Based Three-Part Plan to Improve Memory, Elevate Mood, Enhance Attention, Alleviate Migraine and Menopausal Symptoms, and Boost Mental Energy.* New York: Penguin, 2007.

McDonald, Lyle. *The Ketogenic Diet: A Complete Guide for the Dieter and Practitioner.* Lyle McDonald, 1998.

Moore, Jimmy, and Dr. Eric Westman. *Cholesterol Clarity: What the HDL Is Wrong with My Numbers?* Las Vegas, NV: Victory Belt Publishing, 2013.

Newport, Dr. Mary. *Alzheimer's Disease: What If There Was a Cure?: The Story of Ketones.* Laguna Beach, CA: Basic Health Publications, 2011.

Ottoboni, Dr. Fred, and Dr. Alice Ottoboni. *The Modern Nutritional Diseases: and How to Prevent Them,* Second Edition. Femly, NV: Vincente Books, 2013.

Perlmutter, Dr. David. *Grain Brain: The Surprising Truth about Wheat, Carbs, and Sugar—Your Brain's Silent Killers.* New York: Little, Brown, 2013.

Phinney, Dr. Stephen, and Dr. Jeff Volek. *The Art and Science of Low Carbohydrate Living.* Beyond Obesity, 2011.

Phinney, Dr. Stephen, and Dr. Jeff Volek. *The Art and Science of Low Carbohydrate Performance.* Beyond Obesity, 2012.

Seyfried, Dr. Thomas. *Cancer as a Metabolic Disease: On the Origin, Management, and Prevention of Cancer.* Hoboken, NJ: John Wiley & Sons, 2012.

Skaldeman, Sten Sture. *The Low Carb High Fat Cookbook: 100 Recipes to Lose Weight and Feel Great.* New York: Skyhorse Publishing, 2013.

Snyder, Dr. Deborah. *Keto Kid: Helping Your Child Succeed on the Ketogenic Diet.* New York: Demos Medical Publishing, 2006.

Taubes, Gary. *Good Calories, Bad Calories: Challenging the Conventional Wisdom on Diet, Weight Control, and Disease.* New York: Anchor Books, 2007.

Taubes, Gary. *Why We Get Fat: And What to Do About It.* New York: Anchor Books, 2011.

Tiecholz, Tina. *The Big Fat Surprise: Why Butter, Meat, and Cheese Belong in a Healthy Diet.* New York: Simon & Schuster, 2014.

Volek, Dr. Jeff, and Adam Campbell. *Men's Health TNT Diet: The Explosive New Plan to Blast Fat, Build Muscle, and Get Healthy in 12 Weeks.* New York: Rodale, 2008.

Wahls, Dr. Terry, and Eve Adamson. *The Wahls Protocol: How I Beat Progressive MS Using Paleo Principles and Functional Medicine.* New York: Penguin, 2014.

Westman, Dr. Eric. *A Low Carbohydrate, Ketogenic Diet Manual: No Sugar, No Starch Diet.* Dr. Eric Westman, 2013.

Westman, Dr. Eric, Dr. Stephen D. Phinney, and Dr. Jeff S. Volek. *The New Atkins for a New You.* New York: Fireside, 2010.

Keto Blogs and Websites

Everything About Keto, Reddit: www.reddit.com/r/keto

Ketogenic Diet Resource: www.ketogenic-diet-resource.com

The Charlie Foundation for Ketogenic Therapies: www.charliefoundation.org

The Ketogenic Diet for Health: www.ketotic.org

KetoNutrition: http://ketonutrition.blogspot.com

Ketopia: http://ketopia.com

KetoCook: http://ketocook.com

Ketastic: http://ketastic.com

RunKeto: www.runketo.com

Eat Keto: http://eatketo.com

Kickin' Into Keto: www.ketoblog.net

CavemanKeto: http://cavemanketo.com

KetoDiet: Real Food & Healthy Living: http://ketodietapp.com/Blog

Dr. Dave Unleashed: http://drdaveunleashed.wordpress.com

Ruled.me: www.ruled.me

Matthew's Friends: www.matthewsfriends.org

Dietary Therapies, LLC: Ketogenic Diet for Cancer: http://dietarytherapies.com

Fat for Fuel, My Ketogenic Diet Experiment While Endurance Training: www.sftrails.com/2013/08/fat-for-fuel-my-ketogenic-diet.html

The Ketogenic Diet: www.theketogenicdiet.org

The Eating Academy: http://eatingacademy.com

Eat Keto: http://eatketo.com

A Game of Keto: http://jennynotketo.tumblr.com

WickedStuffed: Whole Food Recipes in 10 Carbs or Less: www.wickedstuffed.com

Defying Age with Food: http://defyingagewithfood.com

Diet Doctor: www.dietdoctor.com

Second Opinions: www.second-opinions.co.uk

Eat Low Carb High Fat: www.eatlowcarbhighfat.com

Films and Documentaries on Ketogenic Diets

Carb-Loaded: A Culture Dying to Eat (coming summer 2014). Produced by Lathe Poland and Eric Carlsen. http://carbloaded.com.

Cereal Killers. Directed by Yolanda Barker. 2013. www.cerealkillersmovie.com.

Fat Head. Directed by Tom Naughton. 2009. www.fathead-movie.com.

". . . First Do No Harm." Directed by Jim Abrahams. 1997. Walt Disney Home Video, 2002. www.amazon.com/First-Do-No-Harm/dp/B000068MBW.

My Big Fat Diet. Directed by Mary Bissell. 2008. http://mybigfatdiet.net.

Keto Calculators

The Low Carb Flexi Diet: www.flexibleketogenic.com

Keto Calculator: http://keto-calculator.ankerl.com

Conversion Charts

Cholesterol Conversion Chart: http://www.onlineconversion.com/cholesterol.htm

Blood Sugar Converter Chart: http://www.onlineconversion.com/blood_sugar.htm

Ketogenic Diet Researchers and Educators

Carl E. Stafstrom, MD, PhD, University of Wisconsin-Madison researcher

Colin Champ, MD, University of Pittsburgh Cancer Institute researcher

David Perlmutter, MD, world-renowned neurologist and author

Dominic D'Agostino, PhD, University of South Florida researcher

Emma Williams, CEO/Founder of Matthew's Friends

Eric Westman, MD, Duke University researcher

Erik Kossoff, MD, Adam Hartman, MD, Eileen Vining, MD, John Freeman MD (retired), The Johns Hopkins Epilepsy Center researchers

Eugene Fine, MD, Albert Einstein College of Medicine researcher

Henri Brunengraber, MD, PhD, Case Western Reserve University researcher

Jeff S. Volek, PhD, University of Connecticut researcher

Jim Abrahams, Executive Director of The Charlie Foundation

Jong Rho, MD, Barrow Neurological Institute researcher

Kieran Clarke, Ph.D., Oxford University researcher

Larry McCleary, MD, former pediatric neurosurgeon at Denver Children's Hospital

Miriam Kalamian, Certified Ketogenic Nutrition Specialist

Peter Attia, MD, physician blogger and researcher

Richard Feinman, PhD, SUNY Downstate (NY) professor and researcher

Richard L. Veech, MD, National Institutes of Health researcher

Sami Hashim, MD, St. Luke's and Roosevelt Hospitals researcher

Samuel Henderson, PhD, Executive Director of Research at Accera (medical food)

Stephen Cunnane, Ph.D., University of *Sherbrooke researcher*

Stephen D. Phinney, MD, physician researcher

Terry Maratos-Flier, Beth Israel Deaconess Medical Center researcher

Theodore VanItallie, MD, St. Luke's-Roosevelt Hospitals researcher

Thomas Seyfried, PhD, Boston College Researcher

Timothy Noakes, MD, University of Cape Town researcher

Ulrike Kammerer, University of Wurzburg researcher

William Davis, MD, world-renowned cardiologist and author

Find a Keto-Friendly Doctor

List of Low-Carb Doctors: http://lowcarbdoctors.blogspot.com

Glossary

Acetoacetate: The primary ketone body found in the urine.

Acetone: The primary ketone body found in the breath.

Adrenal fatigue: A collection of signs and symptoms that occur when the adrenal glands function below the necessary level, resulting in increased levels of stress, fatigue, and depression. People with adrenal fatigue tend to consume caffeinated beverages and products to function.

Antioxidants: Primarily found in vitamins C and E and carotenoids, which include beta-carotene, lycopene, and lutein, these help protect healthy cells from damage caused by free radicals.

ATP (Adenosine triphosphate): The molecular form of energy used by cells.

Autoimmunity: An atypical immune response in which the body attacks its own cells and tissues. This results in autoimmune diseases such as celiac disease, type 1 diabetes, Hashimoto's thyroiditis, Graves' disease, and more.

Beta-hydroxybutyrate: The primary ketone body found in the blood.

C-reactive protein (hsCRP): A test that can detect small amounts of C-reactive protein, a marker of inflammation, in the blood.

Cortisol: A hormone released in response to stress that increases blood sugar levels and suppresses the immune system, among other effects.

Cytokine: Molecule that plays a role in the communication between cells in immune responses in the body and helps repair cells that have become damaged by inflammation, infection, and trauma.

Dyslipidemia: Abnormal amounts of cholesterol or fat in the blood.

Epigenetics: The changes in gene function that do not involve any changes in the DNA sequence. For example, lifestyle changes in diet can play a role in your health despite any genetic tendencies.

Fatty acids: An important source of fuel for the body that leads to large amounts of ATP production, which the body and brain can use in place of glucose.

Gluconeogenesis: The productions of glucose from dietary protein; it takes place primarily in the liver.

Glucose: One of the primary energy sources when the body is a sugar-burner.

Glycogen: Made in the cells of the liver and stored primarily in the muscles, it's a backup energy source that is easily converted into glucose.

Glycolysis: The burning of glucose within the cells.

HDL cholesterol: High-density lipoprotein, a particle in the blood that carries cholesterol from the arteries to the liver.

Hyperglycemia: High blood sugar levels resulting from the consumption of too many carbohydrates or a lack of adequate insulin.

Hypoglycemia: A condition of too-low blood sugar levels that leads to symptoms such as shakiness, dizziness, and changes in mood and behavior.

Hypothyroidism: A condition in which the thyroid gland does not make enough thyroid hormone.

Insulin resistance: A condition in which the body produces insulin but does not use it very effectively.

Insulin sensitivity: The ability of the body to utilize insulin the way it was intended.

Keto-adaptation: A metabolic shift whereby the body uses fat and ketones for fuel instead of glucose. This process can take a few days to several weeks in those who switch to a low-carbohydrate, moderate-protein, high-fat diet.

Ketoacidosis: A very serious, life-threatening medical condition that occurs mostly in type 1 diabetics and some type 2 diabetics who have lost their beta cell function, in which the body has simultaneously high blood sugar levels and very high blood ketone levels. Often confused with ketosis, it is not the same thing.

Ketogenesis: The creation of ketone bodies in the liver from fat and protein.

Ketogenic diet: A low-carbohydrate, moderate-protein, high-fat diet that produces ketone bodies as an alternative means for fueling the body; used therapeutically for a variety of health conditions.

Ketones: The energy by-product that results when the body shifts to burning fat for fuel. These are typically created by consuming a low-carbohydrate, moderate-protein, high-fat diet.

Ketosis: The state in which the body burns fat for fuel in the context of a low-carbohydrate, moderate-protein, high-fat diet.

LDL cholesterol: Low-density lipoprotein, a particle made by the liver that carries cholesterol and fat-soluble vitamins from the liver to the cells. Also refers to the amount of cholesterol carried in the low-density lipoprotein particles in the blood.

Leptin: A hormone made by fat cells that regulates how much fat is stored in the body. It's commonly referred to as the "satiety hormone" because of its role in controlling hunger signals.

Lipogenesis: The creation of fat in the body. This occurs in the liver, muscle, and fat cells.

Lipolysis: The breakdown of fat, which also leads to the generation of ketone bodies.

Lipoprotein: Molecule in the blood that carries cholesterol, triglycerides, and fat-soluble substances throughout the body.

Macronutrient: One of the three major components of food that the human body needs in order to function properly: carbohydrates, proteins, and fats.

Medium-chain triglycerides: Also known as MCTs, these aid in fat oxidation and temporarily increase the production of ketones.

Meta-analysis: An analysis that combines the results of many scientific studies to look for patterns in the data and examine new relationships that may be scientifically relevant for further study.

Metabolic syndrome: A group of conditions, including elevated blood pressure, high blood sugar, increased levels of body fat in the waist, and high cholesterol levels, that combined can predict your risk of heart disease, stroke, and diabetes.

Micronutrient: Any nutrient used by humans in proper minimal levels for optimal physical function.

Mitochondria: Known as the power plants of the cell, these generate ATP for energy. When this process is impaired, it is implicated in a variety of diseases, mostly commonly neurological ones.

Monounsaturated fat: Often referred to as "MUFAs" (monounsaturated fatty acids), these are fats that have one double bond in their carbon chains. One of the healthy fats (along with saturated fat), it's found in foods such as avocados, olive oil, red meat, and whole dairy products.

Myopathy: A muscular disease in which the muscle fibers do not function properly, resulting in muscular weakness.

Polyunsaturated fat: Often referred to as "PUFAs" (polyunsaturated fatty acids), these are fats that have more than one double bond in their carbon chains. As a result, they are chemically unstable and very prone to oxidation, which can lead to the production of free radicals and inflammation in the body. These are found mostly in vegetable oils such as canola, corn, and soybean oil.

Saturated fat: Fatty acids that have no double bonds in their carbon chain; the preferred fat when attempting to get into ketosis.

Standard American Diet: The typical diet of Americans today, composed of around 50 percent carbohydrate, 15 percent protein, and 35 percent fat.

Triglyceride: The major form of stored fat. The breakdown of triglyceride in the liver leads to the generation of ketone bodies.

Type 1 diabetes: The autoimmune destruction of the insulin-producing beta cells in the pancreas, which leads to an increase in blood glucose levels.

Type 2 diabetes: The most common form of diabetes, it is the presence of high blood sugar levels with a diminished capacity of insulin due to severe insulin resistance. It can usually be managed well by consuming a low-carbohydrate, moderate-protein, high-fat diet.

Type 3 diabetes: Another name used by researchers for Alzheimer's disease; in people with Alzheimer's insulin does not respond appropriately in the brain.

VO2 max: The maximum amount of oxygen, in milliliters, an individual can use in one minute per kilogram of body weight.

Acknowledgments

Jimmy Moore: I'm having déjà vu all over again, writing my second book about a year after my last one. But this time around the process was a lot smoother, thanks to the experience I got writing *Cholesterol Clarity* in 2013. I would be remiss if I didn't share my sincerest gratitude to those who helped make this book a reality.

To my wife, Christine, who stands by me daily, offering up encouragement and loving support every step of the way: I cannot imagine going through life without you being a part of it. Well, you and dark chocolate.

To my brilliant coauthor, Dr. Eric Westman, who shared so freely of his time and passed along the tremendous experience he has garnered about ketogenic diets in both research and the clinical realm with patients: "Thank you" just doesn't seem adequate. I know you probably got tired of me sending you a dozen emails and calling you on the telephone every single day for months, but I think the end product is something pretty special, and I hope you are as proud of it as I am. It's an exciting time for the keto message, and I look forward to collaborating with you on future books and projects to help spread the word even more.

To the ketosis experts featured in the "Moment of Clarity" quotes: You've added such depth to the content, and I appreciate your contributions to this book immensely.

To my publishing team, Erich, Michele, Erin, Holly, and everyone who worked behind the scenes at Victory Belt: Thanks for giving me the honor of writing this book. Lives will be changed for the better because people read this book and improved their health. I'm looking forward to writing books for you for many years to come.

Dr. Eric Westman: I am grateful for the education provided by my formal ongoing meetings (the American Society of Bariatric Physicians, the Nutrition and Metabolism Society) and the "in-the-trenches" training that can only be obtained through patient care. This book would not have been possible without the teaching from my patients (who started the Low Carb Support Group) and my ketosis colleagues Stephen D. Phinney and Jeff S. Volek. Most of all, I am grateful to my family and friends for their support.

Index